24.95

WOMEN IN ENGINEERING

SUNY Series in Science, Technology, and Society
Sal Restivo, Editor

WOMEN IN ENGINEERING

Gender, Power, and Workplace Culture

JUDITH S. MCILWEE
J. GREGG ROBINSON

STATE UNIVERSITY OF NEW YORK PRESS

Cover design by Elise Brauckmann.
Cover illustration by Robert McIlwee.

Published by
State University of New York Press, Albany

For information, address State University of New York
Press, State University Plaza, Albany, N.Y., 12246

Production by E. Moore
Marketing by Bernadette LaManna

Library of Congress Cataloging-in-Publication Data

McIlwee, Judith Samsom, 1943–
    Women in engineering : gender, power, and workplace culture / Judith
S. McIlwee, J. Gregg Robinson.
        p.   cm. — (SUNY series in science, technology, and society)
    Includes bibliographical references (p.) and index.
    ISBN 0-7914-0869-8 (CH : acid-free). — ISBN 0-7914-0870-1 (PB : acid-
free)
    1. Women in engineering 2. Women engineers I. Robinson, J.
Gregg, 1949– . II. Title III. Series.
TA157.M342   1992
305.43′62—dc20   91-2050
                                                                      CIP

10 9 8 7 6 5 4

For Mary, Peggy, and Cady Gennette—
three women who have made
a difference in our lives.

CONTENTS

viii   Contents

TABLES

PREFACE

This work is the culmination of a five year collaboration. From the first sketchy ideas, through research design, data collection, coding, analysis, and writing, every step of the process was shared equally. We came to this project via two intellectual paths. Gregg Robinson's previous work was on the professions of the "new middle class." Judith McIlwee had studied the sex segregation of occupations, and women in nontraditional blue-collar jobs. We were both interested in the "high tech revolution" of the 1980s. What effects was it having on the occupational structure, and on the careers of women and men within it? We carried out a small study of high tech assembly workers in one southwest city (Robinson and McIlwee 1989), then turned our attention to engineers.

For Judith this was an occupational group of strategic importance to women's status in the work force and in the family. The subordinate position of women in both spheres is intimately linked to the sex segregation of occupations. Here was a highly paid, rapidly growing profession that women had begun to enter in increasing numbers. Would the pattern of resegregation, so common in other nontraditional occupations, occur here too? If so, what were the factors responsible for it? The movement of women into engineering presented an opportunity to explore the processes by which occupational segregation is maintained or re-created, in spite of efforts to dismantle it.

For Gregg this study provided an opportunity to pursue his long-standing interest in the professions and power. He was particularly interested in the professional culture of engineers: how it is shaped by their location in particular organizational structures, and by the rise of high tech industries. In addition, he saw this research as a way to incorporate the complexity of gender relations into the study of professional power.

Both natives of southern California, we returned home for a year to gather our data. We received invaluable help from individuals and institutions. Thanks to Joseph Gusfield, Hugh Mehan, and Andrew Scull, we were appointed visiting scholars in the department of sociology, University of California, San Diego. Our affiliation there provided us the resources we needed to obtain a sample, and carry out our research successfully. We received funding from the University of Texas at San Antonio, and Stephen F. Austin State University. This was a low-budget operation, however, and we hope it will provide reassurance to others that sociologists can carry out research on a shoestring.

Throughout the process, we have benefited from the insights, advice, and feedback provided by sociologists and engineers. In particular, we thank Joseph Gusfield, Hugh Mehan, David Gartman, Robert Szafran, Rick Nadeau, and Russell Lyon. We owe special thanks to "Ginger," who the reader will meet in the following pages. She was kind enough to read an early version of the manuscript, and to offer her comments and criticisms.

All our respondents gave of their time to fill out a lengthy questionnaire, and many of them sat through an exhaustive (and exhausting) interview, as well. In the process, they provided us not only with answers to our questions, but with information and insights we had not even thought to ask about. We only hope that in some small way the publication of this book will be of help to them and to their colleagues in the profession.

We owe a great deal to those who guided and challenged us through graduate school. In a very real sense, Joseph Gusfield, Randall Collins, Rae Blumberg, Hugh Mehan, and Aaron Cicourel can take credit for what is good in this work.

We would also like to add our names to the long list of authors citing an intellectual debt to C. Wright Mills. Mills's moral stance in sociology is widely emulated by sociologists of our generation. Less often cited is his methodological position. Mills believed that the best of sociology was found in the margin between theoretical erudition and methodological obsession, a margin he referred to as the craft of sociology. We hope that a little of both his moral courage and his sense of craft can be found in this book.

We had help from many who remain unknown to us: the anonymous reviewers who commented on portions of our work for publication in *Social Problems* and *Sociological Quarterly*, and on the entire manuscript. They forced us to clarify and support our arguments and refine our concepts in ways that we think have only improved the finished product. We would also like to thank our editor, Rosalie Robertson. Her advice and encouragement has been invaluable. Of course, any errors, omissions, or inadequacies that remain are ours and ours alone.

Richard Ellis, of the American Association of Engineering Societies, provided us with valuable statistical data on engineers. Students at the University of Texas at San Antonio, Stephen F. Austin State University, and San Diego State University helped us with the coding of questionnaire data.

Finally, we thank each other. We embarked on this project not knowing how well we would work together. We found the process surprisingly positive and productive. Clichéd though it may sound, we complemented each other's strengths and compensated for each other's weaknesses. In combination we produced something far better than either of us could have separately. There were benefits of a more immediate nature as well. We provided each other with someone to listen tirelessly to endless discussions about "the project." We goaded each other to keep going when we were so tired, but had just a few more interviews to code, or just a few more pages to revise. Perhaps most important, we found that it was possible to work together as equals, just as we live together.

1

WOMEN IN ENGINEERING: A PROMISE UNFULFILLED?

Driving the streets of southern California in the mid-1980s is a late model, small pickup truck. As is common in this part of the country, it displays a personalized license plate, which says to the world, "Here I am." The letters on the plate spell INJINER. Not surprising, here in the land of defense contractors and high tech. Engineers populate the area in large numbers, and are in high demand. Nor is it surprising that someone would be proud enough of being an engineer to display it in this way. With the growth of high tech industries in the past decade, engineering has achieved greater visibility in the occupational hierarchy. While engineers still do not enjoy the prestige of doctors and lawyers, America's crisis of competitiveness in the world economy has brought greater attention to the engineers who must develop the technologies of the future. The shortages of engineers projected for the next decade are decried by economists and political leaders. Not surprising, then, that an engineer might want to brag about his chosen profession.

What *is* surprising, however, is that the driver of this pickup is not a man, but a woman. We will call her Bonnie. Bonnie is no different than the thousands of young women who graduated from a major state university in the area in the early 1980s. A native of southern

California, she turned down a job in another state, reluctant to leave the sun and surf that her hometown offers. She is career-oriented and ambitious: she wants to make money, and to move up in the organization. She lives with her boyfriend, who she is planning to marry in a year or so, and wonders how she will be able to incorporate children into her life.

What *is* different about Bonnie is her choice of occupation. Engineering holds the dubious distinction of being the most male-dominated of all the professions. Even fields closely related to it are less male-dominated. In 1988, women constituted 33 percent of computer and mathematical scientists, 24 percent of natural scientists and chemists, but only 7.3 percent of engineers (Vetter and Babco 1989).

During the 1970s and early 1980s the percentage of women receiving engineering degrees grew dramatically, however, and it looked as though engineering would be catching up with these other fields. Between 1970 and 1980 women's share of bachelor's degrees in engineering rose from less than one percent to nearly ten percent, a larger percentage increase than for any other science-related field. This is particularly impressive, given the fact that the occupation itself was growing rapidly during this time (Vetter 1981).

Bonnie is part of that historic development, and she knows it is something to brag about. She enjoys the surprised responses she gets when people realize that *she* is the INJINER referred to on her license plate. There are a number of reasons why women like Bonnie were attracted to engineering in the 1970s and 80s, and which seemed to presage an ever-growing role for them there.

First, engineering as a profession has grown rapidly in the recent past, and will continue to do so in the future. Between 1975 and 1985 the number of graduates from engineering schools doubled (Ellis 1990). Despite this growth, the demand for engineers is projected to increase by another 25 percent between 1988 and 2000. The two specialties on which our study focuses will experience the greatest growth. Electrical engineering, already the largest specialty, will grow by 40 percent. Mechanical engineering, the second largest, will grow by 20 percent (American Assoc. of Engineering Societies 1989a). Serious shortages of engineers are projected over the next several decades, and women and minorities must be drawn upon in larger numbers if we are to meet the need (National Science Foundation 1986; Ivey 1987).

Engineering should be especially attractive to women, for not only does it yield higher salaries than the female-dominated professions, starting salaries for bachelor's degree recipients are higher than for *any* comparable field (College Placement Council 1990). In fact, engineering is one of the five best-paid occupations for women, along with law, medicine, computer science, and educational administration (U.S. Dept. of Labor 1988). Moreover, female engineering graduates receive slightly better starting salaries than men. In 1986, offers to women as a percentage of offers to men were 100.3 percent in electrical engineering, and 100.1 percent in mechanical engineering. Only in the allied health professions did women do as well relative to men (100.3%). They fared less well in all other fields, including computer science, physical science, and mathematics (98%), biology (97%), business administration (95%), economics (92%), and social sciences (85%) (College Placement Council 1986).

This combination of growth and reward makes engineering an attractive field for women. Long confined to "pink-collar ghettoes," where jobs are characterized by low pay and few opportunities for advancement, women are responding eagerly today to careers that offer more.

In addition, the nature of the work involved in engineering has been changing, in ways that would appear to make it more attractive to women. Whereas its traditional image was of rugged, mechanical, outdoor work, engineering today has moved indoors, and involves analytical skill, small scale design, and computer work (Salembier 1971; Hacker 1983). No longer just building "bridges and machinery," engineers are doing work that involves them in a broad range of physical, environmental, and social sciences. In addition, because the newer fields of engineering have had less time to become male-identified, they are seen as more accepting of women (Boyce 1987).

Finally, the "paraengineering" occupations are growing as rapidly as engineering itself, which means that technicians and drafters now do much of the "hands-on" work of engineering, work that is most closely identified with the male gender role. This leaves the more abstract and creative work, along with administrative activities, for engineers (Hacker 1983; U.S. Dept. of Labor 1988).

For all these reasons it was expected that the rapid movement of women into engineering would continue into the 1990s and beyond. However, in the 1980s, the increase in women's share of bachelor's degrees slowed, and by 1989 it had leveled off at 15 percent (American Assoc. of Engineering Societies 1989b). Therefore, it may well be that the surge of women into engineering has peaked, and that the increases seen in the 1970s will not continue into the 1990s.

If that is true, then Bonnie and her female colleagues will constitute not the cutting edge of a new occupational trend, but the sum total of that trend. This means that not just Bonnie, but those who follow her, will remain "tokens" in a heavily male-dominated profession.

Like women in other male-dominated occupations, Bonnie has had to do more than master the intricacies of engineering. She has also had to deal with being one of the first women in that field. This has often meant scrutiny, skepticism, and sexism. Yet she has dealt with these problems and feels confident that she will be moving up soon—first to senior engineer, later to project engineer. One of the central questions in this book is whether she and others like her will actually be able to do that.

In the chapters that follow, we describe the experiences of women like Bonnie, and the men who were their classmates in college. First, however, we must provide some background. In chapter 2 we discuss the status of women in the work force, and in nontraditional occupations. We then examine the major theoretical perspectives that have been used to explain women's occupational status. Finally, we discuss the nature of engineering as a profession, focusing in particular on what we call the "culture of engineering." In chapters 3 through 7 we tell the story of women in engineering today, comparing them throughout to their male colleagues. In chapter 3 we begin with their childhood backgrounds, and the experiences that led them to choose engineering as a college major, and a profession. In chapter 4 we describe their college years, following them in chapters 5 and 6 into the workplace. We describe their experiences as working engineers, and as tokens in a male-dominated work environment. We assess their status in the workplace, and their ability to move up at the same pace as their male counterparts. In chapter 7 we describe the family relationships of married engineers, and the different ways in which work and family interact for women and men.

As we proceed through these chapters we develop a theoretical model to explain the problems and opportunities women find in engineering. We conclude our discussion in chapter 8 by reviewing our model, and considering its implications for theory and public policy.

The findings reported here are based on a study of women and men in engineering, conducted in 1986. We gathered data in the form of questionnaires and in-depth interviews from a random sample of engineering graduates (1976–1985) from two major public universities in southern California. We refer to these schools hereafter as California Elite University (CEU) and Public State University (PSU). We over-sampled women, given their small share of this population. We asked our respondents a wide range of questions, dealing with their back-grounds, college experiences, work experiences, work-related values and attitudes, and family relationships. We explored their experiences and attitudes regarding the entry of women into the profession. (See Appendix A.)

What we found was a complex picture that allows for no easy explanations. Women are doing well in engineering, but not as well as men. Like women in other male-dominated professions, they often find themselves segregated into lower status positions, with less chance of moving into management. Yet depending on the type of organization in which they work, there are significant differences in the opportunities they find. In some workplaces, women lag far behind men, while in others they equal or outpace them.

In an effort to trace the causes of these patterns, we explore the different social worlds through which our respondents have traveled or now reside: childhood, the educational system, the workplace, and the adult family. In the process we develop an explanation, grounded in conflict theory, that synthesizes two major theoretical perspectives on women's work force status: the gender role and structural perspectives. We show how women's careers in engineering are shaped by the interaction of gender-linked attitudes and behaviors, and the structural characteristics of the school, the workplace, and the family.

We argue that interactional resources such as self-confidence and assertiveness, and a fascination with technology and "tinkering," are important to career mobility in engineering. The identification of these characteristics with the male gender role puts women at a disadvantage. But these resources are less important in some organizational settings than others. What seems to matter most is which groups have the power to define the formal and informal criteria for success—what we call the "culture of the workplace." Where engineers as a group are powerful, they are able to define workplace culture in a strongly male-identified way, and women's careers suffer. However, where engineers hold less power, the culture is less male-identified and women do well. The concept of workplace culture forms the analytic heart of our model. It is the medium in which gender behaviors interact with opportunities created by organizational structure.

If the problems that women face in engineering are complex, so are the solutions. Our analysis suggests that if we are to improve the status of women in engineering, we will have to attack it on many fronts. We call for changes in childhood socialization and education processes, in college curricula, in the structures of workplace and family, and in public policy. A tall order, indeed.

Yet changes like these are needed if more than a few women are to succeed in engineering. Unless women are widely and visibly succeeding in the field, there will be little incentive for others to follow their lead. That means that Bonnie's experiences as the only woman engineer in her group will continue to be typical. The woman in engineering will remain a token, always standing out and often falling behind, rather than becoming a routine and well-integrated part of the work group. Rather than a significant path of opportunity for large numbers of women, engineering will continue to be one of those "men's jobs," entered only by the most hardy—or foolhardy—of women.

Given the growth of jobs in engineering and the high pay it offers, whether and how well it accepts women into its ranks is an important social issue. Engineering holds the promise of offering significant career opportunities for large numbers of college-educated women, and thereby helping to improve women's status in the work force. Is that promise being fulfilled? This study represents one of the first major efforts to answer that question.

The experiences of Bonnie and her co-workers are significant in their own right, but they also tell us much about the process of entering nontraditional occupations more generally. By identifying factors that impede or facilitate success in engineering, we can better understand the experiences of women wherever they attempt to navigate the terrain of the male-dominated workplace. Understanding is the necessary foundation of constructive social change, and we hope this book contributes to both.

2

WOMEN'S WORK AND ENGINEERING: THEORETICAL ISSUES

Research on women in the work force flourished in the 1970s and 80s. Virtually every type of work done by women has been studied, from the most traditional to the least. We have learned of the trials and triumphs of housewives and hookers, secretaries and steel workers, managers and miners. The special problems women face in the workplace have also been explored: sexual harassment, discrimination, health hazards, and the competing demands of job and family.

This research has produced fascinating descriptions and disturbing exposés. It has given rise to important theoretical discussions and proposals for policies and programs, as researchers have attempted to explain and find solutions for the problems women face. One of the most serious problems is the pay gap between men and women, which has persisted even as women's numbers in the work force have grown dramatically. Despite the fact that by 1980 most Americans endorsed the concept of equal pay for women, the average woman employed full-time that year earned only about 60 cents for every $1.00 earned by the average man, the same ratio that existed in 1950 (U.S. Dept. of Labor 1983).

One of the major reasons for the pay gap is "occupational segregation" (Treiman and Hartmann 1981; Reskin and Hartmann 1986). Women earn less than men because most women do not work in the same occupations as men. Instead, they are segregated into a narrow range of relatively low-paid, low status occupations, such as clerical and service work, and the "semiprofessions" (e.g., nursing, teaching, and social work) (U.S. Dept. of Labor 1980).

Recognizing the link between occupational segregation and the pay gap, feminists and policy-makers in the 1970s and 80s focused considerable attention on opening "men's" jobs to women. As long as that was where the status, pay, and advancement opportunities were, they reasoned, then women needed help and encouragement to move into those areas. Programs were developed by government, schools, and business to encourage the entry of women into "nontraditional" professions like science, law, and management, and blue-collar jobs like welding, carpentry, and truck driving. Affirmative action regulations provided the legal framework, putting pressure on employers to become active participants in the process.[1]

These efforts achieved some success. During the 1970s there was for the first time a modest but significant decrease in the sex segregation of occupations (Beller 1984). Movement into nontraditional jobs was greatest in professional and managerial occupations, with women making significant gains in fields like accounting, engineering, law, and sales management (Beller and Han 1984). The decline in segregation was followed in the early 1980s by a slight narrowing of the pay gap: women's full-time earnings as a percent of men's increased to 65 percent (U.S. Bureau of the Census 1987).

As women moved into nontraditional occupations, researchers were not far behind. Studies of the "pioneers" in these jobs came out in rapid succession, recounting their experiences and analyzing their successes and failures (Hennig and Jardim 1977; Kanter 1977; Meyer and Lee 1978; Schreiber 1979; Ratner 1980; Walshok 1981; McIlwee 1981, 1982; Harlan and O'Farrell 1982; Deaux and Ullman 1983; Epstein 1983). One of the recurring patterns found in these studies is the phenomenon of "resegregation." As women's numbers increase in an occupation, they often find themselves confined to "female ghettos" within it. Like their sisters in "women's jobs," women in nontraditional jobs hold positions with lower status and visibility, fewer opportunities for promotion, marginality to centers of power, and lower pay, when compared to their male co-workers (Kanter 1977; Harlan and O'Farrell 1982; Epstein 1983). New terms have been coined to describe this phenomenon, like "glass ceiling" and "velvet ghetto" (Cline, et al 1986; Morrison, White and Van Velsor 1987).

Thus, just as segregation begins to wane in one arena, it waxes in another. Why is it so persistent? What forces lie behind the occupational segregation—and resegregation—of women? Much of the theoretical energies of social scientists studying women's work have focused on these problems. Their efforts have taken them in two theoretical directions, which we refer to as the "gender-role" and "structural" perspectives.[2]

The gender-role perspective focuses on the characteristics of individual women and men, and places strong emphasis on gender socialization as the primary determinant of women's work force status. The structural perspective emphasizes the structural features of the workplace and other social institutions. While the two perspectives are often considered mutually exclusive, we propose a synthesis of the two. It is our view that neither approach by itself is adequate to the task of explaining women's experiences in engineering. In the chapters that follow we develop an argument about the specific ways in which these two spheres of social reality intersect in the careers of engineers. In order to lay the groundwork for that discussion, we first examine the major features of the gender-role and structural perspectives, and preview our synthesis of the two.

THE GENDER-ROLE PERSPECTIVE

The gender-role perspective underlies two of the major theories that have been used to explain women's work force status: status attainment theory in sociology, and human capital theory in economics. In addition, much of the research of psychologists and social psychologists on women in the work force assumes this perspective as well.

American sociologists have for the past two decades relied primarily on status attainment theory to explain occupational status and mobility (Blau and Duncan 1967; Ornstein 1976; Sewell and Hauser 1975). Its proponents argue that occupational status is determined by the characteristics one brings into the labor market. Socioeconomic background (usually defined as father's occupation) and educational achievement are the primary determinants, with education being the most important. Although this work concerns itself largely with male status attainment, when women *have* been studied, the findings have been consistent with those for men. That is, women from higher socioeconomic backgrounds, and with higher levels of education, are found in higher status jobs than other women (DeJong, Brawer, and Robin 1971; Treiman and Terrell 1975; McClendon 1976).

Some of these studies have acknowledged the existence of sex-linked occupational segregation and pay inequality, noting that the higher status jobs held by women receive fewer rewards than the higher status jobs held by men (Treiman and Terrell 1975; Featherman and Hauser 1976; McClendon 1976). Status attainment theorists explain these patterns in terms of gender-role socialization. Drawing on Talcott Parsons's functionalist theory of the family (Parsons and Bales 1955), they argue that young men and women internalize different sets of values and aspirations regarding educational and occupational achievement, and regarding the relative importance of family and work activities. For women, the family role is primary, while for men it is the work role. As a result, women exhibit less commitment to the work force, being less likely to seek paid employment, and less likely to work continuously. Moreover, they choose occupations that are less demanding, and therefore more compatible with their family responsibilities. They also choose occupations that involve gender-appropriate (i.e., nurturant, subordinate) activities (Featherman and Hauser 1976; McClendon 1976; Mathaei 1982).

The counterpart of this theory in economics, which has also been influential among sociologists, is human capital theory. According to this perspective, the willingness of individuals to invest in "human capital" such as education, training, and continuity of employment is the major determinant of occupational rewards (Becker 1964; Thurow 1970; Mincer and Polacheck 1974). Sex differences in pay and job type are the result of women's smaller investments in human capital. This, in turn, is explained by their primary commitment to the family, which leads them to limit their human capital investments (Becker 1973), and to seek jobs that demand little commitment and do not penalize them for intermittent work patterns (Sawhill 1973).

Gender-Socialization Research

Both of these theories assume that the underlying force shaping women's (and men's) work behaviors is their gender-role socialization. This assertion finds support in a growing body of research that has illuminated the ways in which gender socialization in the family, schools, and other institutions shapes work-related behaviors and attitudes (Joffe 1971; Hochschild 1973; Maccoby and Jacklin 1974; Rheingold and Cook 1975; Sario, Jacklin, and Tittle 1973; Lever 1978; Weitzman 1979; Gilligan 1982). To begin with, boys and girls learn quite early to view occupations as "male" or "female," and to shape their aspirations accordingly. They carry these perceptions into adulthood (Marini and Brinton 1984; Betz and Fitzgerald 1987).

Moreover, gender socialization encourages men to develop personality characteristics "associated with competency, instrumentality, and achievement" (Betz and Fitzgerald 1987:30). Young boys are oriented toward a future of paid employment, and are taught the importance of "mechanical, technical, and mathematical skills, . . . emotional individuation, and physical and emotional toughness" (England and Farkas 1986:87).

While young girls today see paid employment in their future, their socialization still places primary emphasis on the family role. They are encouraged to develop attributes of nurturance, sensitivity, emotional expressiveness, and physical attractiveness. They emerge from this process with less confidence in their achievement-related abilities, and lower expectancies for success than their male peers (Maccoby and Jacklin 1974; Stake 1979). This appears to be especially true in regard to male-identified activities (Gitelson, Petersen, and Tobin-Richards 1982; Deaux 1984).

As a result, both men and women expect men to be competent, instrumental, assertive, and competitive in the workplace, and to be career-oriented. On the other hand, women are expected by both sexes to be expressive, emotional, and nonassertive, and to value family over career (Broverman, et al. 1972; Hartnett 1977; Sokoloff 1981).

Parsons and other functionalist sociologists saw the outcome of this process as beneficial to society as a whole. Men and women each do "what they do best," and everyone prospers: the individual, the family, and the society (Parsons and Bales 1955). More recent formulations of the gender-role perspective argue that traditional patterns of gender socialization are dysfunctional, wasting human talent and forcing people into roles that may not suit them (Metcalfe 1985; Ireson and Gill 1988). What both interpretations share, however, is an emphasis on the importance of socialization and gender role behaviors as the major source of sex-linked inequality in the work force. As such, their work lends support to the arguments of status attainment and human capital theorists.

Applying these theories to the movement of women into non-traditional occupations, they suggest that a woman would face significant obstacles to her success in those positions, because of the incompatibility of her gender-role orientation to the demands of a male-dominated occupation. She may opt for the less demanding areas of training within the occupation, thus limiting her prospects for mobility and high pay. She may show less commitment to a continuous career, leaving the work force for several years to care for children. She may be unable or unwilling to adopt the aggressive and competitive behaviors of her male co-workers, thus losing out in the struggle for advancement. In addition, she may suffer the hostility and discriminatory treatment of men who resent the violation of appropriate gender roles represented by her presence.[3]

Most analysts of women and engineering have used the gender-role perspective. They have argued that, in addition to the general incompatibility of the female role with professional work, engineering presents special obstacles to women. Engineering is a "thing-oriented" occupation, but "women strongly prefer fields in which they work with people rather than things" (Rossi 1965:1201). Moreover, male engineers are "narrow of interest, stolid, uninterested in cultural things, and not inclined to general intellectual pursuits." In contrast, academically oriented women are characterized by "broad interests, emotional sensitiveness, responsiveness to art and literature, and . . . tolerance of intellectual creativity" (Robin 1969). Moreover, the close identification of technical work with masculinity creates a special contradiction for women. As a result, women engineers express ambivalence toward technical expertise, while men value it highly (Bailyn 1987).

Earlier studies of women who became engineering students and engineers found considerable prejudice and hostility from faculty, students, and co-workers (Bugliarello et al. 1971; Ott and Reese 1975; Hacker 1983). Findings like these have led researchers to conclude that the socialization patterns of both women and men will continue to limit the number of women entering the profession, and will hamper the careers of those who do (Rossi 1965; Perrucci 1970; Burks 1975).

Consistent with these analyses, proposals for change have emphasized the need to alter early socialization patterns, to provide role models and better career counseling for women, and to provide more flexible working conditions for women with families (Rossi 1965; Bugliarello et al. 1971; Ott and Reese 1975).

THE STRUCTURAL PERSPECTIVE

The gender-role perspective, while popular, has been subjected to considerable criticism. A variety of studies have shown that gender socialization alone can explain neither the status nor the behavior of women and men in the workplace. Structural features of the workplace and the larger social system are often more important determinants. For example, historical studies have shown that women's labor force participation, and their choice of particular occupations, is highly responsive to the demand for their labor (Oppenheimer 1970; Glenn and Feldberg 1979; Strober 1984). Opportunities to enter the labor force—or particular occupations—may increase as a result of war, economic expansion, or changes in public policy. Women always respond to these opportunities, often violating gender-role expectations in the process. This happened in World War II, when women were needed to fill "men's jobs" in the factories (Milkman 1987). It happened again in the 1970s when legislation forced the doors of law and medical schools open to women. Despite traditional socialization patterns, women poured in to take advantage of these new opportunities (Epstein 1983). Similarly, when changes in the economy (e.g., high rates of inflation or unemployment) or in family structure (e.g., rising divorce rates) create greater need for the earnings of women, they increase their work force participation in response.

Other studies have shown that the characteristics of jobs are better predictors of work-related attitudes and behaviors than is gender. Jobs that provide real opportunities for mobility and power elicit high levels of commitment and aspiration in both women and men (Gordon 1972; Kanter 1977). Jobs that offer autonomy promote a self-directed orientation (Kohn and Schooler 1983). If women display these traits less commonly than men, it is because the jobs open to them offer fewer incentives to do so. What at first appears to be socialized gender behavior is instead an artifact of the limited opportunities available to women.

Analyses of the relationship between education and earnings show that, while educational achievement pays off in higher earnings for all groups, the payoff is substantially greater for white males than for minorities and women (U.S. Dept. of Labor 1980). In addition, studies that have compared male-female earnings while controlling for a variety of other "human capital" variables (e.g., job-specific training, years and continuity of experience) have been able to account for (at best) less than half the pay gap (Bibb and Form 1977;

Treiman and Hartmann 1981; England 1984). Thus, if we are to understand the occupational status of women, we need to look beyond their gender role characteristics and their investments in human capital.

This diverse group of findings lays the groundwork for an alternative to the gender-role perspective. From a structural perspective, the occupational behavior and status of women and men is determined not so much by the characteristics they bring with them into the workplace, but by the structures they encounter there and in the larger society. Those structures have operated historically to limit women's participation in the work force to low-status jobs, and to reproduce behaviors and attitudes consistent with those positions (Hartman 1976; Anderson 1988; Taylor 1988).

This approach has yielded important insights into the structural basis of work force behaviors and status. It recognizes that human behavior is situationally produced, not just in the early years of family and school socialization, but throughout the life span as we move through a variety of organizational settings. Occupational outcomes are shaped by the structural characteristics of jobs, work groups, organizations, families, and the larger political-economic system.

The structural perspective is not without its problems, however. While insightful, it leaves important questions unanswered. Why are *women* the ones most likely to be found in those low-status, low-mobility jobs that reduce commitment and aspirations? If rewards attach to positions rather than to individuals, why do women who start off in positions comparable to men receive fewer rewards over time? This is a problem documented for women in engineering (Perrucci 1970), and in other nontraditional occupations as well (Brown 1981; Epstein 1983; Rosenfeld 1984).

One answer to these questions provided by a major structural theorist is only partially satisfactory. Kanter (1977) explains the difficulties women face in nontraditional jobs in terms of the dynamics of tokenism. When a woman enters an all male work group, her colleagues judge her more critically and closely, and see her as a woman rather than a co-worker—all of which tend to work against her. The treatment she receives, however, is due not to the fact that she is a woman, but that she is a token (an 0 in a world of Xs). The nature of group dynamics is such that any token would receive similar treatment.

Similarly, she argues that the movement of women into management from the clerical ranks is hindered not by their gender, but by the contradictory requirements of the two positions. To display the qualities of a good secretary (order-taking, subordination, risk avoidance, and a narrow view of the organization) is by definition to display one's lack of suitability for management.

However, these arguments are contradicted by other research that suggests that gender does have an independent impact on occupational experience. For example, there is evidence that male tokens in predominantly female jobs do not experience the same problems, and do not display the same attitudes, as female tokens (Schreiber 1979; Fairhust and Snavely 1983; Zimmer 1988).

Moreover, to identify job requirements as the source of women's occupational status is to beg the question of the *origin* of those requirements. Why, for example, are "good secretaries" and "good managers" defined in those particular—and contradictory—ways? Other studies have documented informal gender bias in hiring and promotion decisions, when objective qualifications of male and female candidates are identical (Betz and Fitzgerald 1987). Thus, there is more at work here than the dynamics of impersonal structures.

A CONFLICT-STRUCTURAL PERSPECTIVE

The structural perspective as we have outlined it operates within the theoretical assumptions of functionalism. Many structural theorists—Kanter included—see a workplace as an impersonal structure, operating in response to its own organizational imperatives, and to the demands of an equally impersonal "environment." The structure and processes of the organization and its subunits (occupations, work groups) shape the behavior and attitudes of individual members. Yet the origin of those structures and processes is left unexamined.

What is missing in this approach is attention to relations of power and self-interest in the organization. Without an understanding of the different groups staffing the organization, and the resources and interests of each, we cannot fully understand the experiences of women in nontraditional occupations. The fact that they are women *does* matter. It is not just the organization, job structures, and small group dynamics with which they must contend. They must also contend with the men who dominate the organization, and who have an interest in maintaining their positions of power and privilege. Thus, it is not enough to examine the structures that shape occupational outcomes. We must look as well to the relations of power that have created and maintained those structures. Only in that context can we understand why particular structures exist, and why the experiences of women and men within them are so often different.

Our approach is also structural, but it is a structuralism grounded in conflict theory rather than functionalism. From a conflict perspective, organizations are "arenas for conflicting interests" (Collins 1975:289), populated by individuals and groups seeking power, status, and economic rewards (Crozier 1964; Perrow 1979; Zey-Ferrell and Aiken 1981). Those with greater organizational resources are able to use them to protect and extend their positions of privilege.

Occupational mobility within such an arena requires both formal and informal resources. Possession of objective prerequisites (academic degrees, background in technical areas, a proven track record in project management, etc.) is only part of the story. Also important are interactional skills such as self-confidence, assertiveness, and self-promotion. Organizations, at least in part, are constituted by relationships between people. Individuals who can manage these relationships well—who are able to impress others with their abilities and talents—are in possession of a resource every bit as valuable as an academic degree or technical expertise (Goffman 1959; Collins 1975; Derber 1979).

Work organizations are also dominated by men, who as a group have an interest in—and the resources for—maintaining their power. This point has been developed both by socialist feminist (Hartmann 1976; Eisenstein 1979; Sokoloff 1981) and conflict theorists (Collins 1991). Given their male dominance, work organizations—especially the powerful positions within them—have long been imbued with a male-identified culture. That is, the values and interactional styles necessary to the achievement of power in the organization parallel the male gender role, with its emphasis on competition, aggression, and single-minded devotion to career (McGregor 1967; Fox and Hesse-Biber 1984).

Our approach to workplace culture draws on both conflict and interactionist discussions of cultural reproduction. The conflict approach to culture focuses on the power relations that allow the values of some groups to become dominant (Collins 1979; Gusfield 1972, 1981; Bourdieu and Passeron 1977; Bordieu 1984). From this perspective, to understand how a culture functions, one must not only describe its values, norms, and styles of discourse, but the relations of power in back of them. Culture is a force in its own right, but one which is itself a function of larger relations of domination. A workplace culture creates an orderly set of practices so that work can be carried out. But it also reflects the differential power of workers, managers, and owners.

Culture is also a force that manifests itself through day-to-day activities and interactions (Goffman 1959, 1967, 1979; Collins 1975, 1981; Derber 1979; Cicourel and Mehan 1985). To believe in a value or conform to a norm is meaningful only insofar as it is obvious to others, and it becomes obvious in interaction. Culture lies in the rituals of day-to-day conformity: the forms of talk, styles of interaction, and modes of dress that signal our belief in it. Culture in this sense is a form of "impression management": we act in such a way as to create an impression in others that we are adhering to a set of values (Goffman 1959, 1967).

This is where the gender-role perspective becomes important. Socialization provides women and men with different interactional resources that they bring with them into the workplace. Those resources do not determine career success directly, however. Instead, they interact with the relations of power and self-interest around which the organization is structured. To the extent that job requirements and career paths are dominated by the interests of men, they will emphasize and reward male gender behaviors. Women, because they display different behaviors, are seen as ill suited for important positions. Therefore, both the structure of organizational power and the culture that flows from that structure tend to favor males for positions yielding high levels of pay, authority, and status, and relegate women to subordinate and poorly rewarded positions.

While work organizations are male-dominated, it also must be said that they are not always male-dominated in the same ways or to the same degree. It is on this point that we distinguish ourselves from some feminist theorists (e.g., Hartmann 1976). Where they posit the existence of an undifferentiated "patriarchy," we argue that it is necessary to look more closely at the structure of particular organizations.[4] Our data suggest that women engineers are more likely to succeed in some workplaces than others, despite the fact that all are male-dominated. What differentiates these organizations is the degree of bureaucratic formalism, the power held by engineers, and the workplace culture that results. Where organization structures and power relations favor women's interests, their gender-linked interactional styles matter less. Where patterns of structure and power work against women, however, their inability to conform to the male-defined culture of the workplace contributes to their subordinate status there.

Finally, there is yet another structure that we must consider if we are to understand women's careers. Theories of organization structure—whether functionalist or conflict—are often too narrow in focus. Socialist feminists, in particular, have argued that to understand women's experiences in the workplace, it is necessary to look beyond it (Hartmann 1976; Sokoloff 1981). Women's subordinate status in the workplace is intimately linked to their subordinate status in the family. Because housework and child care are defined primarily as women's responsibility, men benefit as husbands. They are freed from those tasks, and allowed to concentrate on occupational success. Their greater status and power over their wives is reinforced, since women's family responsibilities limit their ability to pursue high status careers. Men benefit as co-workers, as well, when women's careers are constrained by their family roles.

This view shares some common ground with gender-role theories, which, as we have seen, assert a link between family and work roles. However, socialist feminists—and conflict theorists more generally—formulate the relationship between family and workplace differently. Gender-role theorists see socialized gender characteristics as the primary cause of women's status in both the family and the workplace. Socialist-feminist and conflict theorists focus instead on the ways in which relations of power in the family, the workplace, and political system interact with each other in shaping women's opportunities. It is not gender socialization, but the system of male dominance, that keeps women "in their place." The family, as a set of power relations and as a socializing agency, plays a crucial role in shaping women's status in the workplace. But the attitudes and behaviors women learn in the family are products—as much as causes—of women's subordinate position in both spheres.

In the chapters that follow, we explore the ways in which gender roles and social structures interact to shape the careers of women in engineering. First, however, we examine the profession itself, and the culture associated with it.

THE CULTURE OF ENGINEERING

We have argued that power relations in the workplace allow men to create a cultural climate favoring their interests and their gender-based styles of interaction. Let us tie this discussion more specifically to engineering. Our point of departure is the work of Sally Hacker (1981, 1983). Hacker studied the students and faculty of an east coast engineering institute and found a set of values shared by the men there. She describes a "culture of engineering"—a professional ideology—that stresses the importance of technology over personal relationships; of formal abstract knowledge (particularly complicated math) over inexact humanistic knowledge; and ultimately of male over female traits (Hacker 1981). She argues that this culture is based on a mind/body dualism that stresses the superiority of (rational) thought over (bodily) emotions. This dualism identifies rationality with men, and emotion with women. The culture of engineering places particular stress on the importance of mathematical ability. Math is both the most complicated and the purest form of mental activity. It is also the most "masculine" of subjects.

Hacker's discussion of the culture of engineering is little more than a rough draft of a concept. She is vague about how this culture is produced, and she fails to recognize differences between the university and the workplace. She describes not *the* culture of engineering, but *a* culture of engineering. She accurately describes the value set promulgated in major American universities by university professors. But she generalizes her findings to the profession as a whole. Consequently, she overemphasizes the importance of science, math, and abstraction, while ignoring the orientations of engineers in the workplace.

Our own approach to the culture of engineering draws on the conflict approach to organizations outlined above. The "culture of engineering" consists of the norms and values regarding "correct engineering practice," as defined by (male) engineers. It is created and maintained by the power of engineers in the workplace (or the university) and manifested through daily patterns of interaction. More specifically, the culture of engineering consists of three components. First, and most important, it is an ideology that stresses the centrality of technology, and of engineers as producers of this technology. Second, it stresses the acquisition of organizational power as the base of engineering success. Finally, it requires that interest in technology and organizational power be interactionally "presented" in an appropriate form—a form closely tied to the male gender role. We discuss each of these in turn.

As with any occupational group, engineers share an interest in solidifying their power and prestige within the production process. This means defining ideological relations at work so as to guarantee the prestige and status of engineers. The key for this group is technical knowledge. Engineers alone possess abstract technical knowl-

edge, and it is they above all who benefit from the valuation of this knowledge. Thus, establishing a work environment that is technically oriented, in which technical innovation and creativity is highly valued, and in which promotions are based on displays of technical competence, are their primary concerns.

The emphasis on technology includes not just the abstract and innovative; it extends as well to the more basic and hands-on. Engineers display a fascination with tools, machinery, and gadgets that is more than just a means to an end. There is a strong sense in this culture that the "good engineer" is more than competent in this area; he is obsessed.

This is not to say that engineers are not interested in their organizations, or even that technology is valued to the exclusion of organizational influence. Most engineers *are* oriented toward power in their organizations (Goldner and Ritti 1967; Perrucci 1973; Zussman 1985; Whalley 1986). The means for achieving this power, however, is through control over technology. In our sample there was no contradiction between orientation toward technology and toward the organization. Engineers who stressed the importance of technology were also those most likely to desire organizationally important work (tau c = .13; p=.001). The culture of engineering stresses the centrality of technology to the workplace, and therefore the importance of engineers as producers of that technology. This culture is the means by which engineers attempt to inflate the importance of the "cultural capital" that only they hold (Bourdieu and Passeron 1977). It is the ideology through which they pursue organizational power and influence.

More specifically, this ideology is an important means through which engineers rise into management. The ability to guarantee access to management can be seen as part of a process that Collins (1975, 1979) has referred to as the creation of occupational properties. If high-level management comes to believe that only engineers can manage other engineers, or that engineers make the best managers because of their technical knowledge, this clearly adds to the professional privileges of the occupation, and in that sense expands the occupational boundaries of engineering.

The culture of engineering, however, has to do with more than just the importance of technology and organizational power. As we see in chapter 6, it also values behaviors and orientations consistent with the male gender role. It is here that the gender-role perspective discussed above becomes important. Competence as an engineer is a function of how well one presents an image of an aggressive, competitive, technically oriented person. The *style* of this interactional presentation is as important as its substance. Here gender roles are important. To be taken as an engineer is to look like an engineer, talk like an engineer, and act like an engineer. In most workplaces this means looking, talking, and acting male. Of particular importance in this presentation of self is the image of hands-on competence. There are few things more closely tied to the male gender role than mechanical activities—using tools, tearing apart machinery, and building things. A fascination with, and desire to talk at length about, these activities is part of the interactional display of the culture of engineering that works against women.

The culture of any particular workplace is a function of the relations of power in that organizational setting. The power of engineers—and of the culture of engineering—is limited by organizational structure and the power of management. The interests of engineers always have impact, but not always to the same degree. The culture of engineering is most extensive where the power of engineers is greatest. It is limited where the power of other groups—managers, workers—or organizational requirements interfere with engineer prerogatives.

Success or failure as an engineer is partly determined by how well one maneuvers through the workplace culture. We argue that women experience the least amount of occupational mobility in environments where the workplace is dominated by the culture of engineering, and the greatest amount where the culture of engineering is less pervasive. Where engineers as a group are powerful, the workplace culture takes on a form strongly identified with the male gender role, emphasizing aggressive displays of technical self-confidence and hands-on ability as the criteria for success. As such, it devalues the gender attributes of women, and defines professional competence in strictly "masculine" terms.

On the other hand, in workplaces where engineers are less powerful, the practice of engineering less closely reflects the interests of engineers. This tends to mitigate the emphasis on male-defined displays of technical competence, to the benefit of women. As a result, women succeed because they face a less male-defined professional culture. As we shall see, in highly bureaucratized workplaces, criteria such as time on the job and formal credentials count for more than aggressive displays of technical ability. This improves women's chances of promotion.

It is through this concept of the culture of engineering that we synthesize the structural and gender role perspectives outlined earlier. Gender roles play an important part in our discussion, because they determine in no small part the content of the culture of engineering. But the ability to maintain these gender-based values and forms of interaction depend on the power of engineers. This power, in turn, depends on the structure of the workplace.

The nature and extent of the culture of engineering, therefore, depends on the particular organizational context. In the chapters that follow, we explore this culture and its impact on women in two major organizational settings: the university and the workplace. Before we do so, however, we need to see how these women found their way to engineering in the first place. It is to this discussion that we now turn.

3

PATHS TO ENGINEERING

These were "good girls." Conscientious and disciplined, they were the kind of daughters for which middle-class parents hope. They did their homework and turned it in on time. They were more than just conscientious, however. If there was one thing that set this group apart from so many other good girls that the American middle class has produced, it was their academic performance. They did well in all their classes, but it was in the sciences, and particularly math, that they really stood out.

Though they would eventually enter the most male-dominated profession, these were not gender role rebels. They were involved in nobody's revolution, and were not used to knocking on closed doors or trying to go where parents and teachers told them not to. They were, in fact, quite traditional in their orientations. These young women had both feet on the ground. They had been told, and sincerely believed, that having a stable career, particularly one that would allow a home and family, was what a "good girl" should do.

It is more than a little surprising to find young women like these choosing to enter such a nontraditional occupation as engineering. The gender role perspective discussed in the previous chapter would lead us to expect few women in engineering, and there are. It would also lead us to expect that those who do enter this male-identified field would be gender role rebels: women who somehow escaped or defied the traditional process of socialization. For most of our sample, nothing could be further from the truth. As we shall see, there is no inevitable path from gender role socialization to occupational choice. Whether a young woman becomes an engineer or not has less to do with gender socialization and more to do with academic resources and the structure of opportunities.

In this chapter we examine the factors that produced the initial orientation toward engineering among the women in our sample. We discuss their academic abilities, their practical orientation, the importance of personal relationships, and the social context in which their choices were made. We will see in later chapters that these factors continue to shape their experiences through college and the early years of their careers as well.

Moving up in any occupation is difficult, but it is especially so for a woman entering a nontraditional profession like engineering. We are particularly interested, therefore, in the resources and liabilities that affect a woman's ability to compete. Our data suggest that the paths into engineering are not the same for men and women. Each enter the profession with a distinct set of orientations and abilities. In simplest terms, men become engineers because of a strong orientation toward technology and tinkering, while women are attracted to it because of their strong mathematical skills. These different starting points, in combination with other factors, have a lasting impact on the engineering careers of women and men.

RESOURCES ON THE PATH TO ENGINEERING

Math and Science

Excellence in math and science was a primary factor propelling our female respondents toward engineering. This distinguished them sharply from the men in our sample. When asked why they went into engineering, the three reasons most cited by men were: they had been tinkerers as children; their fathers or other family members had encouraged them; or they had been interested in mechanics or electronics[5]. For women the reasons most often given were: they had been good at math and science; engineering was a practical choice, given its high pay and the abundance of jobs; or they had fathers or other family members who encouraged them (see Table 1).

With the exception of family influences, there is little similarity

TABLE 1
Reasons for Engineering as a Career Choice

Reason	Women	Men
Good at math or science		
N	40	5
Percent	(80)	(17)
Engineering was practical		
N	39	6
Percent	(78)	(20)
Tinkerer		
N	8	17
Percent	(16)	(57)
Interested in mechanics/ electronics		
N	7	8
Percent	(14)	(27)
Father/Family		
N	24	15
Percent	(48)	(50)
Teacher		
N	16	1
Percent	(32)	(3)
Friends		
N	9	3
Percent	(18)	(10)

between the reasons given by women and men. Only 20 percent of the men said they had gone into engineering for practical reasons, and a mere 17 percent cited their skills in math and science. On the other hand, only 16 percent of the women said that tinkering had led them to engineering, and 14 percent cited an interest in mechanics or electronics. Women were drawn to engineering above all because they had done well in math and science; men because they had been tinkerers.

For a man entering the profession of engineering, the process is a "natural" one. It is as if society, their families, and their own personal orientations conspire to point them in this direction. Engineering is an occupation strongly identified with the male gender role, associated as it is with mechanical activity and the creation of technology. Many of our male respondents had fathers who were engineers, scientists, or mechanics. As boys they were in love with machinery or electronics. From the moment they entered school, many knew exactly what they wanted: engineering. Their teachers were more than happy to aid them on a journey with so little ambiguity.

These boys were by and large bright kids, but that was not what distinguished them as a group. Rather, it was their passion for tinkering and technology. Cars, computers, airplanes, stereos, radios—anything that moved or was plugged into an outlet—fascinated them. They loved taking things apart and putting them back together again. Like so many other boys, their socialization had engendered in them a love of tinkering. They did well in school, too. They were good students, but with grease under their fingernails. It was their tinkering orientation and the compatibility of engineering with their developing gender identity that paved such a smooth path for them.

For women the story was quite different. The path to engineering was less obvious and less "natural" for them. Few were tinkerers, and fewer yet had rebuilt a car engine or taken apart a television set. But when it came to school work, and particularly math and science, they excelled. They were more than just competent in school; they were outstanding. It was their academic skills more than anything else that made engineering a possibility for them, despite its male-identified image.

To understand the importance of these abilities to women's entry into engineering, we must briefly discuss the nature of engineering education. Our point of departure is the concept of credentialism. There has been a great deal of research over the last few years exploring the importance of education to occupational achievement. Educational requirements, argue the theorists of credentialism, function not merely as a means of creating a technically competent labor force, but as a means of controlling access to high paying occupations (Collins 1975,1979; Parkin 1979; Johnson 1972; Larson 1977). When eight years of postgraduate training is required of medical students, for example, the result is not only a highly skilled medical profession, but one in which students with middle-class backgrounds will predominate. The time, money, and interpersonal skills required to navigate through this series of classes, exams, and internships favor individuals with the cultural and economic resources that a middle-class background supplies.

This process of creating educational barriers to middle-class jobs is at the heart of credentialism. Professional education is as important for the people it excludes as for the knowledge it imparts. It is a means, above all else, of controlling a labor market.

Our interviews suggest that much of the training received by engineers in college functions as a credential barrier of this sort. When we asked our respondents how much of their math they currently used, the overwhelming majority said it was a tiny proportion. For most, math was used fairly often on the job, but it was low-level math: usually no more than basic algebra.

In the pursuit of an engineering credential, however, math is the most important hurdle. It is the "critical filter" (Hacker 1983) that limits access to engineering by weeding out the largest number of students. As one of our respondents put it: "If you have problems with mathematics, you're gonna have problems with engineering. With the schooling. Maybe not out in the field, but with the schooling you will."

Math courses have to be taken at the right time and in the right sequence. Advanced math is impossible without calculus; calculus cannot be taken before trigonometry; trigonometry requires a knowledge of geometry and algebra; and so forth. It is the cumulative nature of math courses that makes them so crucial for survival in engineering school. It means that at each stage of the preparation process (junior high school, high school, lower division, and upper division), the flexibility and accessibility of the engineering track decreases.

This makes precollege academic preparation particularly important. While deficits in math and science can theoretically be made up in college, it is extremely difficult to do so. There is, therefore, a relatively narrow window of opportunity for entering the engineering educational track. Simply having taken the right math and science classes in junior and senior high school is a tremendous resource.

For example, one of our female respondents was initially oriented toward music. She had been a talented musician, and had won a number of musical honors while still in high school—but she was also very good at math, and had taken all the available courses in it. By the time she graduated from high school, she was worried about the practicality of a music major. She was particularly concerned about finding work after college, and had begun to look for a more practical option:

> It was sort of a funny transition. I was in music and I had always kept up with math courses. . . . I was thinking of what you get if you combine music and math, and I didn't want to go into applied music, or applied math, because it would have the same

kinds of problems as music [no jobs]. . . . So what do you get when you combine them—the only thing I could think was acoustics. . . . I contacted the Acoustical Society of America, and they sent a whole list of schools, and which courses they offered in acoustics. And I just applied to the two that had the most courses.

She applied to two engineering schools. She was accepted at both, chose the one that had the best music department, and became an engineering major. Music eventually lost out to engineering. This choice, however, would have been impossible had she not had a good background in math.

For our purposes, these math (and science) skills are best understood as a resource valuable in the pursuit of an engineering credential. With this resource in hand, a young woman or man can choose engineering. Without it, regardless of intrinsic abilities or interests, a young person has little possibility of entering the pipeline that leads to engineering. The women in engineering today were able to choose that profession because they had persisted in math.

Parental Backgrounds

We do not know just why these young women pursued math and science, when so many other middle-class daughters do not. It could be that their innate talents in this area were too obvious to ignore, and that their parents and teachers had little choice but to encourage them. The fact that they were growing up in the 1970s rather than the 1940s or 50s made it more likely that such talents would be recognized. The women's movement had made that possible, though not inevitable.

Another explanation has to do with the social class backgrounds of these women. Historically, engineering often provided a route into the middle class for the sons of the working class. This is much less true today, however. Most engineers now come from middle-class families. This is certainly true of our respondents. Seventy-eight percent of the sample had fathers in professional, technical, managerial, or sales occupations (see Table 2). The only gender difference was that women were more likely than men to have professional fathers.

Women and men were also quite similar in their mothers' occupations (see Table 2). The majority of both groups had housewife mothers, though this was more common for men than for women. Of

TABLE 2
Parent's Occupational Background: Sample as a Whole, Men/Women

Occupation	Father's Occupation			Mother's Occupation		
	Sample	*Men*	*Women*	*Sample*	*Men*	*Women*
Professional						
N	179	138	41	70	52	18
Percent	(45.8)	(43.8)	(53.9)	(17.7)	(16.4)	(23.4)
Managerial						
N	76	63	13	12	10	2
Percent	(19.4)	(20.0)	(17.1)	(3.0)	(3.1)	(2.6)
Technical or sales						
N	50	41	9	14	11	3
Percent	(12.8)	(13.0)	(11.8)	(3.5)	(3.5)	(3.9)
Clerical						
N	5	5	0	48	37	11
Percent	(1.3)	(1.6)	(0.0)	(12.2)	(11.6)	(14.3)
Craft						
N	35	27	8	0	0	0
Percent	(9.0)	(8.6)	(10.5)	(0.0)	(0.0)	(0.0)
Operative						
N	32	27	5	9	8	1
Percent	(8.2)	(8.6)	(6.6)	(2.3)	(2.5)	(1.3)
Service						
N	7	7	0	5	4	1
Percent	(1.8)	(2.2)	(0.0)	(1.3)	(1.3)	(1.3)
Laborer						
N	7	7	0	0	0	0
Percent	(1.8)	(2.2)	(0.0)	(0.0)	(0.0)	(0.0)
Housewife						
N	0	0	0	237	196	41
Percent	(0.0)	(0.0)	(0.0)	(60.0)	(61.6)	(53.2)
Total	391	315	76	395	318	77
	(100.0)	(80.6)	(19.4)	(100.0)	(80.5)	(19.5)
Kendall's tau-c		$-.07$			$-.06$	
Significance		(.05)			(.07)	

the mothers who were employed, the largest groups were in professional and clerical occupations. Here again, the women were more likely than the men to have had professional mothers.

Thus, while both men and women were children of the middle class, the women were especially likely to be children of the *professional* middle class. If there is any group of parents who would recognize and encourage a daughter's ability in math and science, it would be this group. Academically trained and oriented themselves, we could expect them to encourage the academic performance of their daughters, and to urge them to pursue fields of study in which they excelled, even fields considered nontraditional for women. Indeed, we heard from many of the women we interviewed that their parents expected them to do well in all their studies, and took it for granted that they would go on to college. Most of these parents did not specifically encourage their daughters to become engineers, but the expectation of academic success easily translated into taking more of the classes in which they did best: math and science.

Practical Orientations

Along with their skills in math and science, a second major reason given by women for going into engineering was its practicality. These were the very practical daughters of middle-class families. They were academically gifted, but they were also believers in the bottom line. They wanted to know which occupations were in greatest demand, and which paid the best. To the question, "What made you decide on engineering?," one woman responded:

> Well, I liked mathematics and was very good at it. And they started asking me "Well, what are you going to do with yourself?" I said, "I don't know. What pays the most?" They said, "Engineering." I said, "Okay, I'll do that." . . . I want(ed) lots of money, a Porsche, a dog and a goldfish. All those things that make life important.

By the late 1970s when most of these women were making their career choice, there was a great deal of publicity about the need for engineers. This was the period when high tech entered the public vocabulary, and media attention turned to Silicon Valley. Chips and Apples—neither of them edible—were topics of cocktail party conversation. It was the era of silicon and of Steve Jobs, and of the money to be made in technology. Lots and lots of money. The blush was not yet off the high tech rose. There had been no layoffs in Silicon Valley, and it seemed that the computer industry would be a limitless source of high-paying jobs:

> I had a strong interest and a strong talent in mathematics, problem solving type things, and that was in 1979, right? You know, there's a lot of media stuff about how engineers were doing real well, and there's a real strong need for engineers, so that influenced me to choose engineering.

The practicality of these women also led them into engineering rather than into science or medicine. Medicine was an attractive field for many of them because of its high pay and status, but it required a long period of preparation. Moreover, if one failed to get into medical school, the options left were few. Engineering, in contrast, was a career offering high pay, available jobs, and a short period of preparation. As one woman told us:

> I always wanted to be in science, from the time I was young, although originally I thought I wanted to go to med school. That's why I chose CEU.[6] But when I got there and started getting a better idea of what else there was to do, I called myself undeclared. . . . I still liked the sciences, but as I started approaching the decision to pick a major, I wanted to be sure I picked something I could find work in. . . . [If I didn't get into med school] I probably would work as a lab technician and wouldn't enjoy—you know, thinking five years past college—I would probably be very frustrated. . . . My fiancé was my study partner during the general ed stuff, and he was very interested in engineering, and it kind of scared me. I didn't really know what it meant. But I went to a couple of seminars with him, and started listening to what people were talking about. It sounded very interesting. So I decided to try it, given that I could get a job when I got out and still use the scientific kinds of things.

Some of this practicality can be traced to our respondent's traditional gender role orientations. Most of them assumed that they would marry and raise a family, and that they would have primary responsibility for child rearing. Engineering was doubly practical, because not only did it pay well, it was a job that they could combine with children. Unlike medicine or science, engineering is largely a nine to five occupation. Ironically, their traditional gender roles, combined with their math skills, led these women, not to a "woman's" field, but to one of the most nontraditional professions of all.

Family, Friends, and Teachers

For both men and women, family relationships were important in the choice of engineering as a career. Both were disproportionately the children of engineers or scientists. This was especially true for women: more than a third (35%) had fathers in these occupations, compared with 27 percent of the men.

When asked which people influenced their career choice, nearly 50 percent of both men and women named a family member. For men, however, these were the only people mentioned. Only 13 percent named any other personal relationship (largely friends and teachers) as having influenced them. For women the number of influential people was much larger: 18 percent cited friends, and over 30 percent mentioned a teacher or academic counselor. We look first at the importance of engineer fathers, and then at the other personal relationships involved in women's choice of engineering.

Engineer Fathers. There are a number of reasons why women with engineer fathers might be more likely to become engineers. It is possible that girls growing up in these families would be more oriented toward technology, more comfortable dealing with it, and more likely to have had early mechanical experience than women in nonengineer families. These young women might feel pressure to become engineers in order to please their fathers, especially if they have no brothers. Both of these arguments are plausible, and for some women in our sample they were true. For the majority, however, they were not.

We had only seven women in our interview sample (13%) who could be described as "nontraditional" in their orientation toward machinery or technology. These were women who had experiences with machinery or tools as children (working on cars with their fathers, tearing apart radios, etc.), or who had been strongly oriented toward technology (having expressed a strong interest in electronics, computers, etc.). Of this group of seven, only two had fathers who were engineers, however.

For most of the women with engineer fathers this fact had little effect on their gender socialization. They received little experience with technology or tinkering at home. They did not help their fathers repair cars or fix television sets. Instead they sewed, cooked, helped their mothers around the house, and played with their girlfriends. In this sense, they differed little from other middle-class American girls.

A female mechanical engineer whose father was an engineer spoke for many in our sample when she compared her own mechanical background to that of male engineers:

> Most of the men mechanical engineers that I know, as kids worked on bikes and motorcycles and cars, and they had a lot more confidence in [their] mechanical skills. Whereas I had never dreamed of taking anything apart. It never occurred to me. I wasn't interested. I didn't have things that broke, and so I didn't worry about it.

As children they may have been more aware of engineering as an occupation than women without engineer fathers, but this awareness was abstract and vague. Most described themselves as having been ignorant about engineering. They were not really sure what engineers in general, or their dads in particular, did for a living. They knew that their fathers were involved with technology, and that they worked for large companies, but little else.

It is as if a door was jarred open for these young women, but behind it lay a world they only poorly understood. Having an engineer father meant only that the term "engineer" was not alien to them. It did not mean that they knew what engineers did, or that they had practical experience with electronics or mechanics.

Consider the example of Gina, the daughter of an electrical engineer. As a child, Gina knew her father was an engineer, but had no idea what type. He did not discuss his work with her, and she had little knowledge of what he did. In fact, she had little idea what engineers in general did, before she became one herself.

Gina was not pressured by her father to become an engineer, and had never considered the option before she entered college. Her father did all the things fathers typically do around the house, but that had little to do with Gina. She never fixed radios or repaired the car with him. She described herself as decisively nonmechanical. She loved her father, and wanted to please him, but she did so in the ways of traditional middle-class girls—getting good grades, cleaning her room, being affectionate. These did *not* include helping him tinker around the house.

When she announced her decision to major in engineering at the end of her sophomore year in college, her parents were surprised, but supportive. Her father was particularly pleased:

> I never really got parental influence. . . . I think once I announced the fact that I was going to go into engineering, my dad was ecstatic, but there was never any pressure, or desire to . . . he never said anything to me about, "you're going to be an engineer, aren't you" or "don't you want to be an engineer". . . . He never got into that kind of thing.

Like Gina, few of our respondents with engineer fathers felt direct pressure to become engineers. Their fathers were usually pleased when they decided to follow them into the profession, but, like Gina's father, surprised as well. They wanted their daughters to make something of themselves, and to choose a career that was practical. Beyond that, they provided little guidance.

This leaves us with something of an enigma. A disproportionate share of our sample were daughters of engineers, yet there does not seem to be a direct link between this fact and their choice to become engineers. The answer to this puzzle is deceptively simple. Women from these families are more apt to be *aware* of engineering, and therefore more apt to pursue it.

By the time of their arrival at college, most of these women still knew little about engineering, but, at a minimum, they knew it existed, and that it could provide a good income. This was more than most women—or even men—knew about it. Engineering does not have the prestige or social visibility among the American middle class that the traditional professions or the sciences enjoy. Bright, ambitious American college students are more apt to go into business administration, medicine, or law. In comparison to Europe or Asia, there is much less emphasis on science and math in the American precollege curriculum. As a result, engineering is a career choice about which college-bound students are relatively unaware. In addition, its identification with the male gender role makes it even less visible as a choice for women.

Most of the women in our sample decided on a career at the end of their sophomore year in college. At this point of indecision and confusion, so typical of the undergraduate, the fact that they were simply aware of engineering as an option made the choice more likely. The crucial resource was their math and science background, but given this, the next prerequisite was awareness of the profession. This is where the engineer father played an important role.

Friends and Teachers. Engineer fathers play a strategic role by making their daughters aware of engineering, but they are not the only ones who can do this. One of the factors differentiating men from women was the importance of personal relationships in the choice of engineering. Women were more likely than men to mention other persons as the reason for their choice of engineering. In particular, they named teachers, counselors, and friends as the source of their decision.

This difference is consistent with the gender role perspective. Women are socialized to be more concerned than men with interpersonal relations (Basow 1986). They may, therefore, rely more on the opinions of others in making a career choice, especially a nontraditional one such as engineering. But as we have seen, there is another factor involved as well: whether or not they are conscious of engineering as an option. Men have the advantage of a gender role that makes engineering a more obvious career choice. The young tinkerer is likely to become aware of engineering as if by osmosis, as he explores the world of mechanics and technology. It is unlikely that his nontinkering sister will do the same. Lacking this avenue to awareness of engineering she must reach it by another path. Other people are often the means by which she does so.

Judy, for example, had always done well in math, but she was also gifted in English. Initially, she declared herself a communications major, but she kept up with her math and science, and did well in them. By the end of her sophomore year she still did not know what she wanted to do. A friend in one of her math classes encouraged her to think about engineering. He was an engineering major, and she had been strongly impressed by him:

> He seemed very intelligent, and he really had his goals set out, and he knew where he was going, and what he wanted to do, and I felt so confused and available to anything. . . . He told me "you're taking all these classes and you enjoy them, but . . . you're not in engineering . . . " and I said I don't really know what I want to do and he said, "go talk to my [academic] counselor."

She talked to the counselor, who was very encouraging. She pointed out that Judy had completed all the engineering prerequisites, so it would be easy now to become an engineering major. If she did not like it, she could always quit. That made sense to her. Besides, the choice of engineering seemed so practical. "So, that's kind of how it happened. I never had this burning desire to be an engineer, but a lot of engineers were getting really good jobs, and a lot of communication majors weren't, so I kind of went that way just out of common sense." Carried along by the practicality of the choice, and the respect she had for her friend and the counselor, Judy made the commitment.

Thus, for women more than for men, the choice of engineering depends on the presence of someone to help them take it seriously as an option. A father, a teacher, a boyfriend, or classmate could play this role, but it has to be played by *someone*. Engineering is not an obvious alternative for most women. It takes something, or more commonly someone, to help them take it seriously.

There is a practical point to be made in this discussion of personal relationships. A concerned teacher or counselor can make a difference in the occupational choices of women who are bright and academically-oriented. Even career seminars and lectures about engineering can play an important role. Among our sample were several women who named programs like these as sources of motivation for their decisions.

These kinds of programs, however, often come too late. As we have seen, the crucial period of preparation for engineering takes place well before college. Math and science courses must be taken throughout the secondary school years. If programs or individuals are to be effective in guiding more women into engineering, they must be present at the junior high level and even in the elementary schools.

We can increase the likelihood that young women gifted in math and science will go into engineering by educating teachers and counselors to take them more seriously, and to provide them with a clear understanding of the options available to them. However, there is no reason why less talented women should not also benefit from such encouragement. After all, less talented men enter the occupation all the time. For many men, the math requirements of an engineering major are a somewhat unpleasant hurdle that must be jumped. These men are not academic superstars, but they are competent enough to squeak by. There is no reason that similarly able women should not be encouraged to do the same.

DRIFT AND DETERMINATION

There is a striking sense of drift in the process by which these women chose engineering. Where men were pushed by gender roles, social expectations, and their own inclinations, the decisions of our female respondents seemed almost accidental. Nearly 90 percent of the women we interviewed told us they had no clear idea what engineers did before they entered the field. They had little experience with machinery, and were not particularly oriented toward technology. Nearly half (48%) of the men we interviewed had already decided to become engineers before they graduated from high school. For women the proportion was 24%. The average age for women when they made the decision was 20; for men it was 16.

Most of these women drifted into engineering because they were good in math and the sciences, because someone had suggested engineering to them, and because it seemed a practical option. They were conscious of their own talent, but not sure how to utilize it. Their interest in math and science pointed them toward college and the sciences, but beyond this, they were not sure what to do. Most of them sought to make use of their talents in ways that were "sensible." Thus, they did as their fathers had done, as those around them were doing, or as others suggested.

This sense of drift conflicts with a number of previous discussions of women in nontraditional occupations (Walshok 1981; Berryman and Waite 1985). These studies explain the choice of a nontraditional occupation in terms of nontraditional gender socialization. If a woman becomes a carpenter or an auto mechanic, it is because she likes working with her hands, or is a risk-taker. These characteristics, in turn, are seen as the function of early socialization, often involving a strong relationship with an autonomous and achievement-oriented parent—usually a mother, often a single mother.

We found some women like this among our sample: women who were strongly oriented toward engineering, mechanically inclined, and who identified with an autonomous parent (here usually a father). But it surprised us how few of these there were. As we have said, most of these women were gender role traditionalists, not rebels. There are more accidental and structural factors involved in their decisions than is recognized by the gender role perspective. A woman may drift into engineering simply because she has the proper academic resources, or because a counselor takes her seriously as a potential engineer.

It is worthwhile to briefly consider one of the less traditional women as a point of contrast with the others. Jane already knew in the ninth grade that she was going to become an engineer, long before the rest of our sample had even begun to consider the option. Her father was an electrical engineer, but it was not what he did at work that drew her to engineering. It was what he did at home. Not only did he bring his work home with him, he actively encouraged her to participate. Jane was up to her elbows in tools and machinery throughout her childhood. She and her dad tore things apart and put them together again. She helped him rebuild engines and appliances.

The contrast between Jane and the rest of our sample is striking. She seemed destined to become an engineer: she was in love with technology, and as comfortable in the workshop as in the classroom. Not only was she unafraid of all-male environments, she relished the challenge of confronting them.

Jane was critical of the reasons why most other women went into engineering. She accurately pinpointed the difference between herself and most of the women in our sample:

> I think too many women are in engineering because they are good in math, and I don't really understand that. . . . [T]hey really never did anything to give themselves an idea of what engineering was. That wasn't right, because their knack wasn't there. They didn't like the material."

Jane's comments suggest that the women around her would later experience problems as a result of their ignorance about what engineers do. She was right. But the important point here is that *she* was the exception—not they. Her female classmates shared neither her tinkering orientation nor her clear-eyed view of the profession. While she was marching a straightforward route to a well-known goal, they were traveling a much less certain path.

If it is true that most women drift into engineering, however, it is also true that their choice of engineering *is* determined by larger forces. These women benefited from changes in opportunities and expectations brought about by the 1960s and the women's movement. The women in our sample were not in rebellion against the sex segregation of occupations, yet they took advantage of the earlier rebellion of others. Our respondents were used to fulfilling the expectations of parents and teachers. By the late 1970s, however, these expectations had begun to include higher status occupations for women. As bright math and science students, they were in the right place to benefit from the changes of the preceding decade. They drifted into engineering, but it was changes in social structures that created the current that pulled them.

The importance of this social context can be most clearly seen in the cases of women who became engineers later in life. Having begun their careers in traditionally female occupations (including that of housewife), they found themselves unhappy in these roles. They returned to school in the late 70s and early 80s in search of alternatives, and found themselves attracted to engineering.

Denise is a good example. She graduated with a humanities degree in 1966. As a high school student, she had briefly considered a career in engineering, but had not really taken the idea seriously. After all, it was the early 1960s, and no one else took such an idea seriously for a woman. She was good at math and science, but in college had gone into the humanities. After her divorce in the mid-1970s, she needed to support herself and her son. She knew she did not want to become a secretary—not enough money or satisfaction—but she was unsure what she did want.

She began attending a community college, drifting from class to class, unsure of herself. She took a chemistry class, did well, and the instructor took an interest in her. He encouraged her to think about chemical engineering. At the time, the idea seemed somewhat exotic, but the enthusiasm of the instructor and the sense that the occupation was a growing and important one attracted her.

She decided to transfer to PSU for her last two years, with the idea of engineering in the back of her mind. She did not declare herself an engineering major, however, because she was still uncomfortable with the idea. Her first year there, she attended a seminar that ended her indecision. As part of the PSU career orientation program, the seminar was designed to inform women of opportunities in science and engineering. As she described it, it was largely a "rah rah" session for engineering. It provided enough motivation, however, for her to take the plunge. She declared herself an engineering major shortly thereafter.

What had changed for Denise? It was not Denise herself. She had always had the idea of engineering in the back of her mind. It was the times that had done the changing. The community college instructor's enthusiasm and the career seminar were not there the first time she had gone through college. Denise was taken seriously by that instructor because women across the country were beginning to be taken seriously as scientists and engineers. The seminar would not have taken place had it not been for the decade that followed Denise's graduation in 1966. The times had changed, and Denise was drawn along by those changes.

Sociologists for years have stressed the importance of these kinds of social changes. From Karl Marx to C. Wright Mills they have struggled to fashion metaphors and measures that capture the palpable sense of social structure and the ways in which it determines the decisions of people in their day to day lives. These women are examples of this process. That they must be so talented to be taken seriously as engineering students is still a commentary on the way the cards are stacked, but it is also a demonstration of the changes in how and by whom those cards are shuffled.

These women stand at the end of a long chain of causation. Focusing merely on their own motivations and choices yields an explanation that is both partial and inaccurate. They choose, but from a set of options that is preselected. They struggle, but in an environment in which the arms of combat are already distributed. They possess talent, yet talents must be recognized by individuals and institutions. Most of these women would be horrified at the suggestion that their accomplishments were due to anything other than their own abilities. Yet no less able women in past decades have found themselves unable to realize their talents. The difference lies in changed social structures and opportunities.

GINGER: A CASE IN POINT

To conclude this chapter, we examine in greater depth the experience of one of our respondents. We will follow her throughout the remainder of this book as well. No one person can illustrate all our points, but the woman we call Ginger comes close. If anything, she illustrates some of our points too well. Most of the women in our sample were good in math, but Ginger was outstanding. Most experienced traditional gender role socialization; Ginger's was archetypically so. We use her case as a thread that unites these chapters because she illustrates our points so well, and because her story is so interesting. It is sometimes easy to become lost in all the examples and case histories presented in a book like this. Ginger provides us with the opportunity to follow one person through the process of becoming and being an engineer.

As we said, Ginger was an excellent student. Among a field of very talented women, her performance was second to none. She had a straight A average throughout her entire academic career—from elementary school through college. She was strong in the humanities, good in languages, but it was math that came easiest for her. "I did real well in [math] ever since I was in elementary school; it was something that came naturally to me."

Ginger's family background was different from the majority of our sample, in that she had no family member with any connection to engineering or the sciences. Her father was a real estate developer. Moreover, his contact with Ginger during her adolescence was minimal. Her mother and father were divorced years before, and Ginger lived with her mother. It was her mother who encouraged her to take school seriously and to go to college. Like a lot of women of her generation, Ginger's mother had put family before career. She had started college just after marrying Ginger's father, but soon had her first baby, and was forced to drop out. Like a lot of men of his generation, Ginger's father felt uncomfortable with the idea of his wife working outside the home, so during the period of their marriage she had stayed home with the children. It seems reasonable to speculate that Ginger's mother encouraged her to do well in school because of her own frustrated ambitions. Whatever the reason, that encouragement played an important role in Ginger's academic orientation.

Ginger's father reentered her life shortly before her senior year in high school. Her mother died at the end of her junior year, and she and her two sisters went to live with their father. Given the trauma of their mother's death and the lack of regular contact between him and his daughters, her father decided that the four of them should take an extended vacation together. He loaded them into his RV and they spent the next three months traveling and getting to know one another again.

Ginger valued the chance to renew her relationship with her father, but she also resented the time away from school that the trip involved:

> I was mad. I didn't want to go, I said no, I have to take physics and I have to take chemistry. I was signed up to take chemistry, physics, calculus, all those courses in my senior year, but I didn't. Because I couldn't come in a half year [late] and finish up.

Ginger's father's attitude toward education was much different from her mother's. Traditional, conservative, and without a college education himself, he was not convinced of the value of education in general, and for women in particular. It must have been both confusing and more than a little intimidating for him to deal with his brilliant daughter. By the time he reentered her life, she was, to use her term, a "studybug." He loved her and wanted her to look up to him, but he was a real estate developer and knew nothing about the subjects she was studying:

> He was almost threatened, because he didn't understand. He'd look at my textbooks and he didn't know what they were talking about, and so I think in some ways it almost intimidated him, made him feel like, gosh, he didn't understand what I was doing, and he couldn't help me at it. I couldn't bring the homework home and say, "Hey, could you help me with this?"

His resistance to her education only increased when she declared herself an engineering major:

> [M]y father is definitely a chauvinist. He had four girls, no boys, and you know, I shouldn't be an engineer, because you should be in real estate, number one, and number two, you're going to have to raise a family and babies, you know. So, in fact I was steered away from [engineering] by him.

He was not convinced that any woman, let alone his daughter, should become an engineer. But he loved her, and though he did not approve of her choice, he continued to pay for her college education.

The decision to become an engineer clearly did not come from any home influence. Even her mother had not pushed math and science; she was only concerned about education in the abstract. Not surprisingly, therefore, Ginger was headed toward a traditional female career path until her junior year of college:

> I had actually wanted to be a teacher. . . . I wanted to teach math or Spanish, and so I took like six years of Spanish. I took lots of math, and so I could have gone into either one. CEU didn't [offer] a teaching credential, and so I almost transferred to PSU [where they have a credential program].

She was headed toward teaching, but her math background kept engineering a possibility. On the verge of transferring to PSU, she went to speak to one of the academic counselors at CEU.

> She sat down and asked me what I wanted to do, where I was going to work, and why exactly I wanted to teach. She asked me a lot of good questions, and one of the primary things was that—let's see, my fiancé and I wanted to stay in the area. . . . [She pointed out that] the job market at the time for teaching was pretty saturated, and I would have had a hard time finding a real good job.

The counselor suggested engineering—something Ginger had never considered:

> At that time there were hardly any females in engineering, so I was scared, and I said I don't think I can do that. I'd heard horror stories about Math 105, oh my gosh, the first real intense math class you have to take in engineering. I thought, I can't do it, I'm sorry I don't have the brains for it, even though I had a great GPA. Finally she said, "well, you might as well try it." She said I'd have opportunity wherever I wanted to go. . . . And that's kind of why I made the decision.

Ginger's misgivings about Math 105 were unfounded; so was her fear about "not having the brains" for engineering. In her engineering courses she did as she had always done: she made straight As. But despite her performance, she remained confused about the nature of the profession for which she was preparing. She had made the decision to become an engineer largely on the basis of her counselor's advice, but by the end of her senior year she still had no idea what they did:

> I didn't really know what it meant to be an engineer when I got out. And so I thought what if I don't like this. I mean, I liked the school work, but I knew that it would be different with a real world job, and I thought, "what if I don't like it?" I've spent all this time. . . .

Ginger was intimidated by engineering, at least in part, because like most of our sample she had little hands-on experience as a child:

> I never had experience with hands-on screws, screw drivers, just working on your car, working around the house. . . . I was never in that position at home. My chores were doing the cleaning, and the laundry—those were my chores at home, and I never grew up learning about realities, I mean hands-on applied things at all.

She contrasted her own lack of experience in this area to that of her male classmates:

> I think guys have a little more of that. At least they did in my generation. They had Erector sets, and their science projects, and things like that. So that was a disadvantage, not having that background.

Ginger's story illustrates our argument well. What drew her to engineering was her math ability and the practicality of the discipline. Math came easy to her. She started her academic career headed toward a typically female occupation. Given her traditional gender socialization, it was predictable that her first orientation would be toward teaching. Headed down a traditional path, she was detoured by her own academic ability and a conscientious counselor.

There was nothing driving Ginger toward engineering. She was not in love with the technology, and was uninterested in tinkering. Hers were passions of the mind. She was drawn to engineering because of its connection with math and science. She was pulled by its practicality, and the fact that, in the late 1970s, there seemed to be an endless supply of jobs. She and her fiancé wanted to stay in the local area, and with teaching jobs on the decline in those years, the only hope was to find work in a more marketable discipline.

In the final analysis, however, Ginger became an engineer as a result of changed social institutions and expectations. What made Ginger aware of engineering was a concerned counselor, but what made that counselor concerned were changed attitudes toward women. Had it been ten years earlier, that counselor (or her male counterpart) would have seen Ginger's decision to become a teacher as eminently sensible. But the year was 1978, and the women's movement had made its mark. Attitudes and opportunities had changed.

CONCLUSION

We have seen in this chapter that the path to engineering is quite different for women and men. For men the choice follows naturally from their gender role socialization, which encourages them to tinker and to see engineering as an appropriate career. Our data indicate that men choose engineering as a career because they have been tinkerers as children, and in love with machinery and technology. For women the process is neither so smooth, nor so directly tied to gender socialization. Rather, it reflects a peculiar combination of traditional gender roles, academic skills, and a changing structure of opportunity. As we have seen, their initial choice of engineering is a function of their skills in math, and their practical orientations. That engineering has become a "practical" choice for middle-class women is in no small part the result of changes in attitudes toward women in American society.

When most young women choose engineering, they have little understanding of what engineers do, but this is of little consequence while they are in school. Entry onto the path toward engineering depends above all on ability in math. As we shall see, however, the study of engineering is different than its practice. These women carry strong resources with them as they enter engineering school, but they carry liabilities as well. With their intelligence, their ability in math and science, their practicality and self-discipline, they will excel as engineering students. However, their lack of mechanical background, their unfamiliarity with technology, and their traditional gender socialization will work against them later on. For now, however, their resources overshadow their liabilities.

4

COLLEGE EXPERIENCES

Once enrolled in college engineering programs, these women performed as they had in high school. They were strong students, stimulated by the challenge of a rigorous program. They did well in this competitive atmosphere, often outperforming their male classmates. If success as an engineer were dependent only on academic performance, these women would have been on their way to the "fast track."

Unfortunately, there is more to it than that. As we see in the next chapter, the college programs in which these women excelled did not fully prepare them for the demands of an engineering career. This is in part because their education failed to compensate for their lack of mechanical experiences in childhood. This failure, combined with the male-dominated structure of the engineering school, contributed to feelings of insecurity in these women about their technical abilities. Their academic success was not accompanied by high levels of technical self-confidence. They mastered the curricula, but were still not sure they could "do" engineering. Some of their insecurities were no doubt the products of childhood gender socialization, and were brought with them into the university. However, the structure of the engineering program itself did little to improve their technical self-confidence.

Nevertheless, the college years were good ones for these women. They had the one resource that matters most in engineering school: academic ability. The culture of engineering as defined by faculty stresses the importance of abstract knowledge—math and theory. These women had reached engineering school precisely on the basis of those skills. They would later confront a very different culture, the culture of the engineering workplace. For now, however, what mattered was the perceptions of their professors, and their professors recognized and rewarded their talent, albeit sometimes reluctantly.

These women also reaped the benefits brought by the social movements of the previous two decades. As a result of the struggles for civil rights and women's rights, new laws, university policies, and changing attitudes opened doors to women that had long been closed. Women were still a minority, still tokens in a world of men. But they knew they were legitimate members of their classes, and sensed that the profession held real opportunities for them.

In this chapter we explore the experiences of our female respondents in their college engineering programs. We first discuss the paradox of academic success and insecurity. We then examine the major factors contributing to the lack of self-confidence experienced by women engineering students: the failure of engineering programs to help them compensate for the lack of mechanical experiences in their background; and the male-dominated structure of the engineering school. We describe the interactional experiences of women in that structure—with faculty, and with the male and female students in their classes. We conclude that both their insecurities about their technical skills and their interactional problems were overshadowed during these years by their academic success.

PERFORMANCE AND SELF-CONFIDENCE

Women engineering students nationally are a high achieving group. They enter college with higher SAT math scores than male engineering students (558 vs. 549), and they are more likely to have earned an A average in high school (59% vs. 38%) (National Science Foundation 1986). The women in our sample were no different. Most were strong students in high school, and went on to perform well in their engineering classes, sometimes provoking the surprise of their professors and the resentment of their male peers. Their grade point

averages were as high or higher than men's, and they were disproportionately represented in the engineering honor societies at their
schools.[7]

Making good grades in an engineering program is no easy task.
By all accounts, it is a grueling curriculum presided over by demanding professors. The environment is highly competitive, as students
struggle for the scarce resources of good grades and the good jobs
they bring. Dropout rates are high, and those who make it have little
time for the social life most college students take for granted. As one
woman put it, "Everyone else at school was having a great time and I
felt like the nerd with the calculator on my belt, checking Friday night
labs until midnight." Many of our respondents complained about
how hard they worked in college, especially about all the homework.
The engineering curriculum seems designed to weed people out, and
certain courses in particular have the reputation of "killer courses."
As one woman told us: "In your junior year there's one class that just
murdered people, and they would drop out, and then you think
you've made it through this ultimate test, and you find out there's
another one." These women, however, rose to the challenge.

In fact, "challenge" is the word we heard most often in our
interviews when we asked, "What did you like most about your experience as an engineering major?" One after another of our female
respondents told us the challenge and the experience of mastering
difficult material was precisely what excited them:

> Math was fun, but it had gotten to be not a challenge anymore.
> It was something I didn't have to try at. And all of a sudden here
> was this engineering which I wasn't too sure what it was, and it
> was very challenging. It was definitely a "me or it" situation,
> and I wasn't going to lose. So it was definitely challenging.

Despite the obvious ability of these women to compete and
succeed in a demanding technical curriculum, they had a surprising
lack of self-confidence during their college years. This is a phenomenon found by other researchers as well (Dresselhaus 1985). Slightly
more than half of the women we interviewed told us they felt unsure
of their technical abilities, or they worried frequently about not making it through school. "I thought I was going to flunk out every day,"
said one. "I had very little self-confidence when I got out of school as
far as technical things," said another. The insecurities typically cen-

tered on the technical, hands-on aspects of engineering. One woman told us:

> The labs always frightened me. [Because they were] more experimental. I was always afraid of not being able to come out with the right answer at the end, whereas on paper I'd always be able to.

As we pointed out in chapter 2, research on gender roles has shown that one of the consistent differences between men and women in high school and beyond is in the area of "achievement-related self-confidence." Women's lower levels of self-confidence in this area are partly the result of socialization experiences in childhood, and show up particularly in activities socially defined as "masculine" (Betz and Fitzgerald 1987). Thus, it should not surprise us that women arrive at engineering school with lower levels of self-confidence than men.

Nor should it surprise us that the insecurity felt by these women focused especially on their technical abilities. As we have said, engineering is a profession imbued with a culture of technical know-how. Even engineers who never do anything more mechanical than tapping the keys on a computer keyboard share in the culture of "the tinkerer." This is an area where women's socialization lets them down. Most learn neither the skills nor the vocabulary associated with tinkering. Yet they find themselves preparing for an occupation that carries a strong image of the tinkerer with it. The male students around them value these skills and freely display the vocabulary. Women sense the need to become conversant in this culture, but their college classes provide few opportunities to do so. It is as though they must somehow absorb it by osmosis, without ever being taught.

For most women, however, academic success overshadows their feelings of technical insecurity during their college years. After all, they are succeeding at a demanding curriculum, taking whatever intellectual challenges their professors hand them. Some of them even find their male classmates turning to them for help. As one woman told us:

> I liked the homework-finishing sessions, because I was usually able to do most of the problems . . . and people would find me to find out how to do them. . . . I got more of a pat on the back

from having someone say, "Boy, you explained that better than the teacher did," than I did from getting the homework right.

Most do not yet have a clear sense of what engineers do on the job, and therefore are not aware of the gap between what they are learning in college and what they will be expected to do as practicing engineers. They feel insecure about their technical and mechanical abilities, but these do not win As in their engineering classes. Math and theoretical skills win As, and the women have no lack of either. So the insecurities are there, and they nag, but for most women academic success keeps their self-doubts at bay.

THE CULTURE OF ENGINEERING IN THE UNIVERSITY

As we see in the next chapter, these women will confront a very different environment when they leave college and enter the workplace. Whereas the emphasis in college is on academic performance, math, and theory, the workplace is applications-oriented, and requires hands-on skills. These distinct emphases are related to a difference in what we call the culture of engineering in the two settings. The culture of engineering that prevails in many workplaces emphasizes activities strongly identified with the male gender role: a fascination with technology, expertise as a tinkerer, and an aggressive style of self-presentation. In the university, however, the group with the most power to shape the definition of the culture is the engineering faculty. As a result, the definition of "the good engineer" which prevails there, emphasizes academic over technical skills.

This is true to some extent for other professions as well. The first contact for medical and law students with the culture of the profession comes in school, and it is a highly academic version of it. Like engineers, doctors and lawyers use little of what they learn in school in their day-to-day practice. In engineering, however, the differences between the university and the workplace are more extreme. In the "true" professions, the professional organization (e.g., the American Medical and Bar Associations) has control over the curriculum, and professors are often practitioners as well. The educational process includes considerable hands-on experience as well as course work. Internships and practica expose students to the "real world" of the profession long before they graduate. As a result, there is a significant degree of continuity between the culture of the profession as defined by the university and by its practitioners.

Because the engineering profession is more poorly organized and less powerful, its impact on the educational process is reduced. Engineering associations do not define curricula, and most engineering schools do not offer internships. Because of the variety of workplaces that will employ engineers, highly specific hands-on training is considered inappropriate. Instead, the university teaches the most abstract concepts, leaving specific skills to the employer. This leaves a considerable gap between engineering as defined by the university and as practiced in the workplace. This is especially true in the more elite schools like CEU, where there is a strong emphasis on research.

The culture of engineering as defined in the university is quite compatible with the resources of women students. Here the culture is least dominated by the interests of the working engineer. The emphasis on technical orientation—the image of the tinkerer—is at its weakest. It exists, and the women are aware of it, but it is temporarily overshadowed by the emphasis on math and theory. This makes engineering school a rewarding experience for most of them, even though they are bothered by feelings of doubt about their technical skills.

SOCIAL CHANGES

Women engineering students today also benefit from the changes ushered in by the social movements of the 1960s. Title IX of the Educational Amendments of 1972 prohibited sex discrimination in all federally assisted educational programs. The Women's Educational Equity Act of 1974 provided for the development of materials and programs designed to achieve educational equity for women (U.S. Dept. of Labor 1982). Those changes forced the doors of engineering schools open to women, created the awareness of engineering as a realistic career choice for them, and brought greater acceptance by their professors and fellow students. The more accepting climate of engineering schools today, combined with the academic success women achieve there, helps compensate for the insecurities they feel about their technical competence.

We are *not* saying that women face no problems in their interaction with male faculty and students. As we see shortly, the interactional structure of the engineering school is complex, and in some ways operates to magnify the insecurities of women. But it does not overwhelm them with the feelings of isolation and illegitimacy that it once did.

The experiences of one of our respondents illustrates this contrast for us. Alice has been there—in the engineering school of old, and the engineering school of today as well. Alice graduated with a degree in electrical engineering in 1983, and immediately found a good job with a high tech employer. But this was the end of a much longer journey for her. She had begun her engineering studies fourteen years earlier at a major midwestern university. Like most of our respondents, she had come to engineering by way of excellence in her high school math classes. She did well in college, and especially loved the math and electronics classes. By the beginning of her senior year, however, she began to worry that when she graduated she would not be able to "design anything that worked—not even a simple thing." She did not know a lot about the work engineers did, but she knew "it was a practical field where you made real things." Her fear of taking a job and being expected to design something right away led her to drop out of school one semester short of graduation.

During the next twelve years she worked at a series of technical jobs, starting as an assembler and working her way up to engineering technician. She realized then that she was doing everything engineers did—including "designing things that worked"—but not getting paid what they did. It was only then that she had achieved a level of technical self-confidence that allowed her to return to school and finish her engineering degree.

What she had not realized twelve years earlier was that virtually no one who is about to graduate from engineering school can design something that works. Even with lab classes and project assignments, engineering is learned largely on the job. While male students have to learn to become engineers on the job too, they bring with them a resource created in gender socialization—namely, mechanical experiences. This means that they have worked with tools, built things, and learned a vocabulary that will help them adjust more quickly to the world of the working engineer. Most women have to make the adjustment without the benefit of that head start.

But in this sense, Alice was no different than the women engineering students of today. What *was* different for her was the interactional climate of the engineering school. When she began talking about how she was treated by teachers and students in school, it became clear that the twelve years that separated her two college experiences had made a noticeable difference. When asked what she had liked least about being an engineering student the first time, she responded quickly:

The bias! Against being female. I could give you one very concrete example that I probably will never forget. I walked into a junior level class, sat down in the second row, and as the class came in I realized I was the only female in a class of about 40. The professor walks in, announces the name of the class, and says, "Is everyone sure they're in the right place?" This is a fairly common announcement when an instructor comes in for the first time. He then goes on and says a few more words, then he turns around and looks straight at me, and he says, "This is EE 210. Are you sure you're in the right class?" I looked at him and said, "I'm quite sure." He goes on for another few minutes and asks me again for a third time. That was the worst bias that I've ever seen, but it was *not* the only one.

Alice attributed her decision to drop out of engineering school partly to the sense of isolation and lack of acceptance that she felt there:

> I found no mentor to truly encourage me to stay with it. No one bothered to explain that the function of college was not to teach you to design real things. It was to give you the theoretical background. There was no one I felt comfortable enough to even go and talk to. When I made the decision to drop out, I made it alone.

It was not just the faculty who made her feel so alone. While she found acceptance and encouragement from some students, she also encountered "outright derision" and sexual harassment from others. Nor did she have any female classmates to turn to for support.

In contrast, when she returned to college twelve years later, she found she was no longer alone, and that the men responded to her quite differently than before:

> It was a real pleasure for me to walk into a class and find ten to thirty percent of it female. Not only that, nobody stood up there and asked if we were in the right place. Males didn't seem to care. Very quickly after I got in the program, I had guys asking me if I wanted to be their lab partner, because they realized I had a lot of experience and I knew what I was doing. It didn't matter that I was female. It didn't matter that I was older than anybody else. The students were just interested in getting their degree, and the change in perception of women—it was exciting!

Of course, her positive reception was partly due to the fact that she was now more experienced and more confident of her technical abilities than most of her classmates—male and female. She came in with technical resources that made her attractive as a lab or study partner. Nevertheless, the change in attitudes toward women that she saw was real. It reflected a decade of change in opportunities and gender role definitions.

The student of today benefits from those changes. They have made it easier for women to enter engineering school, and to succeed there, despite their lack of technical background and their insecurity about it. That is not to say, however, that the university could not be doing more to help them overcome that insecurity.

BUILDING SELF-CONFIDENCE AT SCHOOL

A college engineering program can help women build technical self-confidence by providing hands-on experience as part of the curriculum. The two schools from which our respondents came are different in their orientation in this regard. The CEU engineering program is quite theoretical, giving students little hands-on experience. The program at PSU, in contrast, is more practical, providing lab experience and requiring project work. The women we interviewed were aware of the importance of hands-on experience in college. One-third of them said they now wished they had had more of it, and nearly all of these women had attended CEU, which offers the least in this area. For example, one CEU graduate said:

> I would have been better off if I'd had more practical type of classes. While I have a lot of theory base, practical things like designing gears I basically had to teach myself when I ran into the problem at work. Lab work is the kind of thing that . . . would really help out on a job, being exposed to different kinds of test instruments and how to use them, etc.

This is not to say that the PSU students were fully satisfied with the hands-on experience they received. Some felt the labs did not provide enough variety of experience. Others complained that the labs were not as useful as they might have been, because the equipment was outdated and often broken. Nevertheless, the lab work did improve their self-confidence. As one told us, "For those of us who didn't have a lot of hands-on experience—like I had no electronics background—you overcome a lot of fears. I did at least."

In addition, the labs helped them interact more comfortably with their male classmates and later with their colleagues, as explained by one of our respondents:

I had a lab class where we were doing wiring. I'm glad I learned how to do that, so I'm not as afraid basically in dealing with that stuff. And when the guys talk, "Yeah, yeah, you've got to ground this, or do this or that," I know at least what they're talking about.

In addition, women at PSU were frequently recruited into paid internships, which gave them experience in an engineering workplace while still in school. Employment experiences like internships and summer jobs appear to have been especially important in building self-confidence. They not only provided hands-on experience, but gave women a glimpse of the actual work engineers do, as well. Of the women who reported problems with self-confidence in college, the majority (61%) had no engineering-related employment or internships before or during college. In addition, our measure of technical self-confidence in the workplace, which we discuss more fully later, showed a positive association with engineering experience prior to entry into the workforce (tau c=.35; p=.007). Women who now display the most self-confidence in their technical abilities are most likely to have had engineering-related employment before or during college.

Fewer than half of our interview respondents (45%) had the benefit of work experiences, however. Many of those who did not have work experience felt they had missed something important as a result. For example, an electrical engineer told us:

This boyfriend I had used to work in the summers as a programmer and he did hardware stuff outside of school, and I never did any of that. I didn't have any extra training, so I felt kind of behind. . . . If I'd had a general idea of what the electronics world was like, it might have helped because, you know, you're learning transistors and stuff—they didn't mean a thing to me. I didn't know what they looked like, I didn't know what you use them for, but I knew all about the physics of what goes on inside. It's like you learn all this theory and it doesn't mean a lot.

It is clear that universities could do more to help women like these overcome the lack of mechanical background they bring to college. However, women's insecurities are not *only* the result of growing up without tinkering experience, or of engineering programs that fail to provide it for them. It is also the result of their interactional experiences in college. While these experiences have improved considerably in the last two decades, women in an engineering program still find themselves in a social structure that does little to build their sense of competence as future engineers. They are women in a male-dominated environment, preparing for a career in the most male-dominated profession.

THE INTERACTIONAL STRUCTURE OF ENGINEERING SCHOOL

The women in our sample went through college at a time when women constituted from 5 to 30 percent of students in engineering programs, with 10 to 15 percent being typical. This meant that in a class of thirty to forty students, there would be from three to five women. It was not uncommon, however, for a woman to find herself alone, or accompanied by just one other woman. If they were part of an informal study group, as many engineering students are, it was often as the only woman in the group. In short, they were tokens, "O's in a world of X's," to use Rosabeth Kanter's (1977) concept. As Kanter has pointed out, the presence of a token in a group—someone who is visibly different from the others—sets in motion social dynamics that can be detrimental to the self-esteem of the token member. As we said in chapter 2, the concept of tokenism has its limits in explaining the employment status of women. However, it is a useful starting point for our discussion of interaction patterns in the engineering school.

The token is, by definition, highly visible in the social group. The other members are more aware of her presence than they are of each other's. All of her behaviors—good and bad—are noticed. But her actual task performance is often less noticed than her physical characteristics—that which makes her different. The other members are acutely aware of the token's "differentness," and as a result, of their own commonality. Informal boundaries are often drawn between "we" and "she," with majority members excluding the token, or exaggerating their own typical behavior in order to define the boundaries clearly. Either way, the token experiences social isolation.

The token is seen not as an individual, but as representative of her type. Her behaviors are taken as "the way women are," rather than the way *this* woman is. On a token this puts pressures not felt by others. She feels—correctly—that her performance will affect not only how people respond to her, but how they respond to other women in her situation as well. Ironically, the reverse of this process occurs at the same time. The stereotypes about women as a group are assumed to be true of the token woman, whether they fit or not. As a result, her own behaviors are often perceived in exaggerated or distorted forms, in order to maintain the stereotype. The final blow is that the price of acceptance in the group is conformity to a stereotyped role that is comfortable to the majority members. Rather than being accepted as an engineer, she may find acceptance only by playing "mother," "sex object," or "helpless female," for example.

The combined effects of token status, Kanter argues, create stress in the token, make social interaction more difficult, and heighten feelings of insecurity, even though work performance may be unimpaired. We can see this combination of success and insecurity in our respondents' accounts of their school experiences. As we have said, their insecurity was partly the result of their lack of tinkering experience in childhood, and the failure of the university to compensate for it. However, it was also related to their treatment as tokens by their professors and fellow students.[8] It is to these that we now turn.

Interaction with Faculty

In college it is the faculty who hold power. As such, they constitute a crucial resource for students. Attending class regularly and studying conscientiously is, of course, necessary for any student who wants to do well in college. But survival and success are made easier by positive relationships with professors. The ability to talk with them comfortably, both in and out of class, to go to them for help when the subject matter is confusing, and to receive encouragement and support from them, all make survival and success in college more likely for a student. This is particularly true for minorities, whether it be a black student in a largely white college, or a woman in a male-dominated major like engineering.

Treated Just Like the Men, But . . . More than half of the women we interviewed told us of problems they had with their engineering professors. To be sure, they were not alone in this. Engineering faculty members, like college professors generally, can be inaccessible, unhelpful, and even contemptuous in their dealings with students of either sex. As a faculty member at the University of Chicago once remarked, "The faculty did not discriminate between women and men students—they treated them all poorly" (Freeman 1979: 221).

The women we interviewed recognized this as well. Half of them told us they saw no difference in the treatment received by male and female students, and many who reported problems with faculty saw them as unrelated to gender. For example, one woman told us that her major complaint about the engineering program she attended was the attitude of faculty:

> You always got the feeling . . . that the professors were only teaching . . . in order to get their research funds. They really didn't seem to take a tremendous interest in the students. . . . They seemed to take tremendous glee in watching everybody flounder.

However, there are two important distinctions to be made here. First, the same behavior by a faculty member can have a disparate impact on male and female students. As Jo Freeman has pointed out:

> An academic situation that neither encourages nor discourages students of either sex is inherently discriminatory against women because it fails to take into account the differentiating external environments from which women and men students come. . . . Professors don't have to make it a specific point to discourage their female students. Society will do that job for them. All they have to do is fail to encourage them. Professors can discriminate against women without really trying. [Freeman 1979: 221]

This argument applies especially well to women entering a nontraditional field of study like engineering. They are operating in an unfamiliar environment, where they are reminded every day of their minority status. All they have to do is look around them in the classroom or the study group, or at the sex composition of the engineering faculty. Few women have ever done what they are attempting, and the field for which they are training still carries a strong "men only" image. They feel isolated and observed.

They sense that some of their fellow students and professors do not welcome them, or do not take them seriously as future engineers. As one respondent put it:

You stick out like a sore thumb. . . . I'll tell you one thing, you'd never cheat because they're looking at you already. [The male students] were very helpful. The only problem is you wonder, are they helping you or are they trying to meet you outside of school . . . or something like that.

They must deal with these feelings as they struggle to compete in a demanding college program. In short, they bear burdens not shared by their male classmates.

Given this added pressure, women have a special need for time, support, and encouragement from faculty. To be treated exactly as male students are treated, for better or worse, is to be discriminated against, when seen in this larger context. An intimidating or unhelpful professor is a problem for any student, but for the woman in a nontraditional program it can be overwhelming. She is likely to avoid contact with that professor—and perhaps others—as a result. In doing so, she misses out on a valuable resource. A mechanical engineering student expressed this point well:

There were occasions when I was having problems and wasn't really understanding, and I just didn't feel comfortable enough around the professor to go in there and ask questions. I guess I was afraid they would think I was dumb and I couldn't let them know I was dumb, because I was a woman and I was trying to prove that I *wasn't* dumb. . . . Unfortunately, that hurt, because in that last year a lot of stuff I just fell behind in, because I was not willing to ask questions. . . . I didn't want to draw attention.

Nearly a quarter of the women (23%) told us they avoided their professors, and felt intimidated by them. Yet the women in our sample did well in school. Their academic skills generally, and their proficiency in math in particular, were qualities highly valued by their professors. Even faculty members who did not welcome women in their classes or offices had to recognize the talents of these students. Their ability to conform to the culture of engineering, as defined in the university, carried them through. But the lack of faculty support that many encountered did nothing to enhance their self-confidence as future engineers.

Sexism, Subtle and Not so Subtle. The second point to be made regarding women's interaction with faculty is that while faculty often provided the same levels of support—or lack of it—to male and female students, there were also those who treated women differently. More than a quarter of the women we interviewed (28%) reported problems with sexism on the part of at least some of their professors. They often spoke of it hesitantly, because it was subtle. They sensed that they were being treated differently, but it was not always something they could put their finger on. Said one woman:

> I always sort of had the feeling that, as the old cliché goes, being a woman in a man's profession you have to work a little harder. I had to prove that I knew what [the professors] were talking about. And maybe that's part of the reason I didn't like to go talk to professors . . . because their attitude tended to lean a little more towards, "of course you don't understand this. . . ." Not that they ever said anything like that, and maybe I was projecting. But you just never know. So you walk carefully.

Another woman felt vaguely uncomfortable with the way some of her professors talked to her in class: "It was in the way . . . they would call on you, in kind of—the tone in which they said things—more of a fatherly type thing, more a joking kind of thing, or more of a little innuendo or something."

Whether subtle or explicit, the sexism of faculty fell into several basic patterns. Some women felt that because they were women, they were not taken seriously. Both their motivations for entering engineering school and their abilities to survive there were doubted. One of the more explicit examples is the professor who was confused by one of our respondents the first day of class. She apparently did not fit any of his stereotypes about women engineering students, so he said to her, "I can't figure you out. You're not trying to *be* a man, and you're not here just to *get* a man. . . . What *are* you here for?."

More commonly, the response was less blatant. One woman told us, "I think [the teachers] didn't take you seriously unless you were really deadly serious all the time. You had to come in and be very up front and . . . always well composed, and the minute you weren't, I got the feeling that they didn't take you seriously."

Others sensed the discomfort of male faculty members in their presence. One woman recounted her experience of going to her professor's office:

> You'd see them in there palling it up and working with the guys, and I'd walk in there and you could tell they were just intimi-

dated by me. . . . I don't know what it was, but these guys were obviously uncomfortable. Maybe they were waiting for me to fail, or something. I didn't analyze it too closely, but boy, it irritated me. I got no help from any of them.

The issue of women's competence was apparently of no little concern to some faculty members. When one discovered that women outperformed men in his class, he made his surprise known:

One of them once divided up the tests—male and female—and graded them separately, and his purpose was to show that women score lower and that we shouldn't be here, and as it turned out the women had much higher grades. He admitted it in class.

An incident like this praises the ability of women, but at the same time singles them out and belittles them. For it lays bare the operating assumption of the professor: that women are presumed less competent until proven otherwise. This message is not lost on the students. As one woman told us, "I do remember one professor who kind of snidely announced that a woman had gotten the highest grade in an exam, and I think it was just out of pure shock."

It must be said, however, that problems with faculty were by no means universal. Approximately 40 percent of the women we interviewed reported no problems at all with faculty, and most of those who experienced problems with some had positive interactions with others. We heard many comments about professors who were fair, helpful, and encouraging to their women students. Perhaps most important, even those who did not welcome women into the profession could not ignore their achievements. The academic skills of the women constituted a resource that commanded the respect of faculty members, even though it came more grudgingly from some than from others.

Interaction with Students

Judging from the reports of our interview respondents, the interactions of women and men engineering students are a complex mixture of positive and negative. Women clearly find greater acceptance from their male classmates today than they did two decades ago. Nevertheless, they are operating in an environment that is still strongly male-dominated. Their interactions with other students leave them feeling different, observed, and only partially accepted as future members of the profession.

First of all, even when relationships with other students were positive, women were acutely aware of their minority status. For some this created considerable discomfort:

> You get used to being around men all the time, and you're the only woman in the class, but I was never real comfortable with it, because I was always noticed. [Women] stand out, and I guess for the person that doesn't mind being the center of attention, that's fine. But the person who would rather blend in . . . that is difficult.

She was right. Some women liked the attention:

> At first it was kinda like, "Wow, there's a girl in the class!". . . . I liked the extra attention of being a female. I didn't have any problem with it. I enjoyed it.

But whether they liked it or not, all were aware of being women in an overwhelmingly male environment.

Comradery. On the whole, the women in our sample had more positive things to say about their fellow students than about their professors. When asked what they liked most about the college experience, 36 percent included "the comradery with students" in their response. The comments of this woman were typical of many who emphasized the cooperative spirit among students, the sense that "we're all in this together":

> There was a group of about fifteen of us that all knew each other, we all had classes together, so when we were in labs and stuff, we might be there until 2:00 in the morning trying to make something work . . . and if somebody got something that all the rest of us were struggling to get—it was like we were trying to help each other along. And I think that comradery was real good.

Even those who had problems with some students usually had others with whom they got along very well.

There are several factors that help explain women's more favorable perceptions of male students than of faculty members. Perhaps most important is the relationship of power involved. In the university, the power of faculty over students creates distance between the two groups, and solidarity among students. Male and female students have in common an important structural reality: their powerlessness vis-à-vis faculty. They are competing for grades, it is true. But good grades are not as scarce a resource as good jobs and promotions will be later. Students learn that by cooperating with each other, they can *all* get better grades. That is why study groups are so common in a difficult program like engineering. Thus, while they are in school, women and men share a structural position of powerlessness, and a self-interest in cooperation. As a result, women—especially bright women—are likely to find acceptance among their male peers.

Romance and Mutual Attraction. A second factor bringing women and men together is sexual attraction. Many of the women in our sample developed romantic relationships with fellow students. Respondents also talked about the mutual attraction felt between male and female students generally. The men liked having women around, in an environment that was often bereft of them. The women liked being around men as well, especially under such favorable "market conditions." As one put it, "It was great shopping!"

This brings up an obvious difference between women and other minority groups. Blacks and Hispanics are also token members of engineering classes. In fact, their numbers are even smaller than women's (NSF 1986). While women share many experiences in common with these other minority groups, the existence of sexual attraction adds a layer of complexity to their relationship with the dominant group. Intermixed with the dynamics of tokenism and competition is the physical attraction between the sexes. Pushed apart by the first two processes, men and women are at the same time pulled together by the third.

However, the attraction between men and women, while perceived by many of them in positive terms, has its downside. In the context of tokenism, it can undermine a woman's credibility as an engineering student. One of the dynamics of tokenism is the tendency for the majority members of a group to see the token in terms of her social and physical characteristics, rather than in terms of her formal role in the group. That is, she is related to as a woman, rather than as a student and prospective engineer. The existence of sexual attraction between the token and the majority members tends to reinforce that dynamic.

If she were not a token—if she were accepted as a legitimate and equal member of the group—her status as "member of the opposite sex" would merely add another dimension to her interaction with other group members. However, because she *is* a token, she is already seen first as a woman and second as an engineering student. The dynamics of sexual attraction intensify that process. As long as engineering is considered a "man's occupation," the attention that a woman receives because of her "femaleness" tends, by definition, to undermine her credibility as an engineering student.

At the same time, the assumption that engineering is a man's occupation often means that her acceptance as an engineering student undermines her credibility as a woman. Jokes about women engineers are frequently heard in school. They often focus on the idea that physical attractiveness and engineering are mutually exclusive. For example, one joke told to us by a female respondent goes:

What's the difference between a woman engineering student and garbage? Answer: Garbage gets taken out once a week.

So the message women get is that they lose either way. Because they are women, especially if they are attractive, they are not seen as serious engineering students, although they may receive a lot of attention and flattery from male students and teachers. On the other hand, if they *are* serious about engineering, they are seen as unattractive—that is, unfeminine.

These messages constitute part of the interactional terrain that women must navigate in school. That is not to say that they receive these messages from everyone, or that the messages are conveyed so overtly. But they are there, and they form part of the burden carried by women. In addition to the difficulty of the subject matter, the pressures of competition, and the problems with professors that male students face, women must also struggle to establish credibility both as engineering students and as women. This is no easy task, especially since one often comes at the expense of the other.

Mentors. Another aspect of the interaction between female and male students that has both an upside and a downside is the phenomenon of "mentoring." As we said earlier, many women had boyfriends who were engineering students, and they often spoke warmly of these and other men who acted as mentors to them. Often older and more advanced in their studies, these men served as advisors when they were choosing classes, as tutors in difficult subjects, and as important sources of emotional support and encouragement. Said one woman:

> My boyfriend was probably the biggest help. There were times when I was so distraught about the lack of progress I thought I was making, that I was ready to throw my hands up and say, "forget it." And he helped, he kept me on course.

These relationships often resulted in marriage after graduation. In fact, 56 percent of the married women in our sample were married to engineers, and most of these couples had met in college.

Some women had not one mentor, but a whole group of them: the men in their study group who provided help and encouragement. This kind of support can be very important to a woman in an unfamiliar field. The literature on women in nontraditional occupations sings the praises of mentors for the role they play in helping others succeed, and laments the fact that women have less access to them than men (Epstein 1974; Kanter 1977).

We believe, however, that there is reason to be cautious regarding the value of mentors in the careers of women and other minorities. Having someone to encourage you, "show you the ropes," and ease your way through a difficult curriculum may smooth that process. But it may do so at the expense of self-confidence. The mentor may be saying implicitly to the protégé, "You really need my help in order to survive here. You can't do it on your own, so I'll do it for you."

A message like this is more likely to be conveyed when the protégé is a token. When a man becomes mentor to another man in a field dominated by men, an assumption of competence pervades the situation. The mere fact that the newcomer has been granted entry to the school or the workplace is taken as proof of his basic competence, because he displays no social or physical characteristics that set him apart from the majority. The mentoring process merely smooths his progress upward, where he "belongs."

With a token, however, there is no such initial assumption of competence. Because she looks and acts differently than those who dominate the profession, she is seen first as a woman, and in engineering that means that her competence, by definition, is in doubt. Therefore it must be proven, often by performance superior to that of the men around her. Given this, a mentor becomes someone who is doing her a favor, helping her out because she is a woman, and therefore not a likely candidate for success as an engineer—*without his help*, that is.

When a woman senses that she is succeeding only because of her mentor, her success is less likely to build self-confidence. In addition, the mentor's help may prevent the woman from gaining valuable experience on her own. This happened for some of our respondents in their lab classes, where "helpful" men took over:

> Having teammates helps a lot as far as getting the grade, but it probably isn't the best thing for someone who doesn't have hands-on experience being linked up with someone that really does, and can really click through that equipment. . . . One tends to learn less by getting together with people who know more, because you end up watching more than doing.

Self-confidence and hands-on skills are resources women engineering students often lack. A mentor *can* help them develop both, but he can also prevent that development.

Skepticism and Resentment. In addition to these complex "positive-negative" interactions between women and men, we heard many reports of men sending much more straightforward messages to women: that they were not welcome, not taken seriously, or seen as threats. Some men expressed skepticism about their abilities or seriousness:

> There's a tendency to assume that you're wrong, you know, without them having to justify their positions. . . . They interrupt you when you're talking. Don't consider your answer, then present an answer that's almost identical.

The men were keenly aware of the grades women received, and seemed to feel it necessary to do better than the women. When tests were handed back, it was not uncommon to hear men saying, "What did the girl get? Did I beat the girl?" When the women outscored them, as they often did, some men expressed resentment. One woman told us:

> [Some of the male students] think they should be doing better than a female student, and so they would kind of look down on me because I was doing much better than they were. . . . There were people like that, and they would act very cold.

Hostility toward women was especially apparent when the job offers began to come in toward the end of the senior year, and women received good offers. Now the relationships between students were beginning to change. Where they had been members of the same powerless group—"all in it together"—now they were becoming competitors in the full sense of the word. On the job market, there is no room for cooperation. When a woman gets a good offer, it is at the expense of one of her classmates. This new reality was becoming apparent as graduation neared. When we asked one woman how she was treated by the male students in her class, she replied:

> Great. Up until we started getting job offers. Then the females typically were getting offers [with higher pay]. Slightly higher. A few comments were made right from the soul. . . . "Just because she's female she's getting offered more money."

This issue was clearly one that threatened the male students. Because of affirmative action, women engineering students are actively courted by companies with government contracts. As a result, women have had little trouble finding jobs, and have been receiving slightly higher pay than men in their first jobs (College Placement Council 1986). In our interviews, women reported hearing men say things like, "Well, *you* have nothing to worry about. You'll get a good job just because you're a woman."

Resentful as the men may have been, however, they were without the power to do anything about it. It was not they who decided the fate of their female classmates. It was the employers who did the hiring, and the faculty who assigned their grades and wrote letters of recommendation. What matters most at this stage of the engineering career is academic performance, and women's abilities are undeniable. As long as the culture of engineering bears the stamp of the university, women cannot be ignored. Their academic skills, along with affirmative action, constitute a powerful set of resources. Those resources pay off in good jobs, regardless of the attitudes of their male classmates.

Once they enter the workplace, they find a very different world, however. The men in their classes—or men just like them—now become their workplace peers and competitors. Not only is there less incentive for cooperation, but the competition occurs in a very different context. The culture of the engineering workplace is more compatible with the skills and orientations of the men than of the women.

In addition, the attitudes of the men matter more now, because as co-workers they have power they did not have as classmates. As in college, women in the engineering workplace encounter acceptance and hostility, mentorship and harassment. What changes is the structural context in which those behaviors occur. We are getting ahead of ourselves, however. That story will be told in the next two chapters. First, however, we look briefly at women's relationships with each other.

Interaction with Women

While it is not uncommon for a woman to find that she is "one-of-a-kind" in an engineering class, she usually has the company of a few others like herself. As we said, the percentage of women in engineering programs at this period of time ranged from about 5 to 30 percent. Being at one end or the other of that range can make quite a difference. The sense of isolation, of "oddness," is considerably diminished at the upper end of the range, and greatly intensified at its lower end. As one respondent put it:

> When I first started out, it was a lot more lopsided, there was just maybe two or three women in a class of seventy, and towards the end it was much more even . . . it was up to twenty or thirty percent women, which I think was good. [Before], I felt like an oddball.

Several of our respondents told us of the positive role played by other women in their college experience. Said one, "I liked the comradery that developed, especially the women that I met in engineering. I made a lot of good friends." To have even one other woman in a study group composed of men, to occasionally have a female lab partner, or to see a few other women in a class of forty men, provided a welcome break in the overwhelmingly male environment of the engineering school.

Without female professors—and there were none in engineering at either school—these women had no immediate role models to look to for support, guidance, or simply to pattern themselves after. They were creating a new social type—the woman engineer—and had only themselves and each other as resources. Not only that, they were dealing with problems not faced by their male classmates: problems of tokenism, sexism, and self-confidence. Their professors and the men in their classes could provide little help in coping with these problems, in part because they had no experience with them, and in part because they were the cause of them.

Given the important role these women could play for each other, we were frankly surprised that more of them did not appear to see it this way. The sense of isolation was a common theme, but most of our respondents did not emphasize the importance of other women in counteracting that isolation. Similarly, we found less appreciation of the role played by the campus chapter of the Society of Women Engineers (SWE) than we expected. This is an organization dedicated to increasing the numbers of women engineers and providing support and information for those who enter the field. It has both student and professional chapters, both of which engage in recruitment activities at the high school and college level. They also sponsor lectures by women engineers who can function both as role models and conveyors of information.

Many of our respondents had some association with this group, but for most it was minimal, such as attending a few meetings or lectures. Some had been active in the chapter for a while, but discontinued their involvement before they finished college. To be sure, there were a few who were active throughout college, often joining a professional chapter after graduation. For these women, the organization was an important source of support, and provided them with role models—more advanced students, and working engineers. Their work with SWE also provided them with experience in leadership roles, and a social context in which they were, for once, not tokens. As such, it was a resource for building self-confidence as well. These women were not typical of our respondents, however.

As we said in the previous chapter, the women in our sample were, for the most part, neither pathbreakers nor feminists. They found their way to this highly nontraditional college program by way of their talent, their practical orientation, and the opportunities provided by changing social structures. But overall, they were quite traditional in their gender role orientation. Many of them, especially in their college years, were blissfully unaware of the dynamics of tokenism and sexism that swirled around them. Even those who later would develop a consciousness of these issues were quite naive about them at this stage.

If they had little consciousness of the nature and complexity of their status as engineering students, it stands to reason that they had little appreciation of the importance of other women in helping them cope with that status. In fact, we found that some of our respondents saw their female classmates more as liabilities than as assets. They spoke disparagingly of women who got by using their "feminine wiles" rather than through hard work. For example, one woman told us she preferred male lab partners to female:

> It seemed to me they were really willing to put in more effort, whereas—the one female lab partner that I had, she was very smart, but I felt that she wasn't using her own brains, that she would really use more of her feminine influence to get things done for her. And I didn't like that.

Struggling to be taken seriously, these women sought to avoid any association with the flighty, emotional, and manipulative woman of the stereotype, who uses her sexual charms to get what she wants. Nor did they want to be taken for "feminists," hostile to men and seeing sexism everywhere. They sought acceptance and approval *as engineers*, and sensed that too much identification with women—of either the flighty or feminist variety—would undermine that. They wanted to blend in, not build more barriers between themselves and the men whose territory this was. One woman expressed this well, as she explained why she ended her involvement with SWE:

> SWE was important to me the first couple of semesters [as an engineering major]. It was sort of a nest for me to meet other women, because until that time I hadn't met any women who were wanting to go to engineering school. . . . But once I got my feet on the ground, then I pretty much ruthlessly turned my back on them. I decided I'm not a "woman engineer," I'm an engineer.

The identification of engineering with masculinity, and the male-dominated structure of the engineering school, make responses like these predictable. Unfortunately, what women trade off in their desire to be "one of the guys" is an important resource of support and a means of building self-confidence as engineers.

GINGER

We return now to Ginger. As in the previous chapter, she illustrates many of the points we have made here. Ginger is both typical of our female respondents and, at the same time, unique. She exemplifies the combination of excellence and insecurity that we found so common. To be honest, however, she presents a somewhat extreme example of it. Women perform well in engineering school, but few excel as Ginger did. Her grade point average was 4.0 throughout college. Perhaps because of her talent, she was unlike most other students—male and female—in that she preferred studying alone to working in a group. She did not go to others for help, although they frequently came to her. She described herself as a "hermit studybug," going without even the minimal social life of the typical engineering student.

In telling us about her college years, Ginger was surprisingly self-effacing when it came to her obvious brilliance as a student. Where others might use the occasion to brag of their intellect and parade their achievements, she said, "I was very lucky. . . . I was a good student. I knew how to study, I knew all about tests, and . . . math came most naturally." This underplaying of her talent is related to her gender role socialization in two ways.

First, this is a "presentation of self" that is quite compatible with the female gender role in our culture. We associate femininity with being "demure," with the avoidance of bragging and self-promotion. Even if a woman knows her work is outstanding, she should not brag about it. For these are behaviors associated with the male gender role.

Second, Ginger's humility also reflects the fact that her self-confidence did not match her actual level of performance. Research on the attribution of success and failure has shown that women tend to attribute their success to external factors like luck; while men are more likely to attribute theirs to ability (Hansen and O'Leary 1985). Again, this may be partly a matter of socialized styles of self-presentation. But it appears to be related as well to the lower levels of achievement-related self-confidence felt by women (Deaux 1984).

There were other indications of Ginger's lack of self-confidence. For example, she excelled in math above all other subjects—it came "naturally" for her—and one of the things she liked best about college was the theory classes. She clearly had the ability to master highly abstract concepts. Yet she chose to major in mechanical rather than electrical engineering, even though electrical engineering involved more math and theory. As she told us in her interview:

In retrospect, I wish I would have gone into electrical engineering. That's more fascinating to me. It's more theoretical, it's more mathematical. But I was afraid of it. I couldn't see the little current running through the wires. I didn't know how it worked, I never thought of how the lights worked, or anything like that.

Her explanation is not entirely satisfactory. That she was afraid of electrical engineering is clear. She repeated that point several times during the interview. But she implied that there was something about the activities involved in electrical engineering that was at the root of her fear. We believe that was only partly true.

Ginger was typical of the women in our study in that she had no mechanical background in childhood. As she said, "I never had experience with screws, screwdrivers, working on your car, working around the house. . . . My chores were doing the cleaning and the laundry." So it is not surprising that she was intimidated by the workings of a light bulb. But that is not enough to explain her avoidance of electrical engineering. For the field she chose—mechanical engineering—has an even greater identification with tinkering and "hands-on" activity. Mechanical engineering involves the design, testing, and production of mechanical objects. Electrical engineering is more mathematical, theoretical, and computer-based.

If Ginger was afraid of electrical engineering because she had never thought about how a light bulb worked, she should have been just as afraid of mechanical engineering, because she had never worked on a car. We believe the reason has to do with the status differences between the two fields. Electrical engineering stands at the apex of the profession. That has always been true to some extent, but it is even more true since the growth of high tech industry. Because the technology is changing so rapidly, and because the profits of high tech firms are largely dependent on continuous innovation, electrical engineers find themselves in strategic positions within their companies. They have power and status as a result, and the field is known for being highly competitive (Layton 1986; Noble 1977). Mechanical engineers hold less strategic power and lower status, because their work is based on a more stable technology. We discuss this distinction more fully in chapter 6.

Ginger was aware of the differences between the two fields, as well. She spoke of the "elevation" of electrical engineers within the profession. As a woman entering an intensely male-identified occupation, it may have been the position of electrical engineering at the pinnacle of the profession that scared her, more than the nature of the work involved. After all, by the time she was ready to graduate, she still had no concrete idea what engineers did. We believe her choice of a field that was less intrinsically interesting, but also less threatening, is another indication that her sense of herself as technically competent, as able to compete with the best and the brightest, did not match her actual ability.

If Ginger underestimated her own ability, the same cannot be said of her male classmates. As we said earlier, physical attractiveness was somewhat of a liability to the female engineering student, since men took it as evidence of the absence of brains. This was not possible with Ginger, however, despite the fact that she was a very pretty woman. The men were well aware that she outperformed most of them, and she was the target of their resentment as a result. There were some who, as she put it, "weren't proud," and would come to her for help, because "I always knew the material inside and out." But there were others who reacted differently:

> The guys who were more competitive, and who were up there on the curve, and really into being the best in the class—they resented me. No doubt about it. There were comments made in class. People would say . . . things that were mean, really. We'd have a test, and the teacher would be passing back the test and one of the guys would say [sarcastically], "Oh, did Ginger get a perfect score again?" That made me really upset. . . . I think they resented the fact that I did better, especially since I was a female. I didn't see them [saying things like] that with their buddies that may have gotten better scores than them."
>
> [Interviewer: Were the people who had that attitude unfriendly to you in general?]
>
> Yes, definitely. Never came to me, to work problems out together . . . and were unfriendly. I sensed it, definitely. I sensed them talking about me, and so it was hard.

Her way of coping with people like this was to avoid interacting with them. She tried to make sure, for example, that she never ended up with one of them as a lab partner. Her tendency to be a "hermit studybug" was in part an attempt to avoid the sarcasm and unfriendliness that were always possible when she interacted with her classmates. The behavior of these men by no means prevented Ginger from succeeding in school: far from it. But by driving her away, they succeeded in reinforcing her sense of isolation and "differentness," and prevented her from enjoying the casual interactions that are part of the process of learning an occupational culture. This process is especially important for the newcomer in a nontraditional field.

Ginger did have positive relationships with some of her male classmates. Those who were less threatened by her excellence would come to her for help, and she developed a few friendships in the process. She also developed a romantic relationship with a fellow student whom she married just before her senior year. Don was a mechanical engineering major, too, and they took every class together. The circumstances under which they met illustrate the point we made earlier about the tendency for males to take over in lab classes, and the positive-negative nature of male-female interaction. They were assigned to a programing lab together, along with Ginger's friend Linda:

> We were supposed to write programs ourselves, and [Linda and I] had problems with [Don] because he wanted to do it all himself. He wanted to do it his way, and he was just that way. I'd get so mad at him! It's interesting that I ended up marrying him.

In contrast to the problems she reported with the men in her classes, Ginger had none at all with her professors. She would go to them for help, rather than seeking out another student, and she always found them encouraging. This was probably due to the fact that she was such a strong student. We also get a hint from her that the dynamics of male-female attraction may have been involved as well. She said of her professors, "I think they wanted to have females in there. Maybe it was a nice change for them, from teaching males all the time." Given her physical attractiveness, this probably accounts for some of their friendliness toward her as well.

Ginger also enjoyed the comradery of two other women students, to whom she turned, not for help with course work, but to commiserate about their mutual problems:

> We got to be very close, and I think we encouraged each other. That's true, we really did, the three of us, we'd talk about how hard it was and what we were doing, and why should we even be killing ourselves like that?

Despite her superior talent, the encouragement of her professors and her boyfriend, and the support of other women students, these were not easy years for Ginger. Her ignorance about the occupation for which she was preparing, her lack of self-confidence, and the interactional structure in which she found herself all took their toll. When we asked her if she had serious doubts while still in school about her decision to become an engineer, she replied:

> Yes. Because it was so hard, and I spent so much time at it, and I didn't really know what it meant to be an engineer when I got out. I liked the school work, but I knew that was different than a real world job, and I thought, "what if I don't like it? Especially since it was always such an uphill battle. I was the oddball. I was the female, and luckily I did very well. If I hadn't done so well, I would have really been discouraged. I mean, here I was discouraged and I still did well. But I can imagine if I didn't, I would have really felt like a failure, and I would have quit altogether.

Becoming an engineer should not be such an arduous process, especially for someone so talented. Her comment is instructive, however. It reminds us that for the woman entering a nontraditional field, being mediocre is often not enough. There are plenty of mediocre male students who plug along through an engineering program, and become mediocre engineers. There is nothing wrong with that. No field is made up entirely of superstars. But the emotional price of being a woman in a male-dominated program like engineering is such that only the academically strongest are likely to survive.

They survive because they have the positive reinforcement of their performance to counteract the difficulties of the interactional environment. Their academic excellence guarantees success, because academic excellence is central to the culture of engineering in the university. But women with fewer academic talents have fewer resources with which to navigate the male-dominated structure of the engineering program. That structure has become more accepting of women in recent years, but it still creates a burden for them not shared by men. If allowing women to enter engineering means that only the best really have a chance, then the profession is not yet truly open. The door is ajar, and women find more acceptance and less isolation today than they did twenty years ago, but it has yet to open wide.

CONCLUSION

We have seen in this chapter that the college experience was a complex one for our female respondents. They excelled academically and found acceptance from many of their professors and classmates. Yet the highly theoretical education they received failed to make up either for the "tinkering deficit" with which they entered college or for the lack of technical self-confidence that went along with it. Their insecurities were reinforced by the interactional structure of the engineering school as well. Acceptance by faculty and fellow students was neither universal nor unqualified.

Their token status meant that no matter how they were received, they were aware of being different, and of being observed. They felt pressure to prove themselves, to outperform their male classmates in order to be seen as merely competent. They had no female professors to turn to for support or role modeling, and even the comradery of other women students was a mixed blessing in this thoroughly male-dominated environment. In short, in addition to the stresses of a rigorous and competitive program, they experienced problems not faced by their male classmates. We believe that the interactional structure of the engineering school thus served to intensify the insecurities women felt regarding their technical competence.

The concept of tokenism is useful in understanding the experiences of these women. Even though their interactions with faculty and students were positive in many respects, the fact that they were tokens—0s in a world of Xs—created social dynamics that tended to isolate them and contribute to their lack of self-confidence. To fully explain their experiences, however, it is necessary to examine the context of power relations in which tokenism occurs. As we said in chapter 2, token status has a different effect on women than on men, because women are members of a less powerful social group. Tokenism also operates differently in different structural settings.

If we want to fully understand what goes on in social groups, we need to examine the specific activities and interests of *particular* groups. An engineering school is not just any social organization. Nor is it an organization concerned solely with the transmission of knowledge. It serves as a "gatekeeper" to the profession of engineering. Its faculty members have the power to decide what must be learned in order to be considered an engineer, and to weed out those deemed "unfit" for the profession. Their definition of the culture of engineering constitutes the criteria by which students are evaluated. Women are tokens in engineering school, but they are tokens who possess the resources most valued by those with power. As a result, even though their professors often provide little encouragement, and some are openly skeptical or hostile, their academic abilities carry them through.

Engineering is also an occupation that provides valuable re-sources to those who enter it. Engineers are well paid, especially given the limited years of schooling required to enter the profession. Their credentials entitle them to good jobs, and—especially in high tech industries—to considerable status and power in their organiza-tions. The competition for those resources, however, is muted in the college classroom. All the students—male and female—are power-less there. There is competition over grades, but it is not a zero-sum game. Students can help each other get good grades, so along with competition there is an incentive to cooperate. Women are valued members of study groups because they are bright and hardworking.

These points help specify the conditions under which token status is more or less detrimental to work performance and success. Women engineering students do well in college, despite their token status, because that status is offset by (1) their ability to conform to the culture of engineering as defined by faculty; (2) the relative powerlessness of the male students, and (3) the incentives for cooper-ation built into the structure of the engineering program. These fac-tors serve both to diminish the *likelihood* of negative interactions, and to diminish the *importance* of the negative interactions that occur. When a male classmate gives a woman a hard time, it creates emo-tional distress, but as long as she is a strong student, it does not impede her chances of graduating with a good job offer in hand.

That does not mean that there is no cost involved in being a token, however. The academic success of these women is not accom-panied by high levels of technical self-confidence, which is at least partly due to the effects of tokenism. Moreover, the interactional problems women face as tokens increase in importance as their aca-demic abilities decrease. The woman who is only a mediocre student faces greater problems than a mediocre male student. He has only the subject matter with which to contend. She, however, is burdened by her status as a token, in addition to her difficulties with the curric-ulum.

She is unable to counteract her token status with faculty mem-bers because she is unable to conform to the culture of engineering as they define it. She is less able to compensate for her token status with students, because she has less to offer them academically. Moreover, she cannot console herself in the face of their sexism with the knowl-edge that she is getting better grades than they. In short, tokenism does more damage to the woman who is only an average student, because she has fewer resources to counteract it.

For the women with superior talent, however, the compatibility of their academic resources with the university-defined culture of engineering makes these years of success. Their academic achievements help to counteract the tokenism and sexism they experience. They leave engineering school still insecure about their technical abilities, and often with no clear idea what engineers do. But they leave with records of excellence, with the theoretical knowledge to become competent engineers, and with good jobs in hand.

They take it all with them into the workplace—the talent, insecurity, and naivety. They find there a very different world than the one they are leaving. Their lack of self-confidence about their technical abilities becomes a more important issue as they encounter the workplace-defined culture of engineering. More importantly, the particular structures they enter—the relations of power and the opportunities available there—interact with the strengths and weaknesses they bring with them, shaping their careers as engineers.

5

ENCOUNTERING THE ENGINEERING WORKPLACE

Women entered the engineering workplace in growing numbers during the late 1970s and early 1980s. This was a historic development, and the women in our sample were part of it. Still a tiny minority, they now at least had the company of a few other women on the job. Woman engineers were not the oddity they had been a decade earlier. The men hired with them were used to having a few women in their midst—they had been their college classmates. The older engineers they encountered in the workplace had some adjusting to do, and their reactions varied. But the women came in with strong credentials, and were serious about their work. What is more, many companies eagerly recruited them, offering them high starting salaries.

They began their first jobs full of promise and optimism. Even the most practical and traditional among them knew that they were doing something that women had not done before. They were special. How well would the promise of their college years be realized? We look at the workplace experiences of women engineers in this chapter and the next. We see that while women are doing well in their first decade as engineers, they are not doing as well as we would have expected. In particular, they are less likely than their male classmates to be in high-status technical positions, or to be moving into management. There are some important variations on this pattern, however. Women in mechanical engineering, and those working in the aerospace industry have achieved greater equality with men than have their sisters in other areas.

In this chapter we compare the career patterns of women and men, and then consider alternative explanations of the disparities we find. We argue that the gender role perspective, by itself, is of limited value in explaining the career patterns of women engineers. Elements of it are useful, however, when combined with a conflict-structural analysis of the workplace.

EMPLOYMENT PATTERNS

Our respondents graduated from college during the late 1970s and early 1980s—years when the demand for engineers was growing. The majority of them found jobs in two industries: aerospace (34%) and high tech (28%). Aerospace firms produce aircraft and related products for the military, the space program, and private airline companies. High tech companies produce computers, computer-based products, and software.[9] Both industries were growing rapidly during this time, and job prospects for engineering graduates were especially good there. The rest of our respondents went to work for government (10.5%), other manufacturing firms (7%), utility companies (2%), construction (2%), or into consulting (2%).

Most of our respondents found jobs in the same geographical area where they had been educated: southern California. A significant minority (13%), however, migrated to northern California's high tech boomtown, "Silicon Valley" (Santa Clara County).

The work that engineers do is quite varied. As in other professions, some types of work are held in higher esteem than others. In order to fully understand the employment patterns of women and men, we must first become familiar with the prestige ranking within the profession. Engineering can be thought of as a hierarchy organized around two principles: increasing technical and supervisory responsibilities (Perrucci and Gerstl 1969; Perrucci and Rothman 1969; Perrucci 1970).

The heart of engineering is design. Engineers view the conception and design of a product or process as the most important and prestigious aspect of their work. They also see research and development (R & D) as a highly valued activity, given its creativity and technical complexity (Perrucci and Gerstl 1969; Noble 1977; Zussman 1985; Whalley 1986). Ninety-three percent of our respondents agreed that design and R & D were most admired by other engineers, and 52 percent thought they were most valued by management as well. Moreover, design is a prime "jumping off place" for promotion into management (Perrucci 1973; Zussman 1985; Whalley 1986). Because of the similarities between these two fields, and because our sample contained relatively few R & D engineers, we have combined them.

Below design and R & D in both prestige and power in the workplace are activities that either support the design process (analysis or test engineering) or support the production process (manufacturing engineering). Lowest in status are engineering activities that have no contact with either the design or production process. In our sample these were sales and marketing engineers. These positions are outside the technical hierarchy, and are seen by many engineers as work unfitting a "true" engineer.

Just above design are senior and project engineers. They have supervisory responsibilities over other engineers, usually coordinating efforts on a particular project.[10] Finally, there are engineers who have risen into true management. Mid-management has responsibility for an entire part of the productive/administrative process (e.g., program manager). Upper management has achieved corporate-level power (vice-president of a branch; head of a plant, etc.). We included owners of small businesses in the mid-management category.

These differences in status are reflected in income. In our sample, the median income of sales/marketing engineers was $33,330; analysis/production engineers, $33,430; design engineers, $35,180; project managers, $40,940; and middle/upper management, $48,900.

With these distinctions in mind, we can now examine the occupational fortunes of women and men. In Table 3 we see that women were in less prestigious job assignments than men. They were overrepresented in marketing, manufacturing, and analysis, and underrepresented in design and management positions.[11] These findings parallel those of Jagacinski (1987), who found that female engineers had lower levels of supervisory responsibility than males at comparable levels of experience.

How can we explain these patterns? Why do women, so full of talent and promise, fail to progress in their careers as rapidly as their male classmates? Are these patterns the result of women's own choices? Do they just not have "what it takes" to be good engineers?

TABLE 3
Current Job: Men and Women

Current Job	Men	Women
Sales/Marketing		
N	3	5
Percent	(.9)	(6.5)
Manufacturing/Test		
N	67	26
Percent	(20.7)	(34.2)
Design/R&D		
N	188	33
Percent	(58.2)	(43.4)
Senior Engineer		
N	45	10
Percent	(13.9)	(13.2)
Mid-Management		
N	19	2
Percent	(5.9)	(2.6)
Upper Management		
N	1	0
Percent	(.3)	(0.0)
Total	323	76
Kendall's tau-c	−.13	
Signficance	(.001)	

Are they victims of discrimination? We pursue these questions in this chapter and the next, and find that the answers are neither simple nor obvious. As is so often the case in social explanation, there is not one, but a combination of factors shaping the careers of women engineers.

GENDER ROLES IN THE WORKPLACE

We must first remember that the patterns we found among women engineers are not unique. Wherever women have entered male-dominated occupations, the problem of "resegregation" has emerged. The doors open to them, but they find themselves confined to "female ghettos" within, receiving lower pay and status, and on shorter career ladders (Kanter 1977; Harlan and O'Farrell 1982; Epstein 1983).

The explanations most commonly given for this problem reflect the assumptions of the gender role perspective discussed earlier. While the specific arguments vary, they generally emphasize the gender role characteristics brought by women and men into the workplace. Gender socialization leads women to limit their education and aspirations, doubt their competence, behave in ways incompatible with professional success, and to value family over career. Men, on the other hand, learn behaviors that make occupational success likely: competitiveness, assertiveness, and single-minded devotion to the career. They pursue advanced training, display self-confidence, and let nothing stand in their way. Men have also learned to be uncomfortable with the idea of women as their equals—much less their superiors—either at home or at work. They therefore feel threatened and resentful when women enter their occupational terrain.

As a result, women's careers are constrained by their own behaviors and attitudes and by the men around them—their husbands and co-workers. Their willingness to put the needs of their family first, their lack of self-confidence and assertiveness, and the hostility they face from men combine to "keep them in their place." The underlying culprit is the socialization process that implants traditional, gender-linked attitudes and behaviors into young boys and girls.

This is a persuasive argument. We have already seen that the women and men in our sample were quite traditional in their gender role orientations. But is career success determined so straightforwardly by gender role expectations? We pursue this question by looking at each of the major arguments of the gender role perspective, in light of our data.

Education

A major argument of the gender role perspective is that women limit their educational achievements because of the priority they place on their family role, present or future. According to both status attainment and human capital theories, this is a major cause of the lower occupational status of women, given the importance of education in determining occupational standing. Lack of education certainly helps explain why women become secretaries or waitresses, rather than accountants or managers. Similarly, a desire to limit their education to a BS rather than going further helps explain why some become engineers rather than scientists or MDs. However, it is of little help in explaining the relative job standings of the women and men in our study. Both groups received the same education, and the women performed as well as—often better than—their male classmates. Moreover, the women were no less likely than the men to have received advanced degrees in engineering. So their lower occupational standing cannot be accounted for in terms of educational preparation.

Career Continuity

Another major argument of the gender role perspective is that occupational success is achieved through continuity in the workplace. In particular, human capital theory stresses the importance of working year after year without interruption, and staying with the same employer, building seniority and experience. These investments in human capital yield the promotions and pay raises that make for a successful career. Gender role theorists argue that women lose out here because of the interruptions in their work histories. They leave the work force, or take extended absences in order to care for young children. While they are out, their male co-workers take important steps upward. We discuss this issue more fully in chapter 7. The important point here is that the women in our sample had not yet begun to have children in significant numbers, and only two had had any extended absences from the work force. Their patterns of continuity were nearly identical to the men's, and therefore cannot explain their lower job standing.

Not only that, our data suggest that experience and job tenure pays off for men, but not for women. Men who had been out of school longest and with their current employer longest held the highest ranked jobs. In contrast, there was no similar association for women (see Tables 4 and 5). We also have evidence from our interview data that a significant number of women who started their careers in high status design jobs actually experienced *downward mobility* over time. Five of the nineteen interview respondents who started in design positions (26%) moved into lower status positions in analysis, production, or marketing. This was not true for the men. In short, there appear to be different processes at work for men and women. The behaviors that predict success for the former do not do so for the latter.

Work Values

Do women and men have different sets of attitudes toward their careers that can help explain the greater success of men? According to the gender role perspective, they do. Women are argued to be less

TABLE 4
Current Job in Relation to Time since Graduation: Men and Women

Current Job	Men 1 Year	Men 2–3 Years	Men 4–5 Years	Men 6–10 Years	Women 1 Year	Women 2–3 Years	Women 4–5 Years	Women 6–10 Years
Sales/Marketing								
N	1	3	1	1	0	2	2	1
Percent	(4.2)	(2.3)	(1.1)	(1.2)	(0.0)	(6.1)	(11.1)	(4.8)
Manufacturing/Test								
N	5	37	20	6	2	12	6	6
Percent	(20.8)	(28.9)	(22.5)	(7.1)	(50.0)	(36.4)	(33.3)	(28.6)
Design/R&D								
N	17	85	42	42	2	16	5	10
Percent	(70.8)	(66.4)	(47.2)	(50.0)	(50.0)	(48.5)	(27.8)	(47.6)
Senior Engineer								
N	0	2	20	23	0	3	4	3
Percent	(0.0)	(1.6)	(22.5)	(27.4)	(0.0)	(9.1)	(22.2)	(14.3)
Mid-Management								
N	1	1	5	12	0	0	1	1
Percent	(4.2)	(.8)	(5.6)	(14.3)	(0.0)	(0.0)	(5.6)	(4.8)
Upper Management								
N	0	0	1	0	0	0	0	0
Percent	(0.0)	(0.0)	(1.1)	(0.0)	(0.0)	(0.0)	(0.0)	(0.0)
Total	24	128	89	84	4	33	18	21

	Men	Women
Kendall's tau-c	.28	.09
Significance	(.000)	(.15)

TABLE 5
Current Job in Relation to Time at Current Employer: Men and Women

Current Job	Men 1 Year	Men 2–3 Years	Men 4–5 Years	Men 6–10 Years	Women 1 Year	Women 2–3 Years	Women 4–5 Years	Women 6–10 Years
Sales/Marketing								
N	5	0	1	0	3	1	1	0
Percent	(2.4)	(0.0)	(2.3)	(0.0)	(6.3)	(6.7)	(10.0)	(0.0)
Manufacturing/Test								
N	49	11	6	2	15	7	4	0
Percent	(23.3)	(16.4)	(14.0)	(40.0)	(31.3)	(46.7)	(40.0)	(0.0)
Design/R&D								
N	130	34	20	2	23	6	2	1
Percent	(61.9)	(50.7)	(46.5)	(40.0)	(47.9)	(40.0)	(20.0)	(50.0)
Senior Engineer								
N	17	18	9	1	6	1	3	0
Percent	(8.1)	(26.9)	(20.9)	(20.0)	(12.5)	(6.7)	(30.0)	(0.0)
Mid-Management								
N	8	4	7	0	1	0	0	1
Percent	(3.8)	(6.0)	(16.3)	(0.0)	(2.1)	(0.0)	(0.0)	(50.0)
Upper Management								
N	1	0	0	0	0	0	0	0
Percent	(0.5)	(0.0)	(0.0)	(0.0)	(0.0)	(0.0)	(0.0)	(0.0)
Total	210	67	43	5	48	15	10	2

	Men	Women
Kendall's tau-c	.14	−.01
Significance	(.000)	(.43)

TABLE 6
Work Values: Men and Women

Work Value	Sample Mean	Men's Mean	Women's Mean
1. To be treated as a professional by my superiors.	8.81	8.70	9.27*
2. To have the opportunity to explore new ideas about technology or systems	8.26	8.26	8.26
3. To have stability in my life and work	8.06	8.07	8.03
4. To work with others who are outstanding in their technical achievements	8.05	7.99	8.27
5. To work on projects having a direct impact on the business success of my company	7.71	7.78	7.35
6. To help the company build its reputation as a first-class organization	7.46	7.51	7.25
7. To work on projects that you yourself have originated	7.21	7.20	7.28
8. To learn how the business is set up and run	6.22	6.22	6.20
9. To become a first-line manager in your line of work	5.72	5.61	6.13
10. To receive patents on your technical ideas	5.55	5.82	4.41*

*A statistically significant difference between men and women

committed to their careers, to aspire to lower levels of achievement, and to place their families first, all because of gender socialization. However, when we compared the work-related values of the women and men in our sample, we found few significant differences.

On a scale of 0 to 10, with 10 being "extremely important", and 0 being "not important at all", the most important values are ranked in Table 6. Of the ten items appearing in this table, there were only two in which there were statistically significant differences between women and men. Women were *more* likely than men to rate professional treatment by their superiors as very important to them. Women's mean rank on this item was 9.3; men's was 8.7 (Pearson's R=.16; p=.001). This is hardly consistent with the notion that women are less career-oriented than men. It also suggests that women have found professional treatment more difficult to come by than men have, but that is a different issue, and will be discussed in a later section.

The second item that showed a statistically significant gender difference was no. 10. Neither men nor women ranked "receiving patents" highly. But men's mean ranking (5.8) was significantly higher than women's (4.4) (Pearson's R=−.17; p=.000).

Finally, when we asked married engineers what their main source of satisfaction in life was, offering the choice of "family," "work," "both," or "something else," the answers of women and men were highly similar. Most answered "both" (53% of men, 60% of women); women were only slightly more likely to say "family" than men (26% vs. 20%). These differences were not statistically significant.

Thus, the work-related values and attitudes of these women and men are quite similar. Where they differ, the differences are not particularly helpful in explaining their lower job standings. Two earlier studies of engineers reported similar patterns. Perrucci (1970) found essentially the same work-related values among the male and female engineers she studied, and Gardner (1975) found that women shared more values in common with men after ten years in engineering, than they did in school. The gender roles approach could not have predicted findings like these.

Self-Confidence and Assertiveness

The popular literature on women's careers is full of discussions of the inability of women to display the behaviors necessary for success in male-dominated professions (Harragan 1977; Hennig and Jardim 1977; Mitchell and Burdick 1985; Foxworth 1986; Hardesty and Jacobs 1986; McBroom 1986). Two qualities in particular have received attention: self-confidence and assertiveness. Women are told in these books that their lack of these qualities, which results from their gender socialization, makes it harder for them to take charge of their careers and succeed in them.

These discussions are supported by the more scholarly work of gender role theorists, whose research has shown that women emerge from childhood less self-confident about their achievement abilities and less assertive than men (Maccoby and Jacklin 1974; Betz and Fitzgerald 1987). As a result, it is argued, their ability to compete in the male-dominated workplace—where these qualities are required for success—is impeded. A recent study of engineers found lower levels of self-confidence among similarly placed women and men (Bailyn 1987).

This difference in the interactional styles of women and men in engineering has been noted in the sciences as well. According to one recent study:

> [Male] scientists . . . project an image of impersonal authority and absolute confidence in the accuracy, objectivity, and importance of their observations. . . . They will brook neither doubt nor vacillation. . . . [In contrast,] women scientists . . . often call attention to the limitations of their data, to potential flaws in the experimental design . . . taking pains not to overstate their findings. [Namenwirth 1986: 23]

We were struck by the frequency with which our interview respondents spoke of the importance of these qualities in engineering, and of the differences between men and women in this regard. The women were especially aware of the issue: nearly 70 percent made unsolicited comments about it in the interviews. They felt unsure of their technical abilities as engineers, and as a result were less likely to vigorously defend their ideas, or to push for the kind of visible and strategic assignments that lead to promotion. This woman's remarks were typical:

> Every woman I've met has got a lack of confidence, and I don't know why that is. . . . Technically they're exactly the same [as men], but the amount of confidence a woman has in tackling a project versus the amount a man has—it's phenomenal how different it is.
> [Interviewer: Do you see that in yourself?]
> Yeah, definitely. I can be presented with a project and say, "Oh, my God, I can't do this!" That's my first reaction. . . . Whereas I think [a man] at my level would say, "Oh, yeah, great! I'll take that project." Even if he thinks, way down deep inside, "Geez, I don't know if I know how to do this or not."

As we saw earlier, this lack of self-confidence was nothing new. Women were already experiencing it in college, and it was related in part to their lack of tinkering experience in childhood. In school their academic success overshadowed their insecurities in this area, but did not eliminate them. Their schooling did little to help them develop the hands-on skills already acquired by their male classmates. What is more, the reception given them by male students and faculty members often threatened what self-confidence they had.

Once in the workplace, their anxieties about technical proficiency were heightened. They were called upon to perform in ways that had not been required in college—drafting, building prototypes, working with tools. Those who had not had workplace experience during their college years were especially vulnerable. One woman talked about this problem, even though it had not affected her as much as some of the other women she had worked with:

> I had a fairly mechanical background—I always helped boyfriends work on cars, that type of thing. But there are a lot of women who . . . just haven't had the exposure to any number of small mechanical experiences that men have had. And it causes two problems. They blame themselves too heavily for it, and don't see it as just a lack of exposure. And it trips them up all the time. When they don't know pieces of tooling, one from the other, different types of wrenches, that type of thing, it makes them appear as if they're not technically qualified, and that's got nothing to do with technical qualification. It's just a lack of exposure. They haven't had a mechanical background.

At the same time the women marveled at the egotism and assertiveness of the men around them, and saw themselves as lacking by comparison. Discussing the strengths and weaknesses of women as engineers, one woman told us:

> I think they work very hard, and they have a very good academic background. But they lack assertiveness. We get more easily intimidated by men . . . by some of their behavior in meetings. I think intimidation is a big problem. Men are more assertive, more sure of themselves, even if sometimes they have absolutely no ground. And that pays off.

The views of men were quite similar. Many of them acknowledged the competence of women. As one man put it, "Every woman [engineer] I've ever met has been smarter than me." But they saw them as lacking self-confidence about their work, and assertiveness in promoting themselves. When asked about the weaknesses of women engineers compared with men, 33 percent answered, "none"; but 32 percent answered "low self-confidence." One man told us:

They're not assertive enough. And that's why a lot of them don't rise as high. Like one was complaining—she's razor-sharp, Master's from Carnegie Mellon University, but she's not assertive at all. She was griping, why [a man] who started on at the same time is now way up there. I'm not gonna discount the fact that she's a woman. That's still a reality. . . . The prejudice from upper management is not completely squashed, but it's not a big factor, I don't think. I think it's because she's not as assertive.

Thus, our interview data strongly suggest that female engineers have lower levels of self-confidence and assertiveness than men, and that these resources are related to job status. This difference could help explain women's lower status.

In an effort to pursue these possibilities, we assigned scores to our interview respondents for the extent to which they displayed these two attributes. We gave each respondent a score for technical self-confidence and for interactional assertiveness, based on interviewer ratings and content analysis of the interview transcripts (see Appendix). We combined these scores into a single variable, "resources," and found it strongly related to both gender and job status. Resource scores were positively associated with job status (tau $c=.32$; $p=.0001$), and women scored significantly lower than men (tau $c=-.40$; $p=.0004$) (see Tables 7 and 8).

We thus appear to have found an important clue to the occupational fortunes of men and women in engineering. The findings lend weight to the gender role perspective. Men appear to be better prepared by gender socialization to maneuver in the organizational environment of engineering. It is not that men *are* better engineers, but they are better at *appearing* to be better engineers. They are able to make use of their greater self-confidence and assertiveness in promoting themselves, obtaining visible job assignments, and taking risks. As a result, they move up faster and further.

Despite the initial fit of this hypothesis, however, there are important limitations to it as well. First, it should be kept in mind that the association between "resources" and current job is open to more than one causal interpretation. It may indicate, as gender role theory implies, that individuals have made use of the resources they brought into the workplace to achieve a job status commensurate with them. On the other hand, it may indicate a structural process at work: that one's experiences in the workplace, including job status, reinforce—

TABLE 7
Current Job in Relation to Interactional Resources

	Interactional Resources				
	None				A Great Deal
Current Job	0	1	2	3	4
Sales/Marketing					
N	0	3	1	1	0
Percent	(0.0)	(15.8)	(3.8)	(6.3)	(0.0)
Manufacturing/Test					
N	6	8	10	3	0
Percent	(54.5)	(42.1)	(38.5)	(18.8)	(0.0)
Design/R&D					
N	5	6	10	8	5
Percent	(45.5)	(31.6)	(38.5)	(50.0)	(50.0)
Senior Engineer					
N	0	1	5	2	1
Percent	(0.0)	(5.3)	(19.2)	(12.5)	(10.0)
Mid-Management					
N	0	1	0	2	4
Percent	(0.0)	(5.3)	(0.0)	(12.5)	(40.0)
Total	11	19	26	16	10
Kendall's tau-c .31					
Significance (.001)					

or diminish—one's resources. In support of this interpretation, the engineers in our sample who had been in the workforce longest, had the highest resource scores, although the association did not quite achieve statistical significance (tau $c=.13$; $p=.068$).

More importantly, when we look separately at the data for women and men, the limitations of our hypothesis become increasingly troublesome. If these interactional resources contribute to career success, we should see the same patterns within each gender group. Men who are more self-confident and assertive than other men should have higher job status. The same should be true among women. However, the original relationship between resources and current job held up well for men (tau $c=.42$; $p=.002$), but not nearly so well for women (tau $c=.18$; $p=.05$) (see Table 9). Similarly, the association between time in the workforce and resources was very strong for men (tau $c=.35$; $p=.007$), but disappeared completely for women (tau $c=.03$; $p=.400$).

TABLE 8
Interactional Resources: Men and Women

Resource	Men	Women
0		
N	0	11
Percent	(0.0)	(21.2)
1		
N	3	16
Percent	(10.0)	(30.8)
2		
N	8	18
Percent	(26.7)	(34.6)
3		
N	11	5
Percent	(36.7)	(9.6)
4		
N	8	2
Percent	(26.7)	(3.8)
Total n	30	52
Kendall's tau-c	−.59	
Significance	(.000)	

Thus, while the interactional resources that differentiate our female and male respondents may help explain the occupational success of men, they are less helpful in explaining the lower status of women. Women with higher levels of self-confidence and assertiveness are not found in higher status positions as consistently as their male counterparts. Moreover, the work experiences of women are not helping them build these resources, as they are for men. Once again, we find gender role variables more useful in understanding the career patterns of men than women.

SEXISM IN THE WORKPLACE

There is considerable discussion in the literature on women in nontraditional occupations of the sexist treatment women receive. The teasing, hostility, exclusion, patronizing behavior, and sexual harassment in which men often engage in these situations has been widely described, and is generally seen as a serious obstacle to wom-

TABLE 9
Current Job in Relation to Interactional Resources: Men and Women

Current Job	Men None 0	1	2	3	A Great Deal 4	Women None 0	1	2	3	A Great Deal 4
Sales/Marketing										
N	0	0	0	0	0	1	3	0	1	0
Percent	(0.0)	(0.0)	(0.0)	(0.0)	(0.0)	(6.2)	(20.0)	(0.0)	(20.0)	(0.0)
Manufacturing/Test										
N	1	1	4	0	0	8	6	6	1	0
Percent	(33.3)	(20.0)	(40.0)	(0.0)	(0.0)	(50.0)	(40.0)	(40.0)	(20.0)	(0.0)
Design/R&D										
N	2	4	4	4	2	7	4	4	3	0
Percent	(66.7)	(80.0)	(40.0)	(57.1)	(40.0)	(43.8)	(26.7)	(26.7)	(60.0)	(0.0)
Senior Engineer										
N	0	0	2	1	0	0	2	4	0	0
Percent	(0.0)	(0.0)	(20.0)	(14.3)	(0.0)	(0.0)	(13.3)	(26.7)	(0.0)	(0.0)
Mid-Management										
N	0	0	0	2	3	0	0	1	0	1
Percent	(0.0)	(0.0)	(0.0)	(28.6)	(60.0)	(0.0)	(0.0)	(6.7)	(0.0)	(100.0)
Total	3	5	10	7	5	16	15	15	5	1

	Men	Women
Kendall's tau-c	.42	.18
Significance	(.002)	(.05)

en's survival and satisfaction in nontraditional occupations (Meyer and Lee 1978; Schreiber 1979; Deaux and Ullman 1983; Metcalfe 1985). Men's sexist behavior is often explained in terms of their gender socialization. They have learned to expect women to behave in gender-appropriate ways, and to be found in "women's" occupations. Confronting women in their own field, long thought of as "men's work," violates not only their expectations of women, but their view of themselves as well. If women can do what *they* do, even become their bosses, what is left to differentiate them? Having been taught that femininity is to be avoided at all costs, how do they maintain a sense of masculine integrity if women are their equals in the workplace? Moreover, they feel uncomfortable with women as co-workers. They have always interacted differently with women than with men, and now they have to watch what they say and be on guard, because women are around. They can no longer engage in the comfortable, everyday banter they have taken for granted.

As a result, men feel threatened, invaded, and uncomfortable. They react with hostility, subtle or overt, and try to reassert their superiority. They tease, belittle, insult, ignore. They respond with skepticism to women's contributions, or patronize them as "cute little things" who need their help. They assign them tasks that fit their own images of "women's work." They exclude women from casual conversations around the coffee machine, at lunch, or after work. At worst, they engage in outright harassment, sexual or otherwise.

These same behaviors can be explained from a structural perspective as well. As we saw earlier, Kanter (1977) argues that it is not gender socialization, but the sheer dynamics of tokenism that leads to the kinds of interactions just described. It is not because the tokens are women, but because the women are tokens that they are doubted, resented, isolated, and harassed. Our own view is that gender is more important in this process than Kanter acknowledges, given the evidence from other studies that men in token positions do not have the same experiences as women. However, we believe that gender represents not simply a set of socialized role behaviors, but a set of power relations as well. It is not just men's gender socialization that leads them to doubt and resent women in nontraditional roles. It is their interest in protecting their privilege and power as well.

Whether the interpretation is one of gender roles, tokenism, or power relations, the behaviors referred to have been documented wherever women have entered male-dominated occupations. Engineering is no exception. As we saw in the last chapter, women face sexism in engineering school. They encounter it as well in the workplace.

Our interviews showed that the sense of being a minority experienced by women in college was felt at work too, even more strongly. Whereas they usually had a few other women in their classes, they were typically the lone woman in their work group. Even when there were other women engineers in the company, they often had little contact with each other, because they worked in different groups. It was not just the numbers that made them feel different, however. Their interaction with co-workers was a continual reminder of it. All these women encountered sexism from at least some of the men they worked with. The sexism took many forms; here we examine the most common.

Teasing and Joking

Reports of teasing and joking were common in our interviews. The topics typically dealt with women as sexual beings, or as incompetent engineers. For example, Jane, a respondent encountered earlier, told us that she had a particular problem with one of her co-workers:

> I'm not real quick to notice when somebody's putting me down as a female, but this guy purposely wants to smash it in my face, so I just ignore him. He made some comment about a female who graduated first in her class from West Point, and how she must have slept her way to it. [Another time] as I was leaving the building and he was entering, and it was going-home time, I said, "Hey, you're going in the wrong direction." He says, "No, I have to go to work now because you women are going home, and somebody has to pick up the pieces!"

Most women were not terribly bothered by remarks like this, seeing it as "all in fun," or as something they could just ignore. They also learned that the remarks of men were often part of an initial "testing" process, that didn't last long:

> [When I first meet people] they will actually say things like, "Boy, I'd like to do more than shake your hand, honey." But, you know, that gets old real fast, and if you don't bite their head off for it, but just kind of take your lumps, it goes away real fast. And I guess everybody has some kind of initiation, and that's mine.

Nevertheless, this behavior was something men did not have to deal with. However small a problem, it was still a reminder that women were different and in some ways suspect as engineers.

The Patronizing Male

Patronizing behavior—treating women as sweet, helpless, and little girllike—is widespread, especially among older men, whether they be technicians, engineers, or managers. As with teasing, this behavior also singles women out as different, and suggests that they really are not the equals of the men around them. As one 38-year-old woman told us:

> With the older engineers, they always treat you like you're their little daughter, which they don't do to the young male engineers. There's a protectiveness or there's a feeling there where they want to pat you on the head, and you want them to slap you on the back, not pat you on the head.

Younger engineers were capable of similar behavior, though it was less common. In one case, even though the woman was older than her male co-worker, "every time he sees me reach for a screwdriver, he comes over and says, 'here, let me do that for you.' "

Women varied in their response to this kind of behavior. Some were bothered by it, but for most it was not seen as a serious problem. The woman just quoted responded by taking a course to improve her "hardware" skills, so the men around her would have no doubt that she was competent. "I have to get them convinced that it's okay, I know how to run a screwdriver—to pull out a board—splice cables."

Some, however, decided it was best to "play along" with such men:

> You're better off not competing with the males. You can use your own style, if you have the right personality . . . complement the males—that type of thing. Not a good idea to be competitive with them.
>
> [Interviewer: How do they respond?]
>
> They get angry. They don't like competition from females. Yet, if you play it right you can use your femininity to "oh, rescue me—help me," and it works a lot better. I've experimented with this stuff and it works real well. . . . So, why not? If it's gonna help you get your job done, why not?

This kind of manipulation is nothing new. Women, like other powerless groups, have used it throughout history. It is a contradictory process, however. Effective in maintaining smooth working relationships, it nevertheless perpetuates the image of the incompetent woman—the very image women engineers are struggling to overcome.

Mentors

The ease with which many men relate to women as "daughters" would seem to make the mentor relationship a natural one for them. Indeed, women engineers often find a male co-worker or manager who "takes her under his wing" and "shows her the ropes." He helps her make the transition from "knowing" engineering to "doing" engineering, which requires skills not learned in college. He not only teaches her practical skills, but acquaints her with the "ins and outs" of the organizational terrain as well. As we said in the previous chapter, however, the mentor relationship for the woman in a nontraditional field is a complex one, not all positive. While it may provide her with valuable information, support, and contacts, it may do so at the expense of self-confidence. It is, after all, a relationship of unequals, of dependence.

This aspect of the relationship became clear to one of our respondents who thought herself lucky to have acquired a mentor. Until, that is, she decided she was ready to be treated as an equal:

> Shortly after I came on full time, I was given a very difficult project, and [one engineer] took me under his wing. He's been in advanced design for thirty years, and he taught me an awful lot of engineering. . . . As I grew beyond that, there were some real hard times trying to work out a new relationship. When I was no longer . . . looking to him for all the guidance, when I got to a point where I wanted engineering input, but I didn't want somebody meddling in my project, there were some uncomfortable times.
>
> [Interviewer: Were you able to accomplish that?]
>
> Yeah. We worked that out. We now go at each other head-to-head on a more equal basis. It'll never be that comfortable a relationship again, because it just fit before. I needed guidance, he needed somebody to give it to—he needed somebody to mentor. And so now neither of us fills that niche for each other, so it'll never be as comfortable a relationship as it was.

Sexual Harassment: Subtle and Not so Subtle

Just as these men felt comfortable in a fatherly or mentor relationship with women, they also felt free to speak to them in more intimate ways than they would other men. Many respondents told us of their irritation at being called "Honey," "Sweetie," and the like:

> There's a general manager out in the shop that I have to deal with who started off calling me "Darlin," and it just annoys me terribly. To me it was demeaning for him to be that familiar with me. I don't think he would have been that familiar with a male engineer in a similar situation.

This behavior—like teasing and joking—can be considered a mild form of sexual harassment, a problem faced by women in every occupation, traditional and nontraditional alike. Sexual harassment ranges in severity from the sexual crack or endearment to the unwanted "come-on," to actual physical assault. Some of the most overt forms occur where women work around blue-collar workers, such as mechanics and technicians:

> There's an all-pervasive sexual harassment when you have to walk through the shops and hear the whoops and hollers, and whistles. . . . It drains energy. Instead of being able to concentrate on your work—you're on your way to an aircraft, and you know there's a problem, and you're thinking, mulling it over in your mind, and somebody comes up to you and says, "Hi, hon" or whatever, and for that little moment you have to decide, "how should I react, should I call him on this, will I lose respect if I don't call him, will I gain respect?" You just have to make that split-second decision in your mind. "Who is he? Is he a foreman? How do I relate to him?" It drains energy that you want to be putting into your work, and I don't think that the male engineers understand how much energy that drains.

It is not only blue-collar workers who are capable of this behavior, however. Another woman had a problem with a fellow engineer with whom she shared a cubicle:

> He would come in and tell me dirty jokes. What was I supposed to do, laugh at that horrible, disgusting joke that he just told me?

Several women told us of men who "came on" to them, persisting even after the women made it clear they were not interested. Occasionally, the behavior involved physical contact:

> There was one guy who we all complained about. He was an engineer, and he would come up when you're sitting at your desk, and he would put both his hands around you. . . . He would come in and say, "Oh, so dear, how are these doing," and touching you all the time. I think they've given him a lot of warnings that if anything happens again, he's gone.

One reason sexual harassment angers women is because it says they are not professionals, but merely sexual beings. It is not surprising that men who see women this way have a hard time taking them seriously as competent engineers. Along with sexual harassment, even in its mildest forms, frequently goes skepticism. One woman saw this link clearly, as she discussed her relationships with managers:

> I hate being called "honey." They don't recognize you as a professional. That's just a very hard thing for them to do, to understand that yes, you are an engineer and you are capable of making decisions. . . . I've had [situations] where I've gone out in the shop—they were having a problem with a bearing and they wanted me to look at it, and I went out there and said, "It looks fine, go ahead and finish the assembly." They didn't like that. They went back to my boss. They wanted him to go out and look at it. . . . And there's really not a whole lot you can do about it, except insist that you know what you're talking about.

Keeping Women Out

Perhaps the most subtle reminder that these women are different comes when men show their discomfort about being in their presence. As with the more overt types of sexism, this too occurs most often in the early stages of a working relationship:

> My immediate supervisor tended to treat me with kid gloves in the beginning—he wasn't too sure how to deal with me. . . . He would often have a hard time coming to the point he was trying to make, or was very careful about what he was going to say—

he was more hesitant to criticize me . . . didn't want to do anything that was too forward or sounded chauvinistic.

Partly out of this discomfort, perhaps partly out of antagonism,
men often exclude women from their interactions. Many women told
us that they felt left out of social activities, whether at work or otherwise. This woman's complaint was typical:

> There's a lot of social life at [this company], and a lot of times
> you're left out. There'll be a group of people standing around
> and they say, "Yeah, let's go down for lunch—how about you,
> John, you Joe—let's go." You're not one of the boys in that
> sense. . . . Also, when you hear about . . . the things people
> did together on the weekends, and you never even knew about
> it . . . things they knew you could do. Like a bunch would go
> wind surfing.

Several of the women felt that this exclusion from social activities had negative consequences for them in their careers. One
explained it this way:

> A lot of the conversation that comes up in social activities is
> work-related. You miss out on some of the finer points. I think
> its also easier to talk to people [about problems at work] when
> you're on more of a friendly basis, than when its strictly co-
> worker to co-worker. You know, you [need] that common bond
> in order to be able to approach certain subjects. Also, you have a
> tendency to think of people you know and like best when it
> comes to recommending for promotions.

Another felt that what she lost out on most was the "political
stuff." She had no trouble getting the technical information she
needed from her colleagues, but by being excluded from their casual
conversations, she missed out on "the grapevine stuff . . . the little
ins and outs of who's gonna be where—and who has what kind of
attitude towards what decisions. That kind of stuff I get excluded
from a lot."

Sexism in Job Assignments

Exclusion can involve not just informal processes, but formal ones as
well. If women can be left out of conversations and social activities,

they can be passed over for desirable job assignments as well. Many of the women we interviewed complained of managers who stuck them with less challenging, less visible assignments than their male co-workers.

A mechanical engineer working in aerospace found herself receiving poor job assignments compared to others who had no more seniority than she. It was not until she confronted her supervisor assertively that things began to change:

> One of the men I work with graduated at the same time I did. He is a real go-getter, and he was given a lot more responsibility than me. . . . I was never asked to attend meetings, or to manage anything. I did basically routine things, things that I already had the knack of. . . . There was a meeting in Washington that I should have gone to, and there had been several instances before where I had been bypassed. . . . I decided I had to do something. I just basically said, "Hey, start giving me some responsibility. I can do it if you would just let me."
>
> (Interviewer: How did your supervisor respond?)
>
> He said, "Okay," but he was very skeptical. It was up to me to take the jobs, to say, "I'll do this," "I'll do that." He did not give the responsibilities to me—I had to take them.

Standing up for more responsibility also meant refusing to do things that her co-workers and supervisor had come to expect from her, but from no one else:

> They expected me to make coffee . . . to go get supplies . . . run errands. I did that for a while and then I just quit. As long as I would have done it, they would have let me. I just said, "I don't do that anymore."

The questionnaire data showed that women were significantly more likely than men to express dissatisfaction with their job assignments. In particular, they were more likely to be bothered by: (1) a lack of authority to carry out their job; (2) a feeling that their technical training was becoming out of date; and (3) the fact that people at their level had no say in larger matters. These responses suggest that women were finding themselves in less technically challenging jobs, with less authority and autonomy than their male colleagues.

When an engineer is prevented from taking on the more challenging, responsible assignments, she suffers in several ways. Not only is her job less satisfying than it could be, but she is missing out on important learning experiences as well. Moreover, she is not being given the chance to show what she can do. As a result, she is less likely to be seen as someone who should be given more challenges. In short, she is caught in a self-fulfilling prophecy. She is not offered better assignments because her superiors do not see her as someone who can handle them. Without the visibility and the chance to learn new skills, their original perception of her is reinforced.

DOES SEXISM SCUTTLE CAREERS?

Women clearly pay an interactional price for entering new occupational territory. While every respondent had positive things to say about her interactions with the men around her, all had experienced at least some of the problems described here. The issue is not whether these things happen in the male-dominated workplace—it is clear they do. What is important, however, is the *effect* of these interactional problems. Do they constitute a significant obstacle to the success of women in a field like engineering?

We explore this question by looking at the career patterns of women in the two major industry types in our study: aerospace and high tech. These two industries provide an interesting contrast in interactional climate. Aerospace is not thought of as a good area for women in this regard. In our in-depth interviews we heard more complaints about overt sexism in these companies than in any others. A large proportion of this workforce is over fifty and has come out of the military—two factors related to more traditional gender role orientations. Engineers in these firms are also in frequent contact with blue-collar workers, who as a group tend to be the most overt in their displays of sexism.

Probably the most dramatic example of this was reported by Denise, a mechanical engineer working for a large aerospace firm. She had just bought a new car, and as she was on her way out for lunch one day, she stopped by an adjacent building to drop off some paper work:

> I had been in and out of the building for a few days, working on a different type of aircraft. . . . I was away from my car for ten or fifteen minutes. When I came back, a guy who worked out there in the shop had run a hydraulic hangar door into the side of my

car, doing about $900 worth of damage. I hadn't even made the first payment! I had never spoken to him—never seen him . . . [but I found out later that] he had been watching me walk in and out of the shop, and then watched me pull up in my shiny new sports car. . . .

The other guys in the shop had to persuade me that it was done on purpose—I couldn't believe it! I kept getting calls from the guys in the shop [telling me that] this fellow was going around bragging about what he'd done to the bitch engineer's car, and what he was going to do to the bitch when she came back. He had a real problem with a woman in power.

An incident like this would be very unlikely in a high tech workplace, where the interactional climate is more hospitable to women. The men in high tech are younger, there are fewer production workers (and of these a larger share are women), and the university rather than the military has had the strongest socializing impact on both engineers and managers. One of our female respondents had worked in aerospace and still had friends there. She was now working for a high tech firm, and compared the two industries in the following way:

My friends [in aerospace] are harassed a lot more than I would ever be. Being called an "engineerette," being looked at . . . being interrupted . . . and insulted [in meetings]. [Men] always insinuating, "well, you're just gonna get pregnant and have babies. . . . " It's the age of the men, and the military environment. . . . There's men who've been [treating women that way] for twenty, thirty years, and they're not gonna change, and its just kind of accepted. Whereas in [high tech] its much newer. . . . The men are younger and more sensitive to that. . . . There's kind of an unspoken policy there that you're not gonna give women a hard time. Its a much better environment for women.

This perception of high tech industry as less sexist was widely shared among the women in our interview sample. If interactional climate is a significant determinant of career success for women, we would expect them to be doing better in high tech than in aerospace firms. Our data showed otherwise, however. When we looked at engineers employed by high tech firms, we found that the divergence

TABLE 10
Current Job for Men and Women:
High Tech and Aerospace

	Company			
	Hi Tech		Aerospace	
Current Job	Men	Women	Men	Women
Sales/Marketing				
N	1	2	0	0
Percent	(.9)	(11.8)	(0.0)	(0.0)
Manufacturing/Test				
N	16	7	30	9
Percent	(13.7)	(41.2)	(35.7)	(32.1)
Design/R&D				
N	70	6	46	12
Percent	(59.8)	(35.3)	(54.8)	(42.9)
Senior Engineer				
N	18	2	8	7
Percent	(15.4)	(11.8)	(9.5)	(25.0)
Mid-Management				
N	12	0	0	0
Percent	(10.3)	(0.0)	(0.0)	(0.0)
Total	117	17	84	28
Kendall's tau-c	−.19		.10	
Significance	(.0008)		(.130)	

in job standing between men and women was greater there than for the sample as a whole. In contrast, in aerospace the differences between men and women were no longer statistically significant, and the direction of the relationship was reversed. In other words, women had a statistically nonsignificant occupational superiority over their male colleagues in these firms, despite their more sexist atmosphere[12] (see Table 10).

We also found that the relationship between interactional resources (self-confidence and assertiveness) and job status was much stronger for women in aerospace (tau $c = .35$; $p = .06$) than in high tech (tau $c = -.05$; $p = .42$). In high tech, women who scored high on these resources were no more likely to be in higher status positions than women who scored low. In aerospace, however, the more self-confident and assertive women were, like men, most likely to be found in high status positions.

TABLE 11
Current Job for Men and Women:
Electrical and Mechanical Engineers

	Occupation			
	Electrical Engineer		Mechanical Engineer	
Current Job	Men	Women	Men	Women
Sales/Marketing				
N	2	2	1	1
Percent	(1.0)	(6.1)	(.8)	(2.4)
Manufacturing/Test				
N	26	13	41	13
Percent	(13.3)	(39.4)	(32.8)	(31.7)
Design/R&D				
N	127	16	58	17
Percent	(65.1)	(48.5)	(46.4)	(41.5)
Senior Engineer				
N	30	1	15	9
Percent	(15.4)	(3.0)	(12.0)	(22.0)
Mid-Management				
N	9	1	10	1
Percent	(4.6)	(3.0)	(8.0)	(2.0)
Upper Management				
N	1	0	0	0
Percent	(.5)	(0.0)	(0.0)	(0.0)
Total	195	33	125	41
Kendall's tau-c	−.180		.003	
Significance	(.000)		(.48)	

We found similar patterns when we looked at occupational standings for the two engineering specialties included in our sample: electrical and mechanical. As with high tech and aerospace, there is a general perception among engineers that electrical engineering is a better specialty for women than mechanical. Our respondents saw it as abstract, math-based, and "clean" work—associated with computers and lab coats. It was therefore thought to be more suited to women. In contrast, they associated mechanical engineering with the image of the "tinkerer," building prototypes in a shop—an image closely tied to the male gender role. Nationally, more women choose electrical engineering than mechanical, constituting thirteen percent of undergraduate majors in the former, and eleven percent in the latter (American Assoc. of Engineering Societies 1989b).

Yet when we compared the career patterns of our respondents in these two specialties, we found women doing better in mechanical engineering. Among electrical engineers gender inequality was greater than for the sample as a whole, while among mechanical engineers, the inequality disappeared (see Table 11). Male mechanical engineers held a slight edge over women in design jobs, but women outnumbered men in management. Moreover, the relationship between interactional resources and job status was very strong for women in mechanical engineering (tau $c=.40$; $p=.008$), but disappeared for women in electrical engineering (tau $c=.06$; $p=.35$).

What are we to make of these patterns? In order to fully understand them, we need to go beyond gender roles and sexism, and examine the structure of the work organizations in which they are played out. We do that in the next chapter, looking at the relations of power and workplace culture within different organizational environments. We see that the effects of gender role characteristics and sexism are shaped by the organizational context in which they occur. Before leaving the gender role perspective, however, we conclude this chapter with an evaluation of its usefulness in explaining the experiences of women.

CONCLUSION

As we have seen, only a few of the variables emphasized by the gender role perspective are helpful in understanding why women hold lower status positions in engineering than men. Education cannot explain it: their education is the same, and women excel as students. Length of work experience and job tenure predicts job standings for men, but not for women. The work-related values and attitudes of men and women are highly similar, as are their patterns of career continuity.

We appear closest to an explanation when we examine technical self-confidence and the related quality of assertiveness. Women are less likely to have these interactional resources than men, and for the sample as a whole, there is an association between the resources and success as engineers. However, the relationship is stronger for men than for women. In addition, men increase their levels of self-confidence and assertiveness as their careers progress; women do not. Not only that, interactional resources are more important in predicting job standing in aerospace firms than in high tech.

Sexism is a problem to one degree or another for most women engineers. However, women are in the highest status positions, even outranking men, in the very place where sexism is most overt—the aerospace firm. Finally, women are doing better in mechanical than electrical engineering, despite the popular perception that electrical engineering is more compatible with the gender role attributes of women.

Thus, we are left with the conclusion that the gender role perspective is insufficient to the task of understanding the problems women face in engineering. That gender socialization shapes the attitudes and behaviors of men and women differently, we do not doubt. Women and men bring different sets of interactional resources into the workplace. Men interact in sexist ways with their female coworkers. All of these are true—even clichés. While gender role research—and our own—has provided ample documentation of these points, it has not been able to demonstrate a *causal* connection between these gender differences and career outcomes. We believe that by itself, this perspective never will. What is needed is an integration of the gender role and structural perspectives. Some of the gender role variables are important, and do affect women's careers. As we see in the next chapter, however, they do so only in the context of particular organizational structures. We must look first at that context—the resources and power relations of groups within specific engineering workplaces. Then we can integrate the two.

6

THE CULTURE OF
ENGINEERING IN THE WORKPLACE

We saw in the last chapter that the gender role perspective is of limited value to us in our efforts to explain the lower job status of women engineers. The only gender role variables that are useful are the lower levels of self-confidence and assertiveness displayed by women. On the other hand, women working in different industries and engineering specialties are experiencing distinctly different career patterns. Mechanical engineers and those employed by aerospace firms are doing better than electrical engineers and those in high tech, despite the widespread perception that the latter two are more gender-compatible and less sexist than the former. This suggests the need to look beyond the gender role perspective and examine the structure of the organizations in which engineers work. For, as we saw in chapter 2, occupational outcomes are not just a matter of the qualities people bring with them into the workplace. They are also shaped by the relations of power and the resources people find there.

In this chapter we explore the structure of the engineering workplace and its impact on the careers of women. We focus on the two industries where most of our respondents worked, and where we found striking differences in the career patterns of women: high tech and aerospace firms. We also explore, more briefly, career patterns in electrical and mechanical engineering. In the process, we demonstrate the significance of gender-linked interactional styles for women's careers. We argue that self-confidence and assertiveness constitute important interactional resources that can be used to maneuver for career advantage. Yet the usefulness of these resources varies with the power of engineers in the organization. More specifically, the utility of interactional resources is dependent on whether engineers have been successful in dominating the culture of the workplace. Where engineers are powerful, they create work relations that reflect their interests both as engineers and as men. This culture, in turn, becomes a medium through which women must maneuver in order to succeed in their jobs. In short, it is neither gender behavior nor organization structure alone that shapes the engineering career. It is the interaction of the two, mediated by the culture that prevails in a particular workplace.

We begin with a close look at two companies for which many of our respondents worked. They represent the two industry types on which we are focusing. Computer Devices Incorporated is a high tech firm, which employed 8 percent of our respondents. The plant is a medium-sized (approximately 1,500 employees) manufacturer of computer peripherals, and is a branch of one of the country's largest and best known high tech firms. United Missile is no less well known as one of the country's major defense contractors. The plant we studied employs over fifteen thousand workers, and manufactures missile components. Ten percent of our respondents worked there. We turn now to a discussion of the structure, power relations, workplace culture, and experiences of women in each company.

COMPUTER DEVICES INCORPORATED

Everyone connected with Computer Devices Incorporated (CDI) is aware of its reputation as one of the country's premier high tech firms. CDI was founded by engineers, and has always taken pride in its engineering orientation. Nationwide, the company employs over fifty-six thousand workers. Its growth over the last decade has brought many of the tensions associated with increased size and bureaucratization, but the company has managed to preserve much of its original commitment to technology, innovative product design, and engineering.

Among our respondents, CDI had the reputation of being one of *the* places for an engineer to work. Few companies can offer the particular combination of interesting work and good pay found at CDI. The peripherals manufactured at the plant are complicated enough to make for interesting engineering work, and the pay and benefits are among the best in the area. As one woman put it: "CDI is thought of as one of the best companies: the best work environment, benefits, and pay . . . it's a very competitive company."

Staying in this part of southern California was a priority for many of our respondents. Pleasant weather, the ocean, and the amenities of a large city make the area attractive, despite growing levels of congestion and air pollution. Indeed, the attractions of the area lure engineers from all over the country, so there is considerable competition for jobs, especially at a company like CDI. To land a job there is considered a coup.

The CDI plant we studied is located in a suburb about fifteen miles from the center city. The area immediately surrounding the site is open space, but not for long—it is quickly being absorbed by housing developments. Though the plant is a production facility, its physical appearance is more like a research center or an administrative office. The facilities consist of a cluster of one-story glass buildings located in a parklike setting. Cheap to build and energy efficient, these structures, once avant-garde, have become the norm for high tech firms in southern California. The atmosphere at the site is informal: production workers mix with engineers and managers, and all dress casually.

The most prestigious job assignment within CDI, in the view of both engineers and managers, is the design lab. The lab creates prototypes for the peripherals manufactured on site. All engineers at CDI are individually ranked ("stacked") each year, and paid accordingly. Lab work automatically ranks among the highest, and is the standard against which other engineering activities are judged. The status of the lab reflects the company's emphasis on technical innovation and the search for new products.

Lab engineers hold the most prestige, but engineers in general feel valued by the company. As one male engineer who had risen into management put it, "CDI has been a strictly engineering-driven company. The engineers have been given tremendous amounts of freedom and power versus some of the other groups."

The importance of engineers helps to create a strong sense of collegiality among them. When we asked Charlie, an engineer in the lab, what he liked best about CDI, he replied: "sitting around bullshitting with the other people. We have a lot of guys that are really funny and amusing and neat to talk to." Most of his comments about his work activities were made in the plural: we do this, we think that, we made this decision. Charlie and his colleagues had a strong sense of being part of a group. They were proud of what they did, and with whom. There is a conscious sense of community among engineers at CDI—a community that serves as the basis for a common culture as well.

Charlie was in his mid-twenties, married, and the father of an eight-month-old baby. Since the baby's arrival, he had been thinking more about his future. While he fantasized about starting a consulting firm, or becoming a novelist, he felt that, realistically, he would be at CDI for the foreseeable future. Interestingly, rising into management played no role in his schemes. "I'm really not oriented toward management . . . I think of a manager as someone who has these neat lists, and his desk is very pristine. . . . My desk is a mess, and I can never remember what I'm supposed to do from minute to minute." Charlie was good at what he did, enjoyed his work, and felt comfortable in the lab. Why should he trade that for the headaches of management? Besides, where else could he find "such a neat group of guys to hang around"?

This collegiality is consciously encouraged by management. A woman who had worked as a design engineer in the lab told us:

> We socialize a lot, the company encourages the socializing. . . .
> It's part of the written policy. You're supposed to go chitchat
> with people. And you're told to take long coffee breaks and
> wander around and find out what all the other projects are
> doing. Part of your job almost.

This casual and open atmosphere extends to relations between engineers and management as well. Even the lowest level "grunt" engineer is theoretically free to talk to the highest level manager. As Charlie explained it:

> There is an objective in the company charter that says that every
> employee should feel free to speak to anyone above them at any
> time. I think it specifically refers to the division manager [the
> highest level of management on site]. In theory every employee
> is supposed to feel free to walk in the door and say, "Hey, this
> disturbs me," or "I don't like this," or "Why don't we try some-
> thing else?"

This kind of policy is widespread in high tech companies, and is often more a labor relations gimmick than a sign of real openness. Charlie could not think of anyone who had actually gone in and talked to the division manager. Nevertheless, the policy is symbolic of the interactional climate of the workplace. Engineers are relatively unintimidated by management, as illustrated by this anecdote Charlie shared with us: "We had one guy during the Halloween party who dressed up in a Superman suit and jumped on the division manager's desk. Shortly thereafter they decided we shouldn't wear costumes on Halloween to work."

The pride and collegiality of these engineers is also fostered by the autonomy they are given in their work. Officially the policy is "management by objective." That is, a manager tells an engineer only what needs to be done, not how to do it. Such policies are often violated, but it is followed regularly enough at CDI for most of our respondents to see it as standard procedure. At the time of our interview, Charlie was working on a project that he had originated on his own:

> There've been times when I've decided that there was a problem that needed to be addressed and I just started working on it, and I didn't tell anybody about it. Usually it's not as if I'm doing it in secret, because I've talked about it with a lot of my co-workers first, and it becomes apparent that there's something that needs to be done that isn't being done. So you just do it. . . . I started doing that on this temperature control problem I'm working on right now. People said, "wow, you seem to be doing well on this temperature control problem. Why don't you work on that full-time?"

This degree of autonomy is not unusual in the lab, or elsewhere in the plant. A woman in marketing, for example, told us that what she liked most about her job was:

> . . . the independence. I have something that I'm responsible for and I prioritize my day and I decide what my hours are. I have responsibilities, but I decide how I go about them, as long as I'm getting the work done that my manager would like to see me get done.

Engineers were even able to pursue approaches against the wishes of their supervisors. As Charlie told us:

> I've had managers before tell me to do something a certain way, and I've told them it's a stupid way to do it, and they've said do it anyway. . . . If I was really convinced [however] that this was a major error that would cause major problems, I'd probably either just do it the way I thought best anyway and just not tell the guy, or try to talk to his boss about it.

Engineers were in fact encouraged to resist management in the pursuit of product quality:

> In fact, there's a tradition of giving the Rogue Engineer award to the engineer who successfully defied management and got the right answer. . . . It's a miniature elephant head.

This autonomy reflects the fact that engineers hold greater power at CDI than is found in many engineering workplaces. One of the most dramatic examples of this is the selection interview for lab engineers. Candidates undergo a rigorous interview focusing largely on technical knowledge, but the evaluation is done not by management, but by lab engineers. The engineers who conduct the interview take the process, and themselves, very seriously. It is they who decide whether an individual is qualified to enter this elite "technical brotherhood." The interview is a rite of passage in which the criteria for membership are details of the most abstract and technical engineering knowledge, and in which those defining the criteria are one's peers. These engineers have the power to influence access to the most desirable work at CDI. The intensity of this process can be seen in the comments of a woman who worked in manufacturing, but wanted to get into the lab:

> To move into the lab, I have to take another technical interview. See, it's really just awful because what if you don't pass, and your peers are interviewing you? . . . Some of these guys are pompous, they think they're the greatest. I mean, so it's a problem, it's not like [being interviewed by] a manager, it's my peers.

But as technical and competitive as the interview is, the actual work in the lab is surprisingly basic. The prototypes created there, while interesting, are largely variations on existing technologies. They are innovative enough to give engineers autonomy in their work, but not so innovative as to demand the regular use of high-level engineering skills. A woman who had worked in the lab and then transferred out, complained about this: "there's very little design work where you actually sit down and brainstorm a way of making [a product]. . . . You spend fifty percent of your time drafting, [and] doing nonengineering work." In other areas of CDI there is even less high-level engineering. A woman who had worked both in the lab and in manufacturing told us: "in the lab it was about fifty percent hands-on working with parts, in manufacturing probably about eighty percent."

What compensates most engineers for the lack of technical innovation is the chance to practice hands-on engineering—the opportunity to tinker. CDI is not unionized, and, in order to reduce costs, the company employs few technicians. Consequently, engineers do much of the work that technicians normally do:

> The policy at CDI is that you do everything. . . . There are very few engineering technicians. They do not hire them. Engineers are constantly having to build some equipment, and you go down and build it yourself.

For most engineers this hands-on activity is an attractive feature of the job. As we have seen, many of these men began tinkering in childhood, and they relish the opportunity to "get their hands dirty" and "play" with the technology.

Yet lab engineers also place great importance on the design work they do. In their view, "real" engineering means the creation of technology. The further removed engineers are from design, the less respect they receive. This is best illustrated by the attitude of lab engineers toward the group furthest from design: marketing engineers. As Charlie put it: "Well, we have people that we call marketing engineers. They all have engineering degrees and backgrounds, but they don't engineer any more, they market. And we kind of speak derisively when we call them engineers. They're engineers of a sort."

While technical competence and involvement with design are necessary to status at CDI, they are not, by themselves, sufficient. The status of engineers also depends on the way they display this competence. There is a great deal of pressure to conform to the image of the "good" engineer. As a woman who had worked at CDI for four years told us: "that's one thing I learned . . . it's how you're perceived [that's important]. It's an image. It's really how you're perceived that makes a difference."

"Good images" at CDI are strongly linked to the male gender role. Wherever engineers gather, the atmosphere resembles a "technical locker room" populated by "jocks." It is not enough to be quietly competent. Aggressive, competitive displays are the norm. Engineers brag about their technical abilities and the products they produce, and engage in invidious comparisons. As one woman who had worked in the lab put it, "It's a prima donna atmosphere. It's a lot of status-oriented people [who take] pride in their work type of thing: who's smarter than who? Who can have a niftier design than who?" Managers in the lab behave in much the same way. A manufacturing engineer told us: "the lab is thought of as being more prestigious, and . . . there's more risk involved in leading a project [there]. . . . I mean I look at those managers, and they have a certain character about them. A lot of them are a certain cut . . . they are cutthroat and ambitious."

What we are describing here is a workplace culture over which engineers exert strong influence. Engineers at CDI share a distinct set of values and norms, which they believe should be the basis of work relations. What is most important is that their beliefs do influence work relations to a significant degree.

We have focused on the lab engineer, because the characteristics of high tech engineering are displayed there in purest form. But the lab stands at the apex of an engineering-oriented organization. Throughout the plant, engineers hold status and work with considerable autonomy. Whether in the lab or not, engineers at CDI see themselves as members of a technical elite, an exclusive—predominantly men's—club. The emphasis on technology fits well with the tinkering that most of these engineers have done since childhood. The aggressive styles of self-presentation are the kind that boys learn early in life. Everything meshes: workplace culture is reinforced by gender role culture. The sense of symmetry and belonging resonates in the interviews of the men at CDI, as well it should. Engineers had no small hand in creating this workplace culture. Their power at CDI leads quite naturally to an interactional climate that reflects their interests and backgrounds.

One of our respondents, a marketing engineer, told us that CDI was permeated by a "locker room culture." She was referring to the importance of athletics to company social life, but it is a good metaphor for the work culture itself: obsessed with both athletic and technical competition. It is not surprising that men feel at home in such an atmosphere. For women, however, the story is quite different.

WOMEN AT CDI

Unlike men, women at CDI do not flourish, particularly in the lab. Several of the women we interviewed had worked in the lab, and for each of them the experience was a disturbing one. All were bright and competent. They had done well in school, and had been actively recruited by CDI. They had initially been excited about the prospect of working in the lab, but all eventually left it for other areas, deeply dissatisfied with their experiences. Most took demotions in order to get out.

It was not that they were unable to live up to the technical demands placed upon them. While they had difficult experiences in the lab, their problems did not revolve around the abstract, theoretically demanding nature of the work. Most, in fact, complained about the lack of abstract problems to work on. As one told us: "it got old after a while. It was fun and exciting [at first], but once I'd learned how to do it, it seemed like the same machine over and over again."

These women were technically proficient. Their school performance had shown that, as had their ability to handle a demanding technical interview. The problems they experienced in the lab revolved, instead, around the interactional climate there. The atmosphere of aggressive competition that prevails is one in which women are not comfortable. As one woman who had left the lab told us:

> [There's] a lot of competition. A lot of competition. These are very intelligent bright people we're talking about. CDI's a high tech company, and they hire the top ten percent. There's an awful lot of competition. You need to be confident about what you do, and from my own personal point of view, that was a hard thing to find.

Competition was not new to these women, however. They had competed in college, and had done well. What was different was the terms of the competition they now faced. Though acts of technical virtuosity in the lab are rare, the *image* of virtuosity is revered. At CDI the image of hands-on competence is most important. But as we saw in previous chapters, it is here that women are often disadvantaged. One woman spoke for many in our sample when she said: "I had no idea about hardware, screws: does a one-inch screw do the same thing as a half inch screw? I just didn't have a lot of the basics."

The importance of these hands-on skills is related to the problem of self-confidence cited earlier. While these women had done well in college, once they entered the workplace they found their sense of competence threatened by their lack of experience with machinery and tools. A woman who had worked in the lab told us: "That was one of the reasons I felt like I wasn't a good engineer, because I didn't have that background." This was from a woman who had a 3.75 GPA in her major, and who had done well in her work. "My parts always worked. I had the least amount of problems getting my stuff into production, but I . . . didn't like building things. I didn't like it so much that I would go out of my way not to build things."

Her fear of mechanical tasks put her at an initial disadvantage, but many of the skills involved are basic, and quickly learned. The only problem is that a tone and style of interaction has been set. The skill deficits are quickly redressed, but a woman's image with co-workers and her self-esteem have been damaged. She has to play "catch-up" just when she feels most insecure, and when others doubt her competence. She has acquired a reputation as "deviant" from the culture of the workplace. A respondent who was asked if hands-on skill deficits were a major disadvantage replied:

> It's overcome easily. It's overcome in the first year [on the] job. It's just that you really make a fool of yourself . . . a few times, and then you have some uphill climbs with those particular people.

An image like this can be changed, but it is not easy, and it is certainly not a good way to begin a career.

We are not saying that all hands-on engineering skills are learned this quickly. Some skills are extremely demanding, and require years to master. The gap between a design on a piece of paper and a working prototype is often large. Theoretical knowledge of the principles of engineering does not always translate into manufacturable products. These high-level hands-on skills, however, are not the ones that differentiate men from women. Most of the men in our sample entered their first jobs without them as well. This is the "craft" side of engineering, and it requires years for *any* new engineer to master it. The skills that differentiate men from women are the more basic ones discussed above.

A woman is expected to display not only hands-on competence, but self-promotion as well. At CDI "blowing your own horn" is necessary, and knowing when and to whom to blow it is especially important. When we asked one of the women who had left the lab (and CDI) why she had done so, she told us: "A combination of things. . . . The fact that I was not confident about my abilities and didn't blow my own horn, that was part of it. Funny, because the people I worked with would say 'you're a good engineer.'" When asked what she liked least about CDI, she replied:

> The politics, probably. It's a large company and you had to be careful about talking to who and what and where . . . . to do your job you didn't need a lot of politics, but in order to get onto the good projects, to get the good jobs on the projects, a lot of it's politics.

The engineers at CDI all seem to know what kind of person makes it there: bright and technically oriented, but also aggressive and a self-promoter. The last two qualities are at least as important as the first two. They also pose the greatest difficulties for women.

GINGER

We can see the impact of the interpersonal dynamics at CDI in the experiences of Ginger. Her story is particularly instructive in that her career advancement was limited not by any direct and overt discrimination on the part of her managers or peers. The process was complex and subtle, but the outcome no less real.

As we saw earlier, Ginger entered the engineering profession with misgivings. When she graduated she was not sure what engineers did, and she was not sure she would be good at it, whatever it was. There was one thing, however, that she *was* sure of: she wanted to work at CDI. "[CDI] was the only company that I really wanted to work for, and so I went to the on-campus interview, passed that, and got an interview with CDI on site."

She was interested in CDI because of "their reputation, definitely. Their reputation, and also a very good friend of mine, John, who went to work for CDI, said they were a great company to work for. So, knowing that I was staying in the area, CDI was the perfect alternative for me."

Ginger's interest in CDI was partly related to her fear of engineering. She knew she would have a lot to learn about the practice of engineering, and that it would take time:

I wanted to work for a large company, because I didn't have the experience, and I needed that buffer to learn. I needed a company who didn't have to rely on me to produce instantly, like maybe a smaller corporation would. I went into CDI with the intent of working there a couple of years, and then transferring to a smaller corporation.

Ginger's hesitancy about her ability to produce was apparently not shared by the interviewers at CDI. They knew she did not have much hands-on experience, but they were impressed enough by her intelligence and her knowledge of engineering theory to hire her into the lab, after an intensive interview:

[It] was real difficult. It's an all-day interview. You interview with about six people in the lab, and it's technical. But, I did very well. It seemed to be exactly what I was studying. I was very surprised that they were as concerned with all the theory, but definitely most of the questions they asked me were very theoretical. After going through the theory, they went into more of the hands-on, but they totally understood that I didn't have that experience.

Ginger was only the third woman hired into the lab, and she stayed there for three years. She did well in her work, and was respected by management. An advanced engineering degree was an informal prerequisite for moving into management in the lab. Ginger enrolled in a master's program at Stanford University when she started at CDI. After three years she had completed several quarters by video correspondence, and was ready for the on-campus portion of the program. CDI selected a few engineers every year for a fellowship, which allowed them to complete their work at Stanford, all expenses paid. Ginger was chosen for this fellowship, and was planning to take advantage of it:

I was on a very good course. I was one of the few female engineers . . . they had me pegged. I was kind of their token. I think I did well. I *did* do well. I was stacked relatively high, and I had a lot of good experience, and I was going to Stanford to get my master's degree.

Ginger was on her way up. She was on a "fast track." But suddenly she jumped off the track. She decided that she did not want to go to Stanford, and, most surprising of all, that she wanted out of the lab. "All of a sudden I made this change and they thought I was crazy. I was out of my mind. They were losing one of their engineers they had spent three years training. Which, of course, I'm sure they were upset about." Not only were they losing a promising lab engineer, not only was she turning down Stanford and a master's degree, but she wanted to transfer into marketing! "I got a lot of static from my manager saying 'This is not what you should be doing. You're an engineer, you're wasting your talents.'" Marketing, as we have seen, was barely considered an engineering activity by most engineers. From the engineers' perspective, she was taking a giant step down.

Why did she do it? Why did Ginger turn down graduate school? Why was she so anxious to leave the lab that she was willing to take what many considered a demotion in order to do so? The answers to these questions are complicated, but they tell us a great deal about women's experiences at CDI, and in high tech more generally. In order to answer the questions, however, we need to know a little more about Ginger's experiences in the lab.

It would be easy to conclude that Ginger's behavior was simply the result of gender role socialization. At first glance, concepts like fear of success, insufficient career motivation, and lack of self-confidence seem to apply. Ginger, as we have seen, was highly traditional in her gender role orientation, and, for someone so talented, she had a remarkable lack of self-confidence. But the story is more complicated than this.

To fully understand Ginger's experiences, we must appreciate how her gender characteristics interacted with the environment of the lab. As we have seen, the lab was a very competitive place, and Ginger was acutely aware of this:

> The males had a tendency to be very proud of their designs: "This is my design, I'm very possessive of it." And "I did this, and isn't it great, and aren't I neat." [They] felt like they had to be the perfect engineer.

Like the other women who had worked in the lab, Ginger's problem was not with competition per se, but with the style of the competition. Though the interview for the lab had been highly theoretical, Ginger was surprised to learn that everyday practice was anything but: "Probably eighty percent of what I did I relied on my practical experience, maybe twenty percent on what I learned in college." Of that twenty percent most involved basic skills: "how to solve engineering problems is really what I used." While she used math a great deal, most of it involved nothing beyond algebra, and "not the level of math I learned in college by any means."

As we have seen, competence in the lab was measured in no small part by hands-on skills. To be accepted as a good engineer, to compete and be taken seriously, it was not merely the higher engineering skills that were important, but basic mechanical abilities as well. Here Ginger had difficulty, beginning with her first day at work. She was working with an experienced male engineer, and he asked her to hand him a particular tool. She had no idea what he was talking about:

> He just looked at me like, "oh my god, here we go." On my first day! . . . I wanted to quit. I think I went home crying, I just, you know, I said, "what am I in this for?"

This kind of ignorance, of course, did not reflect on her ability as an engineer—she had not been exposed to tools, either as a child or in college, so there was no reason she should be familiar with them. But the experience was an assault on her sense of competence as an engineer, and it confirmed the stereotypes held by many of her co-workers.

Ginger attributed many of her problems in the lab to this lack of experience with hands-on engineering:

> If a man was to graduate at the same time I did, with the same [hands-on] experience level, I don't think it would have been any different. I really don't. I think if that man had more experience in hands-on . . . then he may have earned the credibility of the other engineers faster.

As we have seen, these kinds of hands-on skills are quickly acquired. It does not take a great deal of late night study to learn the names and uses of tools. "I learned it in a few months. I learned all about that stuff, it [was] not a problem." Ginger became competent in this area, but never quite comfortable. But that was all right, because competence was all that was needed to do the job well.

Ginger's problems in the lab, however, were not just due to her lack of hands-on experience, but a more general lack of conformity to the culture of the workplace. Though upper management seemed to be grooming her for promotion, she did not work with management on a day-to-day basis. She worked with other engineers, and she never quite felt accepted by them:

I'd been on a project with the same engineers for about two years and, I'll never forget, one of the engineers had been there about twenty-six years . . . [and he said] "Oh, you're not just another dumb blond." It was like, "well, finally. . . ." But I guess it just took so long. It was so hard to get to that point, and [his comment] just cemented the fact that this man was thinking this for the last two years.

The feeling that she did not belong in the lab resonates through Ginger's interview, and much of it had to do with being female. "In the lab I was the oddball. I wasn't accepted much. I felt uncomfortable and not at ease." When asked what she liked least about her company, Ginger replied: "in the lab I liked it least because it was mostly male-dominated." The males around her seemed to be excruciatingly conscious of her gender:

[There was] this one guy . . . in my mind he was the best engineer in the world, and unfortunately and fortunately I ended up working with him. But he would call me "lady" at first. He did not accept me at all, and he would just call me "lady."

She began to dread her job: "I found myself getting very unhappy—getting up in the morning not liking to go to work, struggling with what I was doing." She wanted out.

Marketing attracted her, but it was not because it was less competitive. It was the style of competition that was different. There was little hands-on engineering there, and the creation or design of technology was much less important. Competition in marketing, therefore, was less engineer-defined. There was less concern with technical abilities, and more with business skills. Marketing engineers performed support operations: if a customer had a problem with a product, a salesperson would work with a marketing engineer to resolve it. Rather than a bunch of boys playing with high-priced toys, it was a bunch of boys and girls seeking to please customers. In order to be accepted in the lab, one had to conform to the image of the "technical jock." In marketing such an image was out of place. It was a more "people-oriented" atmosphere.

In the lab many engineers were uninterested in becoming managers, unless it was in a technical capacity. Roughly half (47%) the lab engineers in our sample indicated little or no interest in gaining a position in management. In contrast, fewer than 10 percent of sales engineers responded similarly. In marketing, management was the goal, and the competition was fierce, as Ginger discovered: "In marketing I had a manager who . . . was out to be the president of the company, so he was out for himself, and he would use some of my ideas, but he'd lie [about it]":

There was also more sexual harassment in marketing:

> In the lab, there was absolutely no sexual harassment. At all. I mean, those guys were there to work. They're engineers, and you know, who cares? In marketing it was a different story.

In spite of all this, Ginger felt more comfortable in her new job. She was able to get out from under her feelings of incompetence, and she felt more accepted.

Marketing was "not as male-dominated. So, I wasn't the odd-ball. I was just another one of the workers." There were more women engineers, salespeople, and managers in this area, and the atmosphere was not as male-defined.

Let us return to our earlier question regarding Ginger's reasons for taking a "demotion" out of the lab. Ginger's initial account of her decision was that she did not like that kind of engineering. She was more people-oriented, and felt estranged by the single-minded technical orientation of the lab. When we pursued this issue with her, however, it became more complex. Ginger found it difficult to put her finger on just exactly what it was that drove her out. If she had enjoyed the technical work more, she would have stayed. But she would have enjoyed it more if she had not felt so isolated and unappreciated. She knew that upper-level management looked kindly on her and was encouraging her to pursue graduate work, but the engineers in the lab seemed unappreciative and distant. She had no mentor, nor even any encouragement from those around her.

Despite these problems, Ginger was attracted by the prospect of becoming a project manager in the lab. If she had seen this as a realistic possibility, she might have stayed. But when she approached her manager about it, he told her simply, "I can't promise you anything." Promotions in the lab are rare, and statements like this are commonplace. In retrospect, Ginger felt that if she had been more confident, and better at promoting herself, she might have stayed and won the promotion she wanted. At the time, however, that seemed highly uncertain, and the lack of encouragement undermined what little confidence she had. She felt, she said, "like a failure."

Ginger's problems were not a matter of simple tokenism. She was clearly a token—an isolated female in a male environment—but that was nothing new to her. At the university she had been one of two or three women in every class she took, but she was compensated by the congruence between her academic resources and the terms of competition. In the lab, Ginger was haunted by feelings of incompetence because her resources were no longer congruent with the interactional culture.

Where does this leave us? Ginger's decision to leave the lab was, in part, the product of her own choices, her own fears. But to say this is to oversimplify. Her choices were shaped, and her fears reinforced, by the interactional climate surrounding her. We believe that this interactional climate was the crucial variable in her decision. She received no encouragement from those around her, and had no mentor to advise her. Her lack of self-confidence and assertiveness was related to her childhood socialization, and especially to her lack of hands-on background. But they were also a product of her daily experiences in the lab. She entered the lab with a deficit in hands-on knowledge, but she acquired these abilities quickly, and performed her job well. Despite her competence, however, she never felt comfortable in the *culture* of the lab.

The lab was an engineer's paradise: interesting work, low levels of supervision, and a significant degree of power over work activities. This autonomy and power allowed engineers to create a work culture that reflected their interests. It was this atmosphere, with its stress on hands-on engineering and its male-defined interactional style, that was Ginger's biggest obstacle. She could become technically competent—and she did—but she would never develop the same enthusiasm for this aspect of the work that her peers displayed, nor would she engage in the requisite style of interaction.

These are not the problems of a single individual or a single workplace. As we saw in chapter 5, women engineers in high tech experienced declining levels of self-confidence over time, while the confidence of their male counterparts was increasing. We can see the reasons for this pattern in Ginger's experiences.

Ginger was unique in one regard, however. Among all the women we interviewed who had worked in the lab, she was the only one who felt that she had any chance of being promoted. In fact, among women throughout CDI there was a general perception that management opportunities for women in the lab were slim. Ginger was so bright that her competence was recognized—at least by upper management—in spite of her lack of conformity to the interactional style of the lab. Other women were not so lucky. That it took someone of Ginger's intelligence to be seen as "lab management material" is a measure of the power of the culture there, and the men who create it.

These differences in interactional style, in technical orientation and self-confidence, would not have such a major impact on women's careers at CDI if engineers did not hold so much power there. As in high tech firms generally, personal reputations and peer evaluations play an important role in mobility. Engineers have to impress their peers as much as please their managers in order to get ahead. Their formal qualifications and time on the job are often not as important as their ability to play interactional games whose rules are defined by engineers. This works to the disadvantage of women, who are uncomfortable in the technical locker room, yet whose advancement is dependent, directly or indirectly, on the judgments of the jocks who inhabit it.

United Missile

The second of our two companies lies at the opposite end of the engineering spectrum. If CDI is engineer-driven, United Missile (UM) is management-driven. It is a workplace characterized by bureaucracy, repetitive work, strict hierarchy, and technical sclerosis. When our UM respondents were asked what they liked best about the company, the most common response was "nothing." When asked what they liked least, the answer was always the same: "the bureaucracy."

Even the physical structure of UM is in contrast with CDI. Where CDI is parklike and suburban, UM is industrial and urban. The UM plant was built in the 1960s, in an area that was at the time on the outskirts of the city. Now, however, it is surrounded by industrial and urban development. The physical grounds are dominated by the production facility, which is composed of several multistoried buildings. There are over fifteen thousand workers on site, making the plant the size of a small city.

The women in our sample held higher status positions at UM than at CDI. This was consistent with our findings for aerospace and high tech more generally. Eighty-four percent of the male CDI engineers in our sample, but only 40 percent of the women, were in design jobs or above. At UM 56 percent of the men and 81 percent of the women were in these higher status positions. At UM mobility is a slow process. The bureaucracy is large, but the company is not growing much, and there is not a lot of turnover at the higher levels. The typical male engineer starting at UM can expect to stay at an entry-level position for several years. What little mobility there is at UM appears to go disproportionately to women. One of our female respondents had been promoted into management within two years of taking her job at UM, much sooner than most of her male colleagues: "I have a supervisory position . . . [but] the next youngest person who holds the same job I do is 40, and I'm 27."

The more favorable status of women at UM is also reflected in their greater job stability. In general, UM is something of an engineering "cattle market." When the company wins a (usually government) contract, it hires large numbers of engineers. When the contract is complete, or funding is cut back, it lays off equally large numbers. These mass hirings and firings lead to occupational insecurity, particularly among entry-level engineers. As a male engineer who had been there for two years put it:

> The aerospace industry is at the mercy of the Congress. They don't like the budget this year, they cut it, and that's it. I think it's one of the most unstable jobs there is. If I had to recommend a type of job to another engineer, especially if he was my friend, I'd highly advise him to go to another industry.

Women feel much less of this insecurity. In fact, one woman chose UM mainly because of its security: "having a family it was probably the more secure job to take—being a woman at UM with defense contracts and so forth, there's a quota, so to speak. They like to take in as many minorities as possible." The women we interviewed at UM were much more likely to rank their job as very secure (71%) than were the men (23%).

Affirmative Action

As the previous quote implies, the most obvious explanation for women's success at UM is affirmative action. The overwhelming majority of our female UM interviewees (72%) felt that their job security and mobility prospects were influenced by affirmative action. With its business largely devoted to defense contracts, UM comes under the purview of affirmative action regulations. As a result, management is eager to recruit, retain, and promote women, in order to fulfill the "goals and timetables" required by affirmative action. This serves as a powerful resource for women.

Though affirmative action is an important factor in women's careers at UM, it is not enough to fully explain their success there. While CDI is not required to do so, it has initiated a voluntary affirmative action program of its own. Thus, the simple existence of an affirmative action program does not distinguish between the two companies. What does distinguish between them, however, is the organization structure within which affirmative action is implemented.

Organization Structure

At UM, affirmative action is more tightly regulated and carries greater weight than at CDI. This in turn reflects fundamental differences in the structure of the two organizations. CDI is an informal workplace, and provides engineers with a great deal of autonomy; UM is formal and its engineers are closely controlled. Rules are everywhere at UM, and there is near mania in their observance. A male design engineer who had quit UM, partly in disgust with the red tape, described his work in the following terms:

> You had to go through so many bureaucratic [procedures]— changing a little note on a drawing would involve meetings, and you would have to go through about four groups to get a drawing released, and there were always scheduling problems. . . . It was not a very enjoyable job at all.

The requirements of federal contracts are a major source of this morass of rules and regulations. Another male engineer told us:

> Aerospace, being that you work for the government, has so many regulations. That's one thing I don't really like about my job: there's very little actual technical engineering. The majority of it is following procedures. We have volumes and volumes of procedures. You cannot do anything here without making sure it's been approved by this procedure or that procedure.

This bureaucratization shows up in the work that engineers do as well. At UM everyone is "pigeonholed," placed into a specialized function that they perform day after day. As one male engineer who had left UM told us: "There was a pigeonhole over at UM, into which I was placed when I arrived, and out of which I climbed when I escaped." Design engineering at UM is both less creative and more constrained than at CDI:

> The design group dealt with drawings. They didn't do any analysis, and so you missed all the analytical thing, which is really the more interesting part . . . and you have to go through so much bureaucratic work. Changing a little note on a drawing would involve meetings and you would have to go through about four groups to get a drawing released."

Many engineers simply check calculations made by other engineers—day after day. A female engineer described her activities in the following manner:

> It was data analysis, so what we did was mostly instrumentation type thing. We kept instrumentation tabs updated. You'd analyze the data looking for anything that was abnormal. . . . I wasn't pleased with the kind of work I was doing.

The bureaucratic nature of UM also means that promotions are based on formal criteria. The majority (67%) of our respondents at UM felt that the most important single factor in promotion was time on the job:

> There's a set progression where you come in and you're an associate engineer for a year. You can't budge for a year. And you're an engineer for five years, and you can't be promoted to the next level for five years, no matter how good you are or how well you do. . . . It is very rigid.

Policies like these seem set in stone. It takes the power of a government contract officer or corporate official to circumvent them. Women are favored in these circumstances.

Not surprisingly, engineers at UM are more highly stratified than at CDI. Where the engineering hierarchy at CDI is relatively flat, with engineers assuming responsibilities often associated with managers and technicians, the division of labor at UM is complex and limiting for engineers. At CDI there are only five different types of engineers; at UM there are nearly twenty. CDI engineers are encouraged to strike out on their own and are given wide discretion; at UM they are on a short leash.

Management at UM is everywhere, and has sole responsibility for most engineering decisions. Only 25 percent of engineers at UM said they had a say in larger matters; at CDI it was 66 percent (tau $c=.53$; $p=.001$). There are no awards for "rogue engineers" at UM; it is not the rogue elephants who do well, but the "weasels":

> It seems that the people who get promoted are the weasels . . . the people who are the boss's favorites, or the people who will do anything you tell them to [in order to] move up quicker. . . . They don't care as much about your technical background as they do about what you will do on command.

There was a feeling among our respondents at UM that management placed little value on creativity or technical innovation. The frustration this produces can be heard in the description one male engineer gave of management:

> They're interested in filling in the little diamonds on their chart. It's: "do it, we don't care if you do it right, we can always clean it up later." So a piece of equipment gets shipped to a base somewhere, and we have to go along with it to fix it, because they don't care if it's designed right. They have to fill in their bubbles for the people right above them.

But it is not just higher order engineering activities that are scarce at UM. Respondents also complained about being unable to do hands-on engineering, because they were limited by company rules. UM is unionized, and there are strict regulations governing which hands-on activities an engineer is allowed to perform. This is a source of considerable irritation to them. As one engineer put it:

> I can't go and do much of anything because the union protects [the technicians]. . . . Sometimes it's you know, you can do it faster yourself rather than telling someone else, but that's the way it goes, you just can't do it.

There is also less comradery among engineers at UM. Socializing after work is uncommon. One of our respondents had left UM to take a job at a high tech firm shortly before our interview. We asked him how much time he spent socializing with co-workers outside of work: "Before, when I was at UM, none. Here [at the high tech firm] the people are really neat. There's a lot of good young engineers here, and so maybe four or five hours a week."

Engineers at UM display little of the pride that is so obvious at CDI. Separated from one another by organizational structure, bogged down in red tape, and dispirited by their lack of power and security, engineers at UM are alienated both from their work and from one another. With neither unity nor power, their influence on work relations suffers. The sphere of engineer influence extends little further than the area around the coffee machine, and is noticeably absent from the culture of the workplace.

For all its frustrations, however, this is an organizational structure that is good for women. As in bureaucracies generally, job descriptions, channels of authority and communication, and criteria for advancement are explicit and standardized. Its formalism means that the "rules of the game" are clear to everyone. The newcomer in a nontraditional field can quickly learn the rules, and can rely on her formal qualifications as she seeks to advance. The limited power of engineers means that rituals of hands-on competence and technical virtuosity count for less. We illustrate these points by looking at the experiences of Carol, a mechanical engineer at UM.

CAROL

Carol's case is interesting both because she had worked at UM for several years, and because she began her career in a high tech firm. For two and a half years after graduating from college, she had worked in a high tech plant as a research engineer. The contrast between the high tech job and UM was a recurring theme in her interview.

Carol had graduated in the late 1970s, excited by the prospect of working in high tech because of the opportunity it offered for creative engineering. Two years later, however, she had become dissatisfied by her lack of advancement. Carol had a strong desire to move into management. She valued the design experience that she received in high tech, but she wanted more than to play with machinery—she wanted to set policy.

She had also been frustrated by seeing men advance who she felt were less competent, but more aggressive than she:

> I worked with some men who I think were pretty dumb, and I wondered how they got through engineering school. And to me, sometimes it seemed that just because they were men they thought they were great, and probably bullshitted their way through [college], the same way they were bullshitting their way through work.

Leaving her high tech job was not an easy decision. She enjoyed the autonomy and creativity of her work, and was not sure she wanted to give that up. She had no illusions about UM: she knew she was not likely to find exciting work there. But she was ambitious and willing to take risks, and she decided to try it. She had heard about a position through a friend who already worked there, and she put in an application only half-seriously. When she was offered the job she hesitated, but took it for one reason: the chance of rising to management:

> It wasn't the engineering that attracted me, because I could see that the engineering work was not that challenging. What attracted me more were the management possibilities. That particular division, the division I'm in, has produced the president of our corporation, and I was interested in seeing if I could work into management.

Carol was hired as a design engineer, but the work at UM contrasted sharply with what she had done previously. At her high tech job:

> It was the kind of a place where they allow people to be as creative as they want to be. By not having a lot of management it allowed the engineers to be their own managers, and to be very flexible. You didn't have all these rules and regulations imposed on you, . . . there was no hierarchy.

This was *not* what she found at UM:

The companies are so different. [At UM] you are constricted by many procedures. . . . Different cost measures and political measures prevent you from always doing the best kind of design. Before it was kind of a paradise: like, "here's the job, go do the right thing."

Carol saw clearly the consequences of this lack of autonomy and power on her colleagues at UM:

Personal power is very important to people in terms of self-esteem, and I think there's very little at this kind of company. [Consequently], people get these bizarre personality distortions because they have so little autonomy or personal power. They get really protective about the most absurd things. [For instance], if your job function is to make sure a paper gets checked in a certain way: the color of the ink has to be just so, and the check has to be so big and so wide.

Besides the lack of power and autonomy, Carol experienced all the other problems with UM that we mentioned earlier. She was now in a bureaucratic workplace, where technical creativity was valued little by management, and engineers felt unappreciated. The experience for Carol was frustrating. She took herself seriously as an engineer, and felt she had something to contribute. But contributions were less important than playing the bureaucratic game: "What I really disliked about the job was that you had to 'group think.' You got pressure and were squashed into not being innovative." The workplace culture little reflected the interests of engineers.

She also encountered the sexism that was so common in aerospace:

Some of the guys put up these girlie calendars, and I would go up to them and say, "You know, I feel really offended by that.' But I wouldn't tell them what to do with it, I just would let them know how I felt. . . . It became a weird little game where this one guy wouldn't take it down, and he loved the fact that it was there. For him it became a point of [honor]. He would say to me, "I would never put something like that up in my home." And I'd say, "Oh, you mean you can be more disgusting at work than you are at home?"

Two things should be evident from this quote. First, this was sexism of the "classic" sort: the degradation of women as sex objects. Second, and as a consequence of the first, Carol did not hesitate to confront it. There was nothing insidious or subtle about the sexism she encountered. These were classic male chauvinists: lewd, crude, and obvious. She knew what they were, and how to respond to them. While these interactions may have been draining and oppressive, they had little impact on her sense of competence. She saw it as *their* problem, not hers.

There were, however, compensations for the sexism and her lack of power: the chances for moving up were good. "It's strange moving up in this company. All you have to do is tell someone that this is what you want and if you're halfway intelligent and female, they're very eager to satisfy." Carol's gamble of taking a job at UM paid off. Within two years of joining the company, she moved into a position in management.

Even as a manager, however, Carol was not entirely happy. She still did not have a great deal of power, and she had to cope with the bureaucratic structure. But there were other aspects of her job that she enjoyed. "I like supervising people . . . because I enjoy seeing them grow and take on their own responsibilities. I enjoy seeing a whole group of people being able to accomplish things."

There was also the security of her job. When asked what she liked best about the company, she replied: "it boils down to the basics. Security. I'm not gonna get laid off. Being a woman I won't get laid off. I can probably totally screw off and they couldn't get rid of me."

Carol was not satisfied with her job, but few workers at UM were. She felt lost in a bureaucracy in which she had little power, and from which she received little appreciation. But this too was common at UM. What was uncommon was the speed with which she moved up, and the security she felt in her job. These compensations were not enough for her, and she was looking for other job possibilities. But they were compensations that few male engineers at UM received. More importantly, few women in high tech experienced them either. Interestingly, though Carol told us that she could always go back to her former (high tech) employer, she chose not to do so. She enjoyed the work more at the other company, but she was not about to trade her managerial position for that enjoyment.

To sum up, the experiences of people like Carol and Ginger give us graphic evidence of the differences between high tech and aerospace firms. At CDI, where innovation is the key to corporate survival, engineers enjoy autonomy and power, including the power to judge their peers. At UM the work is routine and repetitive, and engineers are tightly controlled by management. Engineers at CDI perform a wide range of tasks, including hands-on activities. At UM jobs are narrowly defined, and hands-on activities are performed by technicians. At CDI engineers are a highly cohesive group, proud of their prestige, and competitive in the display of their technical abilities. At UM engineers are disorganized, conscious of their status as one link in a very long chain, and professionally apathetic. Workplace culture at CDI reflects the interests of engineers: an aggressive, technically self-confident, hands-on engineer can expect to do well. At UM the culture is dominated by management and bureaucratic procedure. Engineers with good credentials, who complete projects and have put in their time, do well. Affirmative action speeds up the process for those protected by it.

We believe these differences help explain the contrasting experiences of women in high tech and aerospace. Women move up more quickly than men in aerospace because of affirmative action, but also because the workplace culture is less dominated by engineers and more controlled by management and bureaucratic formalism. Technical self-confidence, aggressive displays of ability, and facility at tinkering mean less than time on the job, project completion, and being on management's good side. Women feel alienated by the bureaucracy and the sexism, but the rules for advancement are clear, and not dependent on the evaluations of their peers. In aerospace, what engineers want is of little importance. They have little say in how their own jobs are defined, let alone in criteria for promotion. Many of them are sexist, but nearly all of them are powerless, and it is power that makes the difference in shaping careers.

ELECTRICAL AND MECHANICAL ENGINEERING

As we said earlier, there is a contrast between electrical and mechanical engineering similar to that between high tech and aerospace.[13] While not wanting to belabor our point, we want to briefly explore the differences between these two specialties, as it provides added support for our argument.

The work that electrical engineers do is innovative, technically sophisticated, and in high demand. In contrast, mechanical engineering has changed little over the past several decades. It is standardized, predictable, and in less demand (Calvert 1967; Noble 1977; Layton 1986). The differences between these two specialties were brought to our attention by one of our respondents, a mechanical engineer. In the margin of his questionnaire, near a question about job satisfaction, he had written a diatribe against electrical engineers. He was upset about their arrogance, their status, and their power.

Our interest was piqued by this unsolicited comment, so we asked our interview respondents about any friction between the two groups. While most engineers described the situation as "a friendly competition," they also admitted that there were status differences between the two specialties, and that this generated conflict. As a mechanical engineer who had risen into management at a high tech firm put it: "I've done some recruiting of candidates for engineering positions—both ME's and EE's—and it seems to me that the EE's that we're hiring are smarter than the ME's." He went on to add:

> ME's feel like they used to be top dog, and now the EE's are taking away the limelight. . . . ME's have pretty boring lives. The kind of jobs they do are designing sheet metal enclosures for card cages for a bunch of PC boards. It's really dull. So resentment is natural.

An electrical engineer agreed with this assessment:

> In our company [mechanical engineers] . . . act almost as a support group. We have an electrical box with all this junk in it—circuit boards. They're the guys that have to package that. . . . It always comes down to decisions that are based on electrical engineering problems. You don't change [the electronics] because the box doesn't fit. . . . So they assume a slightly subservient role.

In control of a highly valued and unpredictable resource, electrical engineers are strategically more important, and enjoy more autonomy and power than mechanical engineers, as a result. One of our survey questions asked if respondents had the ability to perform their work in the way they thought appropriate. Over 55 percent of the electrical engineers, but only 42 percent of the mechanical engineers, answered in the affirmative (tau c=.16; p=.01). When asked if they had input into important decisions at their workplace, 47 percent of the electrical engineers, but only 31 percent of the mechanical engineers, said they did (tau c=.25; p=.01).

The power and importance of electrical engineers also seems to increase their access to promotion. Seventy-nine percent of electrical engineers, but only 62 percent of mechanical engineers, were in design positions or above (tau c=.11; p=.02). An electrical engineer working in an aerospace company told us, "the electrical engineer gets promoted a lot faster than any other kind of engineer." Not surprisingly, these more mobile electrical engineers tended to be more assertive and self-confident than mechanical engineers (tau c's=.12, .22; p's=.1, .03, respectively). In short, the electrical engineer, wherever he works, resembles the engineer in high tech.

As with aerospace and high tech, our respondents' perceptions of women's compatibility with electrical and mechanical engineering conflicted with women's actual achievements in those specialties. When we asked which are the best fields for women engineers, nearly half of our interview respondents (45%) said electrical engineering was best. The reasons they gave were very similar to those expressed about high tech: the men were younger, the work was newer and less male-defined, it was more science- and math-based, and it involved less physical work.

We asked a mechanical engineer at an aerospace firm why she felt that electrical engineering was better for women. Her response was typical of many:

> Because it's growing rapidly. There are a lot of engineers going into the field who are young, and that's very important. And it doesn't require [physical] strength. It doesn't require anything. You don't have to deal with drafting people as much. You deal on a much more intellectual basis with people.

Yet women rose into management more slowly in electrical than mechanical engineering. We believe that the important variable is the power of engineers, and the use of their power to construct a workplace culture congruent with their interests. Electrical engineering, like engineering in high tech, is more innovative, less predictable, and less bureaucratized. These engineers are the elite of the profession. Powerful and high in status, they are more able to define the terms of competition and evaluation than their counterparts in mechanical engineering. It is the power to enforce a culture of aggressive, technically oriented engineering, to create a work style comfortable to them as men, that is crucial.

THE CULTURE OF ENGINEERING AND WOMEN'S CAREERS

We believe that women experience the least occupational mobility in environments where the culture of engineering is most extensive. In contrast, women's mobility is greatest where the culture of engineering is minimized by bureaucratization and affirmative action. Where engineers as a group are powerful, the culture takes on a form strongly identified with the male gender role, emphasizing aggressive displays of technical self-confidence as the criteria for success. As such, it devalues the gender role attributes of women, defining professional competence in strictly masculine terms. On the other hand, in workplaces where engineers are less powerful, the culture is weaker. This tends to mitigate the emphasis on male-defined displays of technical competence, to the benefit of women.

Workplace culture, like any culture, is concerned above all with conformity. The specific values and norms vary from one workplace or occupational group to another. Underlying them all, however, is the demand for conformity to the culture as defined by those in power. Conformity is displayed through interaction and impression management. That is, it is more important to *appear* to conform to a culture than to actually do so. That appearance, of course, must be in culturally approved forms. This helps us understand why women are promoted more slowly than men, despite the similarity of their work values. Whether a woman values promotion, autonomy, or technical challenge is less important than the way in which she displays her interests. The mere fact of value conformity is not enough. Conformity must be properly "presented."

If we account for career success only in terms of performance-based criteria, it is hard to explain why women are not being promoted as quickly as males. Once we recognize the cultural component involved, their difficulties become more understandable. It is women's membership, not their competence, that is at question. They do not conform, or more accurately, do not *appear* to conform, to the culture of the workplace.

Men and women, because of gender socialization, develop different sets of interactional orientations, neither of which is intrinsically superior in terms of work performance. Whether an idea is presented quietly or aggressively, the content is the same. In cultural terms, however, the style of presentation *is* significant. Gender roles are important insofar as they provide an individual with emotional and interactional resources to manage their presentation of self in a work culture. Conceived as resources, gender roles provide cultural tokens of membership, and means of "faking it" where membership is in question.

Nowhere is this more clear than in the importance of hands-on skills to the culture of engineering. In workplaces where this culture dominates, there is a ritualism to these activities. The culture of engineering involves a preoccupation with tinkering that goes beyond the requirements of the job. Vocation becomes avocation, and, in turn, devotion. It is not enough to be competent in the hands-on aspects of engineering: one should be obsessed with them. It is not enough to know the difference between a rod and a piston: one should take obvious joy in this knowledge. The engineer must be ready not only to engage in technical exchanges during work periods, but interested in participating in them during breaks as well. To be seen as a competent engineer means throwing one's self into these rituals of tinkering.

There are, of course, men who lack this background, but they do not start with the added disadvantage of being female. Men begin with assumed membership in the "club." Others take it for granted that they already possess these skills. Since the basic hands-on skills required are acquired relatively easily, even if a man is deficient he can "wing it" until he comes up to speed. There is no such cushion of presumed competence for women. This, in turn, affects their prospects for mobility—particularly in the early years of their careers, when advancement is within the technical ranks, and low-level engineering skills are of greatest strategic value.

This obsession with technology and hands-on activities is responsible in no small way for the problems of women, especially in workplaces where the culture of engineering is strongest. For women like Ginger, the feelings of incompetence that dog them are most often connected to their lack of experience with tinkering. They start with deficits in this area, and even when they have acquired a working knowledge of these skills, they are never quite as comfortable— nor as obsessed—with them as are their male colleagues.

The second area where women's interactional resources make it difficult for them to conform to the culture of engineering is in self-promotion. That the aggressive presentation of competence is seen as the criterion for success as an engineer reflects a particular social definition. That is, it is not enough to *be* competent, or to be *quietly* self-confident regarding one's abilities. Given the predominance of men in engineering, it is not surprising that the display required is strongly identified with the male gender role. Technical proficiency must be displayed in an aggressive and competitive manner; it must be concerned with technical objects, rather than the personal relationships that surround technology; and it must be individualistic rather than solidaristic. Self-promotion is taken as a sign of ability and self-confidence, and those who do not display it are presumed less competent.

Little of this has anything to do with actual job performance. In fact, posturing and competition can diminish technical efficiency by limiting cooperation in the search for the best solution to a problem. It is not efficiency that dictates this cultural style, but the backgrounds and interests of male engineers, and their power.

In this environment, traits associated with the female gender role are devalued simply because they are feminine, regardless of their objective usefulness. There are many female-defined traits that *could* contribute to good engineering and management. Most obviously, women's "people skills" should be an advantage to them. When asked if there was any aspect of engineering in which women were better than men, both men and women agreed that it was people skills. As we have previously pointed out, women's gender role socialization deemphasizes mechanical activities, but stresses personal relationships. Women are socialized to be more conscious of relationships, and, therefore, more effective participants in them.

It is in management that people skills are particularly important. Technical competence is necessary in order to be a competent manager of engineers, but so too is interpersonal sophistication. To be able to produce a piece of technology, or even to promote one's technical accomplishments to superiors, is not identical with the ability to motivate others to produce. Here sensitivity to emotional needs and dynamics is important.

Objectively these should be advantages for women, but in the real world of engineering, and particularly in high tech and electrical engineering where the culture of engineering is strongest, they are not. People skills do not pay off the way they should, because it is male engineers who define the criteria for the good engineer or manager. It is because these are male-dominated workplaces that women's resources do not pay off. Where male engineers are most power-ful, being female exacts the greatest price.

Our analysis of the culture of engineering raises a question about the nature of engineering itself. Is it possible that what we have called a "male-defined approach to engineering" is in fact a necessary and intrinsic aspect of the field? Latour (1987) makes this argument about science. His view is that day-to-day scientific activity (what he calls "science in action") is less the careful, logical, orderly, and self-less pursuit of pure knowledge than it is the messy contest between individuals and interests. That is, science is as much a function of the competition for grants and status as it is the search for insight into the basic mechanisms of nature.

Our description of the culture of engineering—with its competi-tion, posturing, and aggressive self-promotion—sounds suspiciously like Latour's notion of science in action. But if Latour is correct, the culture of engineering is merely a description of what engineering is and must be in the real world. The competition and posturing we describe is not simply the result of male-defined interactional styles, but of the intrinsic nature of engineering. If this is so, it bodes ill for women engineers, given their difficulties in displaying those be-haviors.

There are, however, a number of weaknesses in this argument. First and most important, Latour ignores recent discussions of the sociohistorical bases of technology. Feminists (Keller 1985; Bleier 1986) and labor process scholars (Braverman 1974; Noble 1977; Edwards 1979; Burawoy 1979; Gordon, Edwards, and Reich 1982; Gartman 1986) have pointed out the historically contingent power relations and interests behind the development of technology and science. Much of the competition, posturing, and self-promotion that characterize sci-ence and engineering reflect the styles of the groups who have domi-nated these fields: Western middle-class and upper-middle-class males.

As Latour points out, technological developments and scientific discoveries must be funded, and in order to be funded must be vis-ible. But visibility and the acquisition of funding can be accomplished in more than one way. Given particular sets of power relations and historical conditions, this can become a process of aggressive self-promotion and cutthroat competition. However, other more cooperative styles are no less compatible with the methods of science and engineering. Indeed, feminist scientists argue that scientific developments are *hampered* by the posturing, competition and secrecy that so often pervade the field (Naminworth 1986). Latour mistakes one form of the social basis of science for the intrinsic nature of science itself. We believe that the interactional ingredients of science and engineering are more contingent than he recognizes.

Moreover, even if we assume that some form of competition and self-promotion is necessary in science and engineering, there is no reason that the forms evidenced in places like CDI are the only ones possible. Women engineers have trouble, not so much with competition, but with particular forms of it. After all, they thrive on academic competition in college. In the workplace, it is not that they are unable to come up with the best idea or have the smoothest running project. It is, rather, that they are less likely to present themselves and their ideas in the same way as men. It is the male domination of the workplace and of interaction that hinders these women, not their ability to compete as engineers.

SELF-CONFIDENCE: CAUSAL OR CAUSED?

Finally, let us return to the issue of self-confidence in light of this discussion of the culture of engineering. We should have a sense by now that self-confidence is more complex than many would assume. Simple notions of socialized emotional vulnerability are inadequate to explain the problems of people like Ginger. Women are less confident of their abilities than males, and that plays an important role in their occupational attainment. But self-confidence is as much caused as it is causal. Women like Ginger are lacking in professional self-confidence, but they also face situations that make those deficits anything but surprising.

CDI in general, and the lab in particular, are workplaces in which the resources on which these women are used to relying do not pay off. They are bright, disciplined, and hard working, but these qualities are not as important as they were in school. Anyone operating on such alien turf with resources so little rewarded would feel insecure. Women enter the workplace with insecurity, but they encounter there little that would diminish it, and a great deal that would reinforce it.

Part of the problem of self-confidence is, in fact, really a matter of presentation of self. Even those women who *are* self-confident tend to display it in ways that are not culturally acceptable. Women are not taken as seriously because their style of interaction is not as aggressive, and they tend to promote themselves less, or to do so in less obvious ways. The failures that result from these differences in style have little to do with intrinsic emotional resources, and more to do with the structure of the workplace and the power of males inside it. Many of the women in our sample took their failures of style as failures of competence, thus contributing to their "lack of self-confidence." But this is a vulnerability produced not just by gender role socialization, but by daily interaction in a hostile culture as well.

We do not want to go to the other extreme, however. Self-confidence cannot be simply reduced to structural variables, at least not those associated with the workplace. We have too much evidence that women bring a significant portion of their insecurity in with them, and that it does limit their mobility. We need, however, to recognize the complexity of the issue. We believe that organization structures and power relations are the most important variables, but that interactional styles, particularly if they are conceived as resources, play a role as well. Self-confidence and assertiveness emerge out of, and are maintained by, social structures, but once they exist, they become causal variables in their own right. We are left, then, with the interplay of organization structures and interactional resources. Previous discussions of women in nontraditional occupations have too often chosen one side or the other of this dialectic. A full explanation, however, lies in the intersection of the two.

7

THE FAMILY AND
THE ENGINEERING CAREER

Our portrait of women in engineering remains incomplete without a look at their family lives. These are women for whom the family is not an abstraction or a future plan, but a reality: the majority are married, and many are planning to have children soon, though few as yet are parents. We cannot fully understand their experiences in the workplace without considering the ways in which family and work structures interact. Like the workplace, the family is a structure of power relationships, opportunities and constraints. What happens in the family affects the work lives of both women and men, but in different ways. Historically, the family has represented a resource in the careers of men, but an obstacle for women. Does that pattern hold true for the bright, career-oriented women becoming engineers today? Will they be able to "have it all," succeeding at work *and* as wives and mothers too? Or will they have to choose one over the other, as generations of women before them have had to do?

We explore the family lives of engineers in this chapter, examining the impact of marriage and children on the careers of the women and men in our sample. We see that for women engineers today, the relationship between work and family is complex. As they attempt to navigate the culture of engineering and establish their careers, their families represent both a resource and a liability. Before turning to the data, however, we place our discussion in its theoretical context.

POWER AND PRIORITIES IN MARRIAGE

From a conflict perspective, the family is a structure of unequal relationships—in particular, a structure of male dominance (Scanzoni 1972; Collins 1985). Feminist scholars have developed this perspective most fully (Morgan 1970; Gornick and Moran 1971; Hartmann 1976, 1981; Eisenstein 1979; Sokoloff 1981; Wilkie 1988). They have critically examined women's role in the family, and the links between family and workplace. They argue that men benefit from women's traditional family role as husbands, co-workers, and employers. Because housework and child care are defined primarily as women's responsibility, men benefit as husbands. They are freed from those tasks, and allowed to concentrate on occupational success. The family thus constitutes an important resource for them in their career development. Moreover, as the primary breadwinner in the family, men's careers take priority over their wive's, and their position as "head of the family" is reinforced.

Men also benefit as co-workers when women's family responsibilities limit their ability to compete for high-status positions in the workplace. Thus, these jobs are effectively reserved for men. The occupational segregation that results also allows men to maintain positions of authority and higher status over women in the workplace, which reinforces their dominant position in society.

Finally, men benefit as employers. As long as women's primary role is in the family, they constitute an attractive and flexible source of labor for employers. They can be hired for low pay, and laid off when demand is slack. In the meantime, employers can demand high levels of commitment from their male employees, on the assumption that their wives (whether employed or not) are taking responsibility for family and household needs.

From this perspective, gender socialization is important, because it prepares women and men to accept and value their traditional roles. But it is the system of power—not gender socialization—that fundamentally shapes women's lives (Hartmann 1976; Eisenstein 1979; Sokoloff 1981). Their role in the family is primary, and their opportunities in the workplace are limited, not simply because they have been socialized to think and behave accordingly. It is, rather, because men—as husbands, co-workers, and employers—have both an interest in maintaining women's traditional roles and the power to make it happen.

The power that men hold in all major social institutions enables them to maintain a "cultural mandate" or ideology that women are primarily responsible for the well-being of home and family. This mandate pervades the workplace, schools, mass media, and family, and is transmitted through the socializing activities of these institutions. In this sense, socialization is an important mechanism in maintaining women's subordination, but one that does not exist in a vacuum. It has its source in, and is sustained by, the ongoing relations of power in each of those institutions.

THE FAMILY AND THE PROFESSIONAL WOMAN

We move from this general framework to the family lives of engineers by looking briefly at some recent studies of "dual-career families." There has been considerable interest in these families in the past two decades, as their numbers have steadily grown. Women in dual-career families are neither occasional workers nor housewives, as was typical of married women in the past. They are career-oriented professionals, married to professional men. Do the family roles of these women limit their occupational advancement? Do the pay and status they receive in the workplace translate into equality in their family relationships? In other words, are they exceptions to the general patterns found in a male-dominated society, or are they too constrained by the cultural mandates and traditional family structures of that society?

Research on dual-career couples indicates that the men in these families (compared to husbands of nonprofessional women) are more likely to approve of egalitarian marriages, and are more willing to accommodate to the demands of the woman's career (Betz and Fitzgerald 1987).

In addition, professional women, especially those in male-dominated careers like management, medicine, and law, are less traditional in their gender attitudes. They are less likely than other women to see the family as their primary role in life, or to see their own careers as less important than their husbands' (Scanzoni 1975; Regan and Roland 1985; Betz and Fitzgerald 1987). As a result, professional women are more likely than other women to marry late or not at all.

Those who do marry are more likely to postpone childbearing, or to avoid it altogether.

For the married professional woman, then, we would expect to find a family structure conducive to career success. After all, she has the clout that comes from a high-status, high-paid job. She and her husband both have less traditional attitudes regarding gender and family roles. She should be able to translate all that into family arrangements that support her career. What we find, however, is a very mixed picture. Professional couples may espouse egalitarian ideals, and professional women may hold less traditional gender attitudes, but when actual behaviors are observed, tradition and inequality persist (Pepitone-Rockwell 1980; Nieva 1985; Betz and Fitzgerald 1987).

Professional women are more likely than their husbands to make sacrifices that affect their careers adversely, like taking part-time work, withdrawing temporarily from the labor force to care for children, or moving (or staying) in response to the demands of the husband's career. These patterns are especially apparent when the couple has children.

At first glance, these findings appear to undermine the conflict perspective on the family. The social and economic resources of the professional woman should provide her with marital power equal to her husband's. Yet they do not. Upon closer examination, however, we can see two reasons for the persistence of traditional patterns. First, the family is not an isolated unit, but exists in a larger social context: the system of male dominance that shapes the attitudes and behaviors of individuals. The earning power and occupational status of professional women gives them more marital power than most women, but does not negate the effects of that larger system of power—and the cultural mandate that it supports.

Second, the assumption that professional couples are equal in social and economic resources is often incorrect. While they may hold roughly similar levels of occupational status—both are professionals—the woman often has less education, is less advanced in her career, holds a lower status position, and earns less money than her husband (Martin, Berry, and Jacobsen 1975; Butler and Paisley 1977; Bryson and Bryson 1980). We argue in this chapter that these differences are important in understanding the family relations of professional couples. Along with the pervasive cultural mandate of women's family role, they help explain the traditional patterns found in the dual-career family.

How does all this affect the careers of professional women? Do their traditional roles in the family limit their success in the work-place? A variety of studies have produced a variety of answers to this question. There is evidence that the persistence of traditional patterns in the professional family works to the detriment of the wife's career (Butler and Paisley 1977; Bryson and Bryson 1980).

Among scientists and engineers, women have higher unem-ployment rates than men, and the differences seem primarily due to the restricted job searches of women. Because of family respon-sibilities, the need to remain in a particular geographic location, or to work part-time, women are less able to pursue job opportunities as freely as men (Finn 1983). Women's family responsibilities have also been found to hinder their upward mobility in science careers:

> While men are able to give almost complete priority to further-ing their careers, women scientists fit their careers around fam-ily commitments. The most frequent reason for men to change jobs is to gain promotion, while that for women is to accommo-date to a move by their husband. The consequence is that the career prospects of women scientists are increasingly dimin-ished at almost every change of job, with few surviving to reach the senior positions. [Martin and Irvine 1982]

Alice Rossi (1965) argued that women's temporary withdrawal from the labor force during the childbearing years is especially dam-aging to a career in science or engineering:

> Not only is training for such fields a long and difficult process, but the pace of technological and scientific knowledge has been so rapid that even those who remain in these fields have difficul-ty keeping up, let alone those who return . . . after a break. [p. 1199]

Yet there is other evidence that marriage and children do *not* adversely affect the careers of professional women. First, some stud-ies have found that marriage and children are associated with greater career success and satisfaction among professional women (Martin, Berry, and Jacobsen 1975; Epstein 1983; McBroom 1986).

Second, studies of publication productivity in a variety of pro-fessional fields have found that marital status and the presence of children have either no effect, a negative effect, or a positive effect on publication productivity among women (Fox and Faver 1985; Cole and Zuckerman 1987)!

Thus, research on professional women has yet to clearly sort out the effects of family life on career patterns. It remains an important question, however, especially in light of recent trends. More and more women are combining professional careers, marriage, and children. They are, in fact, attempting to "have it all." We can see the magnitude of change occurring by comparing two studies of women in science. In 1960, according to census data on scientists and engineers, four-fifths of employed men but only two-fifths of employed women were married. What is more, the dropout rates among women aged 25 to 44 ranged between 30 and 50 percent (compared to 1 to 2% for men) (Rossi 1965). In contrast, a 1987 study found high rates of marriage, childbearing, *and continued employment* among women scientists (Cole and Zuckerman 1987). Three-fourths of a national sample of employed women scientists were married, and two-thirds of these women had children.

These patterns are being replicated in other professional fields as well. Thus, it is increasingly important to understand the impact of family on women's careers. Our data can contribute to this process, albeit in a limited way. Our sample is composed largely of young engineers in the early stages of their careers. None of our respondents had been out of school more than ten years, and most were in the early stages of family-building. In particular, they were only beginning to have children in significant numbers. We will have to await follow-up studies to see the emergence of clear-cut patterns among this sample. We do have preliminary evidence, however, that family life has complex effects on the careers of women engineers: it works as both resource and obstacle.

We also have evidence that the particular set of power and status relations within the professional marriage affects that process in important ways. We believe that the conflict perspective is useful in understanding these patterns, but that family power relations need to be examined more closely than they have in the past. Merely to note that both partners in a marriage are professionals, and to conclude therefore that they are equal in resources, is to miss important details. What is needed is an examination of relative levels of education, job status, and career stage within a marriage. To the extent that there is inequality there, we can expect to find inequality in the work-family roles of each partner as well.

TABLE 12
The Family and the Engineering Career: Men and Women

Family Status	Men	Women
Married		
N	145	43
Percent	(44)	(54)
Of Married Respondents:		
Children at home:		
N	88	12
Percent	(27)	(15)
Married to professional		
N	115	70
Percent	(35)	(88)
Married to engineer		
N	13	43
Percent	(4)	(54)
Total	329	79

THE MARRIED ENGINEER: RESOURCE OR LIABILITY?

The women in our study, like other professional women today, displayed no inclination to avoid marriage. Even though they were in the early stages of their careers, more than half (54%) were already married. In fact, they were more likely to be married than the men (44%). The married women were somewhat less likely than the men to have children, however (15% and 27%). But many of the women who were not yet mothers were planning to have children within a few years.

While women and men were quite similar in their propensity to marry, the marriages themselves were strikingly different. The difference lay in the relative status relationships of husband and wife. Women were most likely to be married to "status superiors"; men to "status inferiors" (see Table 12).

The overwhelming majority (88%) of married women in our sample were married to professional men. Sixty-one percent of these two-professional marriages were actually two-engineer marriages. What is more, judging from our interview data, the husbands were typically older, more advanced in their careers, and held higher educational degrees. Many of these couples met in college, where he was closer to graduation, encouraged her to major in engineering, and helped her with her studies. Women who did not meet their husbands in college usually met them on their first job. The men had been on the job a longer time, and "knew the ropes."

This scenario rarely applied to the men in our sample. Only about one-third (35%) of the married men had professional wives, and only 12 percent of these were married to engineers. The majority of married men had wives who held nonprofessional jobs (30%), or were housewives (35%). Men's marriages followed traditional patterns in other ways as well. Whether married to professionals, nonprofessionals, or housewives, the men were most often older and more advanced in their careers. Thus, the marriages of male and female engineers involve different sets of power and status relationships. As a result, their marriages interact differently with their careers. For the woman married to a "status superior," marriage provides both resources and liabilities.

Women Married to Engineers: Resources and Liabilities

Marriage by itself has no significant effect on the career patterns of engineers, at least as judged by our measures of income and job standing. The married engineers in our sample had higher incomes and higher status jobs than single ones, but when we controlled for length of time in engineering, the relationships disappeared. Thus, it is not marriage per se, but the fact that married engineers are further along in their careers than singles that creates the difference.

However, when we looked not at marital status but at *type of marriage*, we found an interesting pattern. When we compared women married to engineers with all other married women, we found the former group earning higher salaries (tau c=.202; p=.12) and holding somewhat higher status jobs (tau c=.104; p=.26). The differences did not achieve statistical significance, but the pattern was there. In particular, women married to engineers were more likely to hold management positions (27%) than were women married to nonengineers (15%). When we looked just at women without children, the pattern was even stronger (tau c=.50; p=.05 for income; tau c=.27; p=.18 for job status). Thus, marriage to an engineer does appear to provide a career advantage, particularly for women without children. In order to understand why this is so, we need to consider the marital relationship itself.

A woman married to an engineer, especially when he is more

advanced in his career, has a "built-in" mentor to give support, advice, and information, and to provide her with useful contacts. These are things that mentors typically do for their protégés, and women in nontraditional occupations often suffer from the lack of such help. We can speculate that this husband-mentor relationship serves as a resource to women as they leave college and move into the early stages of their careers. Most married men have no such advantage, because they are not married to engineers, and even if they are, their wives are usually behind them in their careers. If a man has the benefit of a mentor, it is not likely to be his wife.

If women married to engineers reap some benefits from having a "built-in mentor," they suffer from it as well. We were surprised to find significantly lower levels of technical self-confidence displayed by these women than by other married women. Our evidence for this comes both from the interviews and the questionnaires. Looking first at the interview data, there was no difference between married and single women in our measure of technical self-confidence. There was a sharp difference, however, between women married to engineers and other married women (tau $c = -.32$; $p = .04$). Women married to engineers also scored lower on several indicators related to technical self-confidence in the questionnaire. For example:

> How important to you is it to:
> establish a reputation as an authority in your field? (tau $c = -.30$; $p = .03$)
> receive patents on your technical ideas? (tau $c = -.37$; $p = .02$)
> be evaluated only on the basis of your technical contributions? (tau $c = -.38$; $p = .01$)
> have the respect of your colleagues for your technical ability? (tau $c = -.30$; $p = .02$)

Women married to engineers were significantly less likely than other married women to rate these things as very important to them. These findings lend support to the argument that for women in a nontraditional occupation, a mentor is not solely an advantage. A woman may benefit from the contacts and advice of a mentor, but she may do so at the expense of her self-confidence. She is always aware of his greater knowledge and experience, and is dependent on him as well. How can she be sure that she could succeed on her own, if she has someone who, as one respondent put it, is "making sure I'm not going to fail"?

TABLE 13
Willingness to Move for Promotion:
Men and Women

Conditions under which respondent would move	Men	Women
Only if spouse was sure of obtaining a satisfactory position		
N	30	25
Percent	(35.7)	(67.6)
If spouse had *some* chance of obtaining a satisfactory position		
N	34	8
Percent	(40.5)	(21.6)
Whether or not spouse had prospects for a satisfactory position		
N	20	4
Percent	(23.8)	(10.8)
Total	84	37
Kendall's tau-c		−.28
Significance		(.001)

    The mentor-spouse relationships these women have with their husbands also appear to affect the relative importance of the two careers. Women engineers are in general more likely than men to subordinate their careers to their spouses', but women married to engineers are especially likely to do so. We asked respondents whose spouse was employed under which circumstances they would move to a different city in order to take a better job: *only* if their spouse could be sure of getting a good job as well; if there was *some chance* their spouse could get a good job; or *whether or not* their spouse could get a job there. As a group, women were much more likely than men to take the needs of their spouses into account (see Table 13). Sixty-eight percent of the women, but only 36 percent of the men, said they would move only if they could be sure their spouse could get a good job. Nearly one-fourth (24%) of the men were willing to move whether or not their spouse could find a job, compared to only 11 percent of the women.

    This difference reflects the kinds of marriages men and women have. Men are less likely to take the career needs of their wives into account, because their wives generally have lower-status, lower-paid jobs. We see this when we look at the responses of men with atypical marriages—those married to women with professional jobs. Their answers are significantly different from men married to nonprofessional women (tau c= −.323; p=.003), and they more closely resemble the answers of women. Only 9 percent would move regardless of their spouse's chances. In contrast, 39 percent of men married to nonprofessional women would move without taking their wive's opportunities into account!

Women married to engineers were even less willing than other women to move unless their spouse could be assured of finding a good job (tau c= −.25; p=.05). When we add this finding to the lower levels of technical self-confidence expressed by these women, we are left with the conclusion that being married to an engineer creates a particular pattern of deference, dependence, and insecurity among women engineers, at the same time that it yields some concrete benefits. How this combination of resources and liabilities will affect their careers over the years is a matter of speculation. It seems quite possible, however, that the liabilities will gradually erode the resources. In a marriage where the husband holds greater occupational status, his career is defined as primary, and she doubts her technical abilities, her career may well stagnate as his progresses. This is especially likely as children enter the picture. As we have already seen, the income and job advantages of marriage to an engineer are strongest among women without children. To the extent that children are defined as women's responsibility, they will add to the liabilities already present in the marriage. If marriage by itself is not a clear detriment to the careers of women engineers, children are a different story.

CHILDREN AND CAREERS

As we have seen, men are unlikely to take their wives' career needs into account when offered a job in another city, unless their wives hold jobs equal in status to their own. The only other variable that affects their decisions in this regard is whether or not they have children. Men with children at home were far more likely to say they would move whether or not their wife could find a job (40%) than men without children (10%). This suggests that, from the man's perspective, the presence of children gives his career even greater priority. For women, however, having children has no impact on their willingness to move. They are reluctant to disrupt their husbands' careers either way. This difference brings us to a discussion of the effects of children on the careers of engineers.

Despite all the change in gender role attitudes in the past twenty years, the role of mother remains overwhelmingly associated with women. The cultural mandate that women must mother is firmly in place, even though fathers are fully qualified to do everything but bear and nurse children. The birth of a child in most families means that the woman—not the man—will make major changes in her life. She will have to decide whether to leave the work force for several months or several years. She will have to decide whether to work part-time or full-time. If she continues to work, she will have to arrange care for her child, and figure out what to do when the child is sick. She will have to decide whether to try for a promotion to a more demanding position, or to hold back until her children need less of her time. She will have to decide, when her work is piling up or her boss asks her to stay late, whether to slight her work or her children. She will, in short, have the major responsibility for the well-being of her child(ren), whether she continues in her career or not.

Responsibility for children usually goes hand in hand with responsibility for housework. Study after study has shown that employed women do nearly as much housework as housewives, while their husbands do only slightly more than men whose wives are not employed. There is even less innate connection between women and housework than between women and child rearing. Yet fathers participate even less in housework than in caring for their children (Hochschild and Machung 1989; Model 1982; Pleck 1977).

We found these patterns quite clearly among the engineers we interviewed. Whether married or single, parents or not, most were aware that children presented dilemmas for women much more than for men. In this section we look at several families who were dealing with the issue in one way or another: planning, having, or deciding not to have children. In the process, we explore the links between family power relations, household division of labor, and the careers of engineers.

As with the sample as a whole, most of the married women we interviewed had professional husbands, who were typically engineers. He was usually older and more advanced in his career than she. In addition, he often held a higher educational degree. Thus, while on the surface the marriage appeared to be one of equals, in terms of status and earning power he held the advantage. As a result, while both partners were career-oriented, his career took priority.

Most of these couples had no children, and daily life was much the same for husband and wife: busy workdays, time together in the evening and on weekends, and shared household activities. There were differences, though they were often small in magnitude. He worked more overtime, she did more work around the house. When it came to the question of having children, however, the differences were striking. Both women and men assumed that children would affect the wife's career, but not the husband's.

Sandra and Jack illustrate these patterns well. They met in college, where he was majoring in electrical engineering, she in mechanical. He was a year closer to graduation than she. He became her boyfriend and mentor, helping her with homework, and giving moral support when she felt discouraged. She looked up to him and thought of him as brighter and more ambitious than she. Thus, early in their relationship a pattern of inequality was established. He assumed a position of leadership and higher status, even though on the surface they were equals.

This pattern was reinforced after they left college and married. Sandra went to work for the government, in an aircraft rework facility, Jack for a small high tech company. Both were career-oriented, but for Jack it was a much more single-minded pursuit than for Sandra. He poured himself into his work: besides his regular job, he had a consulting business with several other engineers, and taught part-time at a community college. He regularly worked six-day weeks, and arrived home at 8:00 P.M. on weekdays. He earned considerably more money than Sandra, and both saw him as the primary breadwinner in the family.

In contrast, Sandra was consciously shaping a career for herself that was compatible with family responsibilities. She loved her work, and found the intellectual challenge stimulating. She wanted to remain a "working engineer," rather than moving into management, partly because she liked the technical work, but also because she wanted no more than a 40-hour workweek. Her job required little overtime, and she valued that. She also valued the fact that as a civil service employee, she could progress in her career without *having* to go into management:

> That's one of the neat things about civil service . . . you can be a respectable engineer, and get promotions, and you're not a failure if you didn't go on into upper management. Whereas I think in a lot of the outside world, you are. If you're just a good engineer, you're a failure. . . . I think its a real neat job for a woman, because almost all the time I can be home by five, even

if I put in an extra hour. Whereas, my husband's not home yet. But he's a young engineer—you know, go-getter.

Here we see that for Sandra there was a clear difference between she and her husband. He was a "go-getter," reaching for the top. She wanted to be a respectable engineer. This difference is tied to her role in the family. As she put it: "If I were competing with him for salary, it'd be difficult. Who'd take care of us? We'd need another wife."

She wanted to be home by five, and took major responsibility for the household and meals. It was not that Jack made no contribution there. He washed the dinner dishes, did the vacuuming, and went with Sandra to shop for groceries. Sandra proudly described him as "the best housekeeper ever," and insisted that "he does at least half the chores."

But she clearly did more. In fact, she described herself as "running around in a frenzy" when she got home from work, "to make sure everything is done and the house immaculate." What she did not do herself, she planned and organized, because "he couldn't possibly do both. He has too many hours at work, and I enjoy it." His longer work hours often exempted him, not just from the planning, but from the doing as well: "when he's working a lot of overtime, I try not to give him too many projects when he comes home. . . . I don't harangue him that I'm doing too much."

Sandra's workday was often interrupted by family responsibilities as well. She complained in the interview about having to make phone calls during the day, to deal with banks, repair shops, and the like. She was clearly unhappy with this, yet she rationalized it as inevitable, given the greater demands of his job:

> I feel like, "I have a job too—I can't talk on the phone and get the dryer fixed." . . . I feel a little dumped on sometimes. But I am a little more flexible at work. I usually can find fifteen minutes to go hide, and make a personal phone call.

Sandra and Jack were planning to have children within the next year, and this fact was an important part of *Sandra's* attitude toward her career. She wanted a forty-hour week, not just to be home for her husband, but for her children. However, she had no intention of abandoning her career to become a full-time mother. In fact, she spoke derisively of women who do that:

It's very popular now for the young professional woman to become totally organic, and nurse her babies until they're five, and
stay at home, and the husband makes enough money so they
can still have a Volvo. . . . Now the woman who was good-
looking and handled a job and her husband and everything else,
is at home and fat and can't handle the kid . . . and the house is
a mess . . . because they kind of give up on things.

It was important to her to continue with her career full-time, but
she also took it for granted that raising children would be primarily
her responsibility. The only realistic way to do both, in her mind, was
to limit her career ambitions:

I don't think I have to be the super mom. That's why I view my
career as a little scaled down. I don't want to make it to the top.
I'm not interested in running the corporation. It [would be] a
really challenging and wonderful job, but I really do want to be
home when my kids get home from school.

Sandra had carefully thought through her strategy for combining career and family. She was postponing children until she had a
position she was happy with, and that would allow her some flexibility in her schedule. Implicit in her plans was the assumption that
successfully managing career and family would be *her* responsibility,
not Jack's:

[I want to] be senior enough to be able to negotiate a little bit
about my working hours, and to know that I like this job and I
don't need to start looking for other jobs. That would be difficult
to do while you're also trying to manage baby-sitters and small
children and all.

Like Sandra, most of the engineers we interviewed assumed
that children were primarily the responsibility of women. It was the
woman who would have to accommodate her career to the demands
and needs of a child. She would have to decide whether to work part-
time, full-time, or to leave her career altogether. This decision would
be complicated by her earning power as an engineer—could they
afford to lose part or all of her salary? Important as that question was,
however, it was not the crucial issue for the women we interviewed.
They were struggling most of all with their role and responsibilities as

mother, and whether or not that was compatible with a career. They sensed that children would come at the expense of *their* careers, not their husbands'. For some, like Sandra, this seemed both expected and accepted. For others it was a source of turmoil.

Cathy was strongly oriented toward rising into management, but also certain that she wanted children. In fact, when we interviewed her, she was pregnant with her first. She and her husband, Tom, who was an engineer with a more advanced degree than she, were planning to have two children, and she wanted them as close together as possible. She assumed that she would have to be out of the work force temporarily, and hoped that by having two children close together, she could limit her absence to about three years.

Cathy was not sure, however, that her strategy would be successful. She had real doubts about her ability to rise into management, and saw her family as the major obstacle. When asked why, she replied:

> [It is because of] the time demands of a family, and the importance I put on it. In order to get into management, you have to promote yourself within the company, and get yourself into a position where you have the respect and support of the people around you. . . . [They want] someone who will take on extra work, who will jump in and solve something without being asked. . . . There's a time conflict there between my work and my family.

Cathy never mentioned the possibility that Tom could or should share the raising of their children. They had already established a relationship in which his career was primary. When we asked if she would be willing to move to another city for a better job, she responded quickly, "I wouldn't take it." When asked what would happen if her husband were offered the same opportunity, she said, "We would probably take it," explaining:

> I feel my career is diversified enough that I can move to different types of companies and be able to go on. His is a very defined stepladder that he needs to get to where he wants to be.

Consistent with the higher priority placed on Tom's career, he was largely exempt from household responsibilities. When they were first married, Cathy did all the cooking and housework. That created conflict between them, and they solved the problem by hiring a maid to do the housecleaning. Tom agreed to cook dinner two nights a week. That left Cathy with less work, but still more than Tom. She cooked three nights a week, did the dishes, laundry, and grocery shopping. Incidentally, this is a pattern we found among many of our respondents: a maid is hired to resolve conflicts about housework, which absolves the husband of responsibility. The wife, however, does most of the chores not taken over by the maid.

Cathy's sense of being torn between two worlds—career or children—was something we heard over and over in our interviews with women. Many doubted that they could do both well, yet did not want to give up either one. For the men it was not a matter of choice. They could have both.

To be sure, some of the men we interviewed expressed concerns about the effects of a family on their career, but with two important differences. First, this was clearly not the burning issue that it was for women. Most of the women talked at length about career vs. family issues, often with considerable feeling. When the men talked about it at all, their comments were brief, and without intensity. Second, the men's worries revolved not around career disruption, but around money. They saw children and even marriage as bringing financial pressures with them—pressures that rested primarily on *their* shoulders. When we asked one man whether his career had affected his decisions about marriage or having children, he replied:

> Yes. I didn't want to get married until I was out of college—in order to be able to support whatever happened. And I don't want to have kids until I can afford one house on one salary . . . and that's going to take a couple more years.

This respondent was married to an engineer, and liked the fact that they had work interests in common. But it was clear that he saw himself as the breadwinner, and her career as dispensable. The cultural mandate that men provide and women nurture was evident in this interview, as in many others. Our male respondents knew that the demands of their career would interfere with the time they would have with their families, but as one put it, "I'll have to live with that." They also knew that having a family would affect their wives much more than they.

There were a few exceptions to the patterns described here, but very few. Of the seventeen women we interviewed who were married to men with greater occupational status than they, only three appeared to have relationships in which both careers were equally valued. These women were strongly dedicated to their careers, and willing to make only minimal concessions to accommodate children—or none at all. One woman had already made the choice between motherhood and career. Like generations of professional women before her, she had decided against having children at all.

The second woman thought she could have both, but only by relying on outside resources. Her plan was to hire live-in help to do most of the work. As an alternative, she thought she could do some of her work at home, without jeopardizing her career.

Notice that neither of these women considered their husbands responsible for raising children. Even though they were unusual in their degree of career-orientation, their solutions to the question of children were, in that sense, quite traditional. The husband's career was left undisturbed, and the assumption that raising children is women's work survived intact.

Only the third respondent deviated from this pattern. She told us that she and her husband—a chemist with a PhD—saw children as the responsibility of *both* parents, and they were grappling with the question of how to work that out. They were unique in even asking the question, "*who* would stay home with the child?" They had yet to come up with an answer, and were putting the decision off for now. Whether they will actually arrive at an arrangement involving shared parenting remains to be seen.

Until now, we have been talking about women for whom parenthood lies in the future (if at all). As sociologists have long been aware, it is never safe to assume that what people say they intend to do is in fact what they will do. For a small group of our respondents, however, the future is here—they already have children. By looking at their lives, we catch a disturbing glimpse of what lies ahead for the others. It is a picture of careers scaled back, or on indefinite hold, while husbands pursue their own ambitions unthwarted. For the few who attempt to "do it all," combining full-time engineering with child rearing, it is a picture of stress, overwork, and frustrated aspirations.

JULIE: A CAREER ABANDONED

Julie provides us with an example of a woman who withdrew from the labor force in order to care for her children. She had worked

for United Missile since she graduated from school eight years previously. For the last three of those years she had been a senior engineer, doing thermodynamic analysis. She continued to work full-time
after her first baby was born. When the second came along, however,
she found it too difficult to continue with her work. As she put it,
"With one child it was manageable. With two, I didn't think I could
keep my sanity." When we interviewed her, she had been away from
her job for a year, since the birth of her second child. Her older child
was four years old. She was married to Bob, who had a master's
degree in computer science. He worked at home much of the time,
and had very flexible hours.

Julie, in contrast, had no flexibility in her hours at UM, and was
often required to work overtime. This was part of the reason why she
decided to leave her job. "The job was demanding too much. Par for
the course at UM is ten hours [a week] overtime. I mean you don't
work forty hours a week usually." Despite the greater flexibility of
Bob's job, however, the idea that he could take over more of the child
care did not seem to have occurred to them. In fact, when Julie went
through periods of working a lot of overtime, it was not Bob, but
Bob's mother who took care of their little girl.

While Julie was still employed, she and Bob took turns picking
their daughter up from her baby-sitter, cooking dinner, and washing
dishes. Other than that, he did little, except for some yard work. Julie
did the grocery shopping and laundry, and they had a maid to clean
the house. As with other couples, the maid was a solution to the
conflicts they had over Bob's unwillingness to do more housework.
Bob's mother came over and got their daughter up in the morning,
while he slept in, and took care of the child during the day. Julie did
all the work of getting their daughter ready for bed at night:

> I did all of it. I still do. I give them baths, and put them to bed. I
> do the part that isn't very much fun. And my husband always
> plays with the kids. He does that now. Now that we've got two,
> he'll take one to play with, and I'll take the other one up and
> give her a bath, put her to bed. Then I'll take the other one, and
> do the same thing.

Another source of concern for Julie was the quality of care her
daughter was receiving. She spent the day with Bob's mother, and
had no contact with other children. Julie was worried about the child's
social development. She went two afternoons a week to a day-care

center, but Julie was dissatisfied with that too. Looking back on it, she felt that she could have found a better center. At the time, however, she was so busy with her job and family responsibilities that she had no time to even *think* about what would be best, let alone look into other alternatives. When the second baby was born, she felt she had no choice but to leave her job. "I just didn't know how I was going to work it out logistically." The burden was clearly on her to work it out, and she chose the only way she thought possible.

Julie wanted to return to work, but she could not foresee a time when she would be able to work full-time. Even in ten years, she said she hoped she would be working part-time, as a "job-shopper." This is not uncommon work for engineers. It involves hiring on with a company for a limited period of time, to work on a specific project. It is not a viable way to build a career, however. Julie was still interested in engineering, but she had given up on the idea of a career. She saw no realistic way to continue with it, given the demands of her family.

GINGER: A CAREER SCALED BACK

Ginger found a different way out of the dilemma of parenthood, and stopped short of giving up her career. She continued to work full-time for six months after her first baby was born, but then left her job at CDI and went to work part-time for her husband Don. He had his own business, designing and developing residential properties. Since they both worked at home, this meant she could spend more time with their baby daughter. She worked four hours a day, while the baby was being cared for by a neighbor.

We need to back up, however. It was not just the birth of her baby that changed Ginger's career path. Well before becoming a mother, her relationship with her husband was affecting the choices she made about her work. The reader will recall that Ginger met Don in college. Her first introduction to him was in a lab class, where he infuriated her by his domineering attitude. They became romantically involved, however, and married after graduation. We interviewed her six years later, ten months after the birth of their first child. She was happily married, and crazy about her baby. However, she had made significant sacrifices in her career, while her husband had not.

As we saw earlier, Ginger had been a brilliant student, and had landed a job in the design lab at CDI, which was as close as an engineer could come to "starting at the top." From there she moved downward, transferring to a lower status position in marketing, where she eventually was promoted to a supervisory position. She then left the company altogether, to work part-time for her husband.

Ginger's path was not just the result of her marriage and motherhood. The design lab where she started was a hostile environment for women, and few stayed there. But her family role was a factor as well. At several key points in Ginger's career she limited her aspirations, at least partly in response to her husband's advice, or to the demands of his career. Just after they were married, in their senior year of college, Ginger received a full graduate fellowship to pursue doctoral studies in engineering. She enjoyed her engineering studies, especially the theoretical aspects, and wanted to become a university professor. Her husband, however, suggested that she "see what engineering is like first—see what the real world's like." She took his advice, and dropped her plans for graduate study. Whether he intended it or not, Don had dissuaded her from aspiring to a higher occupational status than his own.

As we saw earlier, when Ginger was working in the design lab at CDI, management offered her a paid leave of absence and a fellowship to complete her master's degree in engineering at Stanford University. This would have improved her chances of becoming a manager in the lab. Her decision to turn down the opportunity was based on several factors, most of which had to do with her disillusionment with her job. Also contributing to her decision, however, was the fact that her husband's occupational fortunes were tied to the area where they lived. He had a business there, and they would be separated while she went to school. Like so many women engineers, especially those with engineer husbands, Ginger was reluctant to make such a move, even temporarily.

After her baby was born, Ginger tried to continue with full-time work. She and Don did not want their baby to spend all day with a sitter, and they tried a nontraditional arrangement. Don cared for the baby half-day, and took her to a baby-sitter for the other half-day. This solution was not satisfactory to either one of them, however. The baby interfered too much with Don's work, and Ginger wanted more time with her. She was working sixty-hour weeks at the time, including commuting time, and was not happy about spending so much time away from her baby.

CDI was of no help to her. As another woman who worked there told us:

Well [CDI's attitude is] basically, "you've gotten yourself in this situation, you resolve it." You get strictly the disability [leave]—anything else is non-paid. There's no part-time, there's no job sharing, there's no child-care support or referral.

Ginger said that she probably would have stayed at CDI if she could have worked fewer hours. But with no flexibility in her job, she decided to leave the company altogether, and work part-time for Don. The baby then spent half the day with her mother, and the other half with the baby-sitter, while Ginger worked.

In assessing decisions like these, it is never easy to be certain of all the reasons, or to identify the most important. If Ginger had not been about to marry Don, would she have gone to graduate school before going to work at CDI? If she had not been married, would she have gone to graduate school when she had her second chance, despite the problems she was having in the lab? Or if she had felt better about her job in the lab, would she have gone to graduate school, even though it meant leaving Don temporarily? If CDI had made part-time work possible for her, would she have stayed on there, with Don sharing equally in the baby's care? We cannot be sure of the answers to these questions. The best we can do is to suggest that her relationship with her husband, the lack of support from her employer, and the cultural mandate that women mother, all contributed to the decisions she made.

CYNTHIA: "HAVING IT ALL"

Cynthia provides an example of another alternative for the career woman/mother. She was the personification of the "superwoman." She had married Ralph thirteen years earlier, shortly after graduating from college. Since then she had worked full-time, while simultaneously bearing and caring for three children, and completing a master's degree in engineering. She never took more than thirteen weeks maternity leave for the births of any of her children.

Ralph had done graduate work as well. He studied four years for a PhD in chemistry, but did not pass his qualifying exams. Since then he had turned to computer systems work, and was now a systems project manager, designing hardware and software.

In contrast, six years after receiving her master's degree, Cynthia was still a senior engineer, doing analysis and testing. She was frustrated by the fact that she had little opportunity to do design work, and that she was not moving up any faster:

> I want to go up the line. I don't want to stay where I am. I don't want to be pigeonholed off somewhere. I want power.

She attributed her problems in part to the politics of the workplace: the fact that as a woman she was excluded from the "old boys' network." She also felt, however, that having children—who were now eight, four, and one years old—had held her back:

> I had been pretty good at setting goals for myself up until the time I had children, and my children have taken front seat to a lot of things, and have clouded some of my professional objectives.

Small wonder! Cynthia shouldered the full responsibility of caring for her children and her household. Ralph tolerated few infringements from his family on his career. Cynthia put it in a nutshell, when we asked her how Ralph felt about being married to an engineer: "I think he's proud of it, as long as it doesn't interfere with his life."

That seemed to be his attitude toward everything connected with his family. From the time she got the kids up in the morning until she put them to bed at night, it was Cynthia who did *everything*. Just listening to her describe her day, which went nonstop from 4:30 in the morning until after 10 at night, was exhausting. On weekends she cleaned the house, did the laundry and grocery shopping. She did all the cooking and dishwashing. Throughout all this, Ralph was consumed with his career, and unavailable even to pick the children up from day-care when Cynthia had to work late. As she put it:

> He usually works at the office 'til 8 or 9 at night, and consults two out of four weekends. . . . He's a compulsive workaholic and does not like working in the house or around the house.

What happened when someone had to be home with a sick child? Here Ralph could occasionally help, because he could work at home on his computer. This was a mixed blessing, though:

I'm not always so sure what kind of care the kids get when Ralph is home because he has a very unique talent for tuning everything out, but at least there is *someone* there.

Now that her children were getting a little older, Cynthia was facing additional problems:

My older boy was in soccer and little league this year, and next year I'm gonna have two boys in soccer, and they schedule practices at 4:00 in the afternoon. That's just impossible. Last year I took vacation time to do it. . . . Next year we're gonna have to find someone to take them to school and pick them up and get them to the practices. I just can't do it.

Not surprisingly, Ralph's lack of participation in family life was a source of conflict between them. When we asked how that conflict was resolved, Cynthia replied calmly:

I blow my top and he ignores me. . . . Oh, occasionally he'll surprise me and do something around the house, but to a large extent—I may be able to guilt-trip him, but he has a high threshold for guilt. I don't know. I'm trying to get the kids to help. They don't like that, but. . . .

Cynthia's family role clearly played a part in her lack of progress at work. What is surprising is that she was doing as well in her career as she was, given the overwhelming burden she carried at home. But how many women have this kind of stamina and spirit? If it takes a woman like Cynthia to successfully combine a full-time engineering career with children, then the number who do so will remain small, indeed. Her case may be an extreme one—we certainly hope so. But we must entertain the possibility that Cynthia portends the future for some of the women in our sample who will have children in the next few years. Married to men more advanced in their careers and often more highly educated than they, already defining their careers as subordinate to their husbands', there is little likelihood that they will be in a position to bargain for equal sharing of the parental role when it arrives.

THE DEVIANT CASE: ATYPICAL STATUS RELATIONSHIPS

What about couples whose marriages do not follow the typical pattern—women whose husbands are less educated and hold lower-status jobs? If we are correct in our argument about the importance of power relations in the family, then we would expect to find differences in the way these women balance career and family. That is, women married to "status inferiors" should be less traditional in this regard. There were few of these women in our sample, as among engineers generally: 12 percent of the married respondents in both our questionnaire and interview samples. This meant only three of the women we interviewed fell into this category. Our discussion of them falls into the sociological tradition of "deviant case analysis": the qualitative examination of individual cases which do not fit a prevailing pattern.

None of these women had children.[14] However, when we looked at their marriages, we found some interesting patterns. Two of the three couples exhibited a significant degree of equality, and even role-reversal in their relationships. We focus here on Denise and Stuart to illustrate this.

Stuart was a sales manager with a high school education. He earned more money than Denise, but they both knew that could change in the future. She had only received her engineering degree two years earlier, and was strongly motivated toward rising into management. In fact, it was Denise who was the hard-driven careerist in the family. As she put it, "I'll never be a forty-hour a week person." When we asked her if Stuart saw any disadvantages in being married to an engineer, she said:

Only that I'm gone so much, and I'm so work-oriented. Even when I'm home, he complains, "You're here, but you're not really here—you're a million miles away!" And he has problems with that. . . . It's all the things that I used to associate with a woman complaining about her husband.

Denise and Stuart shared housework equally. The only conflicts they had about that arose when he thought *she* was not doing her half. They hired a maid, which solved the problem.

When asked about her willingness to move in order to take a better job, Denise told us that both she and Stuart had had offers, which they had turned down. Neither was willing to jeopardize the other's career. Thus, we see in this couple a distinctly different kind of relationship. Her career is as important in shaping family life as his—maybe more so. We believe this is more than just coincidence, or a matter of individual idiosyncrasies. Few of the married couples with traditional status relationships displayed these patterns. Yet two of three couples with atypical status relationships did. The third couple, Barbara and Jim, were more traditional, but not entirely so.

Jim was a lab technician with a high school education, and Barbara was strongly career-oriented. She wanted to become a project manager, but she viewed her family as the biggest obstacle to achieving her career goals:

> I think family is a big potential obstacle, because I don't know how I'm gonna want to divide my time, once there are children. I work extra hours now on my own, and take classes once in a while still, where I don't think I'll have time to do that any more. That might hinder my advancement. . . . To me it's not just a job. If I had chosen something that was just a job, I would more easily give it up to have a family.

She and Jim were planning to start having children soon, and wanted three. Barbara wanted to continue working full-time, and she worried about the inflexibility of her current job, which was in a test department:

> In test there's a lot of freedom during some periods, but a lot of times you're bound by the tests, and you have to stay close by. If we have children there could be some problems then. I'd need more flexibility, so I'd be freer to come and go from work if I had to.

Barbara did not see Jim as having significant responsibility for integrating children into his career. Like the women married to status superiors, she saw it as her problem. Her relationship with Jim was not like theirs in every respect, however. She expressed more willingness to move for the sake of her career than they did. When we asked her if a move would be out of the question unless there was a good opportunity for him, she replied:

> That's a good question. I wouldn't say it'd be out of the question. I'd say it'd be less likely, but it wouldn't be out of the

question. We could probably do it as a temporary thing. He could do some other kind of work temporarily.

Thus, his work did not take precedence over hers, because his was more like a job than a career. He could do something else, at least temporarily. If, on the other hand, he wanted to move for a better job, she "would have to find something related to engineering," because hers was a career. The status difference in their jobs thus gave Barbara a resource not shared by most married women. In her case, however, it was not enough to override *all* the traditional assumptions about women's role in the family. She would be responsible for the children when they came, and she was now responsible for more of the housework than Jim was. They shared chores, but as she put it, "I tend to do more."

This division of housework was not an arrangement she was satisfied with, however. They had regular conflicts over it, and when we asked Barbara what she would change about her family life if she could, she replied, "more even sharing of housework." It remains to be seen whether her dissatisfaction will lead to the common solution of hiring a maid, or whether she would prevail on Jim to do more. It is also possible that when they actually begin to have children, her desire for greater equality will spill over into this arena as well. Given the importance of her career to her, and given the greater status and earning power of her work, it is possible that she will begin to want more shared parenting than she now envisioned. This is, of course, speculation, and we have no way of knowing what will happen in the future. We do know, however, that her status superiority over her husband provides her with resources in her marriage not available to most women engineers.

For the women in this group—even for Barbara, though to a lesser extent—their greater occupational or educational status gives them an unusual degree of power in their marriages. That power makes it *less* likely that their family roles will conflict with their career goals. In this sense, they experience the family-career relationship more like men traditionally have: they can have both. That they *will* have both is not guaranteed, however. The cultural mandate that children are the responsibility of women is pervasive, and will affect even these women to some degree.

In addition to these few women, we found two men in our interview sample who had atypical status relationships in their marriages. They had wives with more education than they, and one had higher occupational status as well. Their marriages displayed patterns consistent with what we have already seen. Both men had given up jobs to move for the sake of their wive's careers, indicating the high priority placed on the latter. Household tasks were fairly evenly divided. Moreover, the earning capacity of their wives freed these men from some of the pressure of the breadwinner role felt by most husbands.

Kurt was a mechanical engineer, whose wife Jan had recently become an attorney. He was attracted to the idea of starting his own business, and felt free to take the risks involved:

> My wife is a professional, and therefore [my] setting up a business and failing would not damage our overall ability to live comfortably. I don't have the pressures that a lot of people have. . . . They get locked in because they get a wife and kids, house, and they cannot afford to be without a paycheck for a month.

Bill, married to a civil engineer with a master's degree in construction management, also felt that marriage gave him freedom:

> If I'd gotten laid off last year, I wasn't going to be in difficult straits. I could live until I'm 65 on her salary. Not that it would be fair, but. . . . I wasn't like some people who maybe have kids and are the only one working.

However, Bill worried about what would happen if they had children, apparently assuming that their family income would be diminished:

> I think we will try to have some children. She'll be thirty-three in September and I suppose we should have them soon, but we're cautious people. I don't want to have children and be poverty-stricken at the same time.

Both Bill and Kurt expressed interest in having children, and thought it would be difficult. Neither discussed the possible options for raising children, and it was unclear whether they assumed their wives would bear this responsibility. The fact that they did not clearly state that assumption, as did most of the other men, probably reflects the unusual status relationships involved in these two marriages. How the question of children will be resolved for these two couples remains to be seen. However, the high status and earning power of the women at least makes it more likely that their careers will not automatically be seen as dispensable.

These generalizations about atypical status relationships remain tentative, because of the small number of them in our sample, which reflects their rarity in society as well. The pattern of women married to older, better educated men in higher status occupations is pervasive. Yet it may be that—short of broader social changes—reversing that pattern is one of the few means available to women to achieve a more equitable integration of career and family roles. Marriage to a status inferior does not guarantee role equity, as we saw with Barbara and Jim. But it provides a resource that at least makes it possible. It is a resource that can counteract the prevailing cultural mandate that assigns women responsibility for the family, and demands of men complete devotion to the career.

The paradox, of course, is that short of fundamental social changes, it is unlikely that marriages like these will be anything but exceptions to the norm. The tendency for women to marry men who are status superiors is part and parcel of a system of male dominance—both a reflection and reinforcement of that system. As long as men dominate the major institutions of society, both men and women will see couples like Barbara and Jim as deviant, and there will be no strong incentives for others to follow in their path. Barbara told us, in fact, that Jim was sensitive about her occupational status in social situations:

> If we're at an engineering dinner, for some club or something, people ask him what he does. People are always asking if he's an engineer too. He works for a company called Allied Engineering, so people think he's an engineer too, and he has to explain that he's not, that he's a lab tech. That's difficult for him.

The sense of stigma felt by couples like this may even create a response that counteracts the power resource the women hold. To reclaim their legitimacy, one or both of them may cling to traditional roles. This may explain some of the traditionalism we found in Barbara and Jim's marriage.

CONCLUSION

We have seen in this chapter that the family structure of the married woman engineer is much like that of other professional women. While it may be more egalitarian than the families of nonprofessional women, it still assigns her a greater share of household responsibility, and defines her career as less important than his. In the absence of children, the differences are often small, and may have minimal impact on her career. Indeed, given the likelihood that she is married to an engineer, she will reap the benefits of a "built-in mentor," who can provide advice, contacts, and other support that may be missing in the workplace. As a result, marriage may mean better job assignments and higher pay, even though these may be accompanied by lower levels of technical self-confidence and a greater willingness to subordinate her career to her husband's. At least in the early stages of her career, for the woman without children, marriage does not appear to be a significant liability, and for women married to engineers it provides some concrete resources.

When children enter the picture, however, it changes considerably. Whether children existed in their imaginations or their daily lives, the women in our sample saw them as *their* responsibility—not their husbands'. Nor was it only the women who saw it this way: their husbands and employers generally agreed. As a result, it was the women who would have to adjust their careers to the needs of their families, which for most would mean an interrupted, scaled back, or abandoned career. The marital resources they reaped from their status as professionals were not enough to counter the greater occupational status of their husbands, the inflexibility of their employers, or the cultural mandate of the larger society.

The only significant exceptions to this pattern were women married to lower status men. This suggests that part of the problem lies in the status relationships within the two-professional marriage. When a woman marries a man older, more advanced in his career, and more highly educated—as is most often the case—she may gain a mentor, but she does not gain full equality in the marriage. Not only does her self-confidence suffer, but her career is defined as less important than his. The difference in career primacy may lie hidden until the birth of a child. Then the greater resources of the husband, supported by the cultural mandate that women mother, come into play. As a result, his career flourishes, while hers stagnates or is abandoned altogether.

Even when she has greater occupational resources than her husband, it is by no means certain that equality will prevail. It is probably *more* likely, but the few women and men in our sample with atypical status relationships did not yet have children, and thus had not been tested in that regard. Those who do have children in the future will encounter strong pressures to revert to tradition from employers, co-workers, family, and friends.

We have seen in this chapter that we cannot consider the family in isolation from the workplace, or from the larger system of power and culture in which both are imbedded. The same is true of the workplace and the engineering school. Resources derived in one sphere are made use of in others. Constraints imposed here limit options there. Gender-linked social expectations permeate all simultaneously. What happens in the family, the workplace, and the university is a product of organizational power relations and resources, gender role behavior, and the structure of external institutions. Women's careers in engineering are shaped by the complex interplay of all of these.

In our concluding chapter, we discuss the theoretical and practical implications of the findings presented here and in the preceding chapters. We argue that, just as women's careers are shaped in complex ways by their experiences in family, school, and workplace, so improving their status in engineering will require multiple and wide-ranging changes in all these institutions.

8

CONCLUSION

We have followed the women and men in our sample on a long and complex journey: from childhood, through college, and into the first decade of their careers. We conclude by considering the practical and theoretical implications of our analysis. We first discuss what can be done to improve women's status in engineering, focusing especially on government policy. Second, we explore the implications of our conflict-structural approach for discussions of women in nontraditional occupations more generally.

It should be said at the outset that our conclusions and recommendations are not constrained by what is considered "practical" in today's political climate. As a result, some may appear utopian and unrealistic. We believe, however, that social analysis needs both realism *and vision*. If we are to move beyond the point at which we now stand, we need to speak in terms of what *could be*, not simply what is. Without vision, social analysis too easily becomes capitulation to the status quo. We believe we are in good company in this position. After all, the best of sociology has often been accused of being either subversive or utopian (Giddens 1987). With or without such precedent, simple honesty leaves us no choice but to follow the implications of our data. Before we turn to this task, however, we review the findings and arguments of the preceding chapters.

SUMMARY OF FINDINGS

The decision to become an engineer was influenced most importantly by a woman's skills in math and science. Most members of our
sample were traditional in their gender role orientations, and ignorant about engineering as a profession. Their interest in this occupation, however, was often kindled by an enthusiastic teacher or counselor, an engineer father, or a supportive boyfriend. In turn, it was
changing attitudes and social structures that helped these people take
women seriously as math and science students. The changes of the
1960s and 70s had worked their way into the consciousness of the
middle class, bringing the recognition that women too could become
scientists and engineers.

The decision to become an engineer was made later for women
than it was for men: typically in their second or third year of college.
Given this late entrance, having taken the right preparatory courses
was essential. Engineering presupposes algebra, trigonometry, calculus, physics, and chemistry. Most had already taken these courses
and done well in them. As a result, it was possible for them to choose
engineering halfway through college, and to survive a demanding
curriculum.

They worked hard as engineering majors, and thrived on the
academic challenge. Though they encountered resentment and hostility from some male students and faculty, they did well in their
studies. Their classmates may have felt threatened and resentful toward them, but they did not have the power to hold them back. Their
professors held that power, but they valued academic performance
above all else, and could not ignore the talents of these women students.

There was one area, however, where the background of these
women was weak. Most of our sample had little mechanical experience as children, and consequently felt insecure about their technical,
hands-on competence. Their college experiences did little to remedy
this deficit. While in college, however, their lack of self-confidence in
this area was overshadowed by their success in their studies. That
would change when they entered the workplace.

Upon graduation, these women were quickly hired, receiving
starting salaries as good or better than their male classmates. However, within the first ten years of their careers, they were occupying
lower status positions than the men. Women were less often design
and R & D engineers, and more often production and sales engineers.

They were less likely to be moving into supervisory positions as senior engineers, or into middle management. This was despite their obvious talents, and the fact that their education, work-related values, and work continuity patterns were virtually identical to the men's.

This pattern was complicated by other factors, however. In high tech firms and electrical engineering, women did much worse than men, while in aerospace and mechanical engineering they did as well or better.

Overt sexism did not seem to be the crucial factor explaining these patterns. While women in all workplaces faced at least some degree of sexual harassment, exclusion, patronization, and hostility, there was actually more of this in aerospace firms, where they were most successful. Where women fared more poorly it was related to the technical, hands-on nature of the work, and most importantly to the power of engineers in the workplace. Where women experienced greater occupational mobility, engineers were less powerful, and the workplace was dominated by management and bureaucratic formalism, which included affirmative action policies.

Where male engineers held power, work relations reflected their interests. The "culture of engineering," which prevailed in these workplaces, put a premium on male-defined styles of interaction: aggressive displays of technical ability, self-promotion, and self-confidence. In an environment like this, women felt a sense of incompetence that they had not experienced in college. Their mobility was slowed, not because they were not good at their jobs, but because they were not good at the male-defined interactional rituals demanded.

There was in these workplaces a complex interplay of structure and gender role. Structures were primary, because they defined power relations. Power relations in turn shaped the culture of the workplace. Once created, the culture became a reality sui generis, which engineers, both male and female, had to navigate in order to succeed in their careers. Gender roles were significant, because they influenced the content of the culture and served as interactional resources in navigating it. Where workplace culture was defined by engineers, it was imbued with the technical and interactional orientation associated with the male gender role. Women were disadvantaged as a result.

The relationship between structure and gender role also operated in the family lives of engineers. Most of our respondents were married, but the marriages of women and men were quite different. Women were typically married to men who were superior to them in educational and occupational status. A surprising number were married to engineers. These engineer husbands tended to be older, more advanced in their careers, and, consequently, to be better paid, and in higher positions than their wives. This situation created both advantages and disadvantages.

On the one hand, their more advanced husbands functioned as mentors, providing advice, information, and support. Women in these marriages were rising into management more rapidly than other women, and earning higher salaries. On the other hand, their careers were given second priority to their husbands, and they displayed lower levels of technical self-confidence than other married women.

This situation was created as much by the structure of the family as by gender socialization. The greater status of husbands gave them more power in the family. In addition, the mentor role played by these older, higher-status men placed women in a dependent situation, which undermined both their power and their self-confidence. These tendencies were muted among our respondents, because they were still early in their careers, and most were childless. The experiences of the few women who did have children suggested that the arrival of children intensifies the negative effects of marriage to a higher-status man. It was among these women that we saw careers stalled, scaled back, or abandoned altogether.

Structure and gender role, power relations and interactional resources—these were the recurring themes of our discussion. What we call a conflict-structural perspective describes a dialectic between organizational structure and gender role, but it is a weighted dialectic. Each of these elements holds autonomous importance, but structure is primary. It defines the power relations that determine the nature of workplace culture and the kinds of interaction peculiar to it. Merely looking at institutional structure ignores interpersonal and interactional issues, but focusing solely on the latter misses the forces that create them.

IMPLICATIONS FOR WOMEN'S STATUS IN ENGINEERING

The implications of our study for women's future in engineering are both disturbing and hopeful. We begin with the bad news. Women's enrollments in engineering programs around the country appear to have peaked, or at least slowed dramatically in their growth. In contrast, the number of women entering other nontraditional professions like law, medicine, and accounting continues to climb. It seems clear that young women do not yet perceive engineering as a viable career alternative, despite the opportunities and rewards it offers. We believe there are a number of reasons for this. First, engineering has a more male-identified image than most other professions. Engineering is more like the male-dominated blue-collar occupations in this regard. Most Americans do not know precisely what engineers do, but the general image they have is of a technically and mathematically oriented, asocial type: in short, the "nerd." According to the stereotype, the nerd loves to tinker, to invent, and to spend long nights hunched over a slide rule—or in more recent imagery, a computer keyboard. He is devoid of social skills, or of concern for his appearance. Hardly an image to inspire the emulation of a teenage girl!

While there are important grains of truth to this stereotype, both engineering and engineers are more diverse than that. Some engineering work fits the stereotype well. But what most engineers do is less technically and mathematically challenging than they like to admit, and more social and administrative than hands-on. But young engineers-to-be do not learn that until they enter the workplace. And the image itself is no doubt a factor in deterring young women from seriously considering it as an alternative at all.

Improving Educational Opportunities

Part of the problem, then, is the image of engineering as inherently masculine, an image that is only partly accurate. The inaccuracies of the image can be changed through active efforts at recruitment and education in the elementary and secondary schools. This is part of the good news that comes out of our study. The Society of Women Engineers conducts a speaker's program that sends women into the schools to talk about what they do, and to encourage girls to think about engineering as a career choice. Among our sample were several women who named programs like these as sources of motivation for their decisions. But SWE cannot reach enough women by itself. School systems need to incorporate information about science and technology careers for women into school curricula *at all grade levels*. In addition, if teachers, counselors, and parents are educated about opportunities for women in engineering, and about the actual nature of the work, they can play an important role in the recruitment process.

As we have seen, however, the image of engineering as a masculine activity is partly real. There *are* aspects of the work that fit better with male than with female gender socialization. In particular, young girls are encouraged neither to tinker nor to pursue math. While the debate continues regarding the biological versus social bases of gender differences in math and visual-spatial skills, it is clear that most women, like most men, can become competent in both areas. It is also clear that young girls receive fewer opportunities and challenges in math and mechanics, either at home or in school. This is a situation highly amenable to change. More good news.

Providing girls and young women with a sense of the importance of math and mechanical skills, and with opportunities to develop those skills, would go a long way toward enlarging their horizons, both occupationally and socially. Math in particular is crucial, and not just for engineering careers. It has been estimated that the failure of most high school and college women to take advanced math courses excludes them from 75 percent of all college majors (Sells 1978). As we have seen, excellence in math is currently the most common route into engineering for women, and competence in math is essential for pursuing an engineering major. By increasing the number of women who are comfortable and competent in this area, we make engineering a more viable choice for them. In order to do that, however, we must be more aggressive in encouraging young women to take math courses throughout the precollege years.

We can increase the likelihood that young women gifted in math and science will go into engineering by educating teachers and counselors to take them more seriously, and to provide them with a clear understanding of the options available to them. However, there is no reason why less talented women should not also benefit from such encouragement. After all, less talented men enter the occupation regularly. For many men, the math requirements of an engineering major are a somewhat unpleasant hurdle that must be jumped. These men are not academic superstars, but they are competent enough to squeak by. Parents and teachers should encourage similarly able women to do the same.

Mechanical know-how is much less important than math in college. It becomes more important on the job, depending on the kind of engineering involved. It remains most important, however, as part of engineers' presentation of self. Whether or not they actually build prototypes or tinker with equipment on the job, they need to be able to present themselves as someone who is capable of doing so. By providing opportunities to learn and enjoy mechanical skills, we make it more possible for women to feel comfortable on the job, and to interact self-confidently with the men around them.

As we have seen, technical self-confidence is an important asset in the making of an engineering career. We believe it plays a role earlier as well. As long as engineering carries with it the "tinkering" image, young women will not be drawn to it unless they see themselves as capable of tinkering too. Being a whiz at math is enough to compensate a woman for her lack of mechanical background, at least while she is in school. But as long as this is the only kind of woman who becomes an engineer, their number will remain small. We need to make engineering for women more like it is for men: accessible to the average student, as well as the exceptional one. As with men, engineering should be seen as a realistic choice for the woman who is *reasonably* competent at math *and* mechanics. In order to make that happen, we need to make sure that the *average* college-bound woman has had opportunities and encouragement in both areas. This means integrating mechanical experiences into the curriculum, rather than limiting them to special courses, or extracurricular activities. Girls and young women from preschool on should be learning to use tools, to build and repair, and to understand mechanical principles. Parents, of course, can play a crucial role in this, and education efforts should target them as well. But if we want to reach the largest number of young women most quickly, the emphasis should be on changes in school curricula.

In the meantime, universities could do much more to help the current generation of young women overcome the lack of mechanical background they bring to college. If they are serious about increasing opportunities for women, engineering schools need to recognize the "tinkering deficit" produced by female gender socialization, and develop compensatory programs to provide women with the resources they were denied in childhood. It does not take long to learn these things. There is nothing mystical or very difficult about using tools and performing basic mechanical activities. Familiarity and self-confidence can be gained quickly. But it takes a supportive, nonthreatening environment, away from the judgments of people who take such skills for granted. Programs like these could easily be made part of every woman's training in engineering school. They could be offered as well to nonmajors, to encourage women to consider a technical major, and to bolster technical skills and self-confidence as early as possible. Beyond that, more extensive lab opportunities and internship requirements in the regular curriculum, and more part-time student-engineer positions in local industries would be invaluable to women.

Strengthening Affirmative Action

The image of engineering, and the background required for it, are not the only problems we face in recruiting women. There is also the matter of the opportunities actually available there. We have seen that, while engineering is a good occupation for women, they face significant obstacles to acceptance, especially in high-status positions. Engineering will become a truly popular choice for women only when they see other women accepted and allowed real opportunities for mobility in the profession. Career opportunities must be visibly available not just to the brightest and most assertive woman, but to the average woman—just as they are available to the average man.

Our study found that women are more successful in some organizational settings than others. They do better in bureaucratically structured organizations that evaluate engineers on the basis of formal qualifications and achievements, provide special resources for women (affirmative action), and limit the power of engineers. That is the good news. The bad news is that these organizations—primarily aerospace defense contractors—also provide engineers with some of the least satisfying work available today. Compared with high tech engineering, aerospace jobs rank low on autonomy, creativity, and variety, and high on red tape. The limited power of engineers in these firms means they are less able to shape the work culture to suit their (male) interests. Women benefit from that as women, but not as engineers. In short, women engineers today often face an unpleasant choice: opportunity in a less satisfying work environment or frustration in a more satisfying one.

What is needed is to make the resources women find in aerospace available in other types of organizations as well. The most realistic way to limit the power of engineers in industries like high tech is to offset it with a power resource from outside the organization. Affirmative action is the most obvious and effective resource available today. Where affirmative action is institutional policy, procedures for hiring and promotion are formal and explicit. The greater emphasis on credentials, seniority, and written evaluations works to the advantage of women, especially when they are confronting a male-defined workplace culture. By expanding the scope of affirmative action regulations, and strengthening their enforcement, we could go a long way toward creating the visible opportunities necessary to make engineering an attractive career for women.

The visibility of those opportunities will in turn encourage young women to acquire the skills necessary for success in engineering. It will be easier for teachers, counselors, and parents to persuade young women to continue their math studies, and to take courses involving hands-on technical skills, if they can point to concrete payoffs that await them in engineering. Without expanding women's opportunities in the engineering workplace, we cannot hope to attract large numbers of well-prepared women to it.

We recognize that our call for an expansion of affirmative action comes at a time when it is being scaled back, undermined, and attacked from the highest levels of government. In the 1980s the executive branch of the government was overtly hostile to affirmative action, and the Supreme Court ambivalent. As a result, its scope has been narrowed, and enforcement has lagged. Corporate leaders have gotten the message, and many have let their own efforts lapse. The active recruitment of women and minorities into engineering that occurred during the 1970s is much less in evidence today.

Nevertheless, the experiences of the women in our study are testimony to the effectiveness of this embattled policy. Our data suggest strongly that affirmative action does work. For the women in our sample, this program has produced exactly what its framers intended: it has allowed competent members of a minority group to succeed in spite of resistance to them. That may be the best news of all. The experiences of our respondents also raise questions about some of the common arguments against affirmative action.

One argument is that affirmative action is counterproductive: that it stigmatizes participants and promotes unqualified individuals who then go on to fail. We found no evidence for this. Affirmative action served as a resource to bright women who would have otherwise been ignored or defeated by the resistance of peers and managers. The women and men in our sample were equals in engineering knowledge. They were much more likely to be equals in job assignments and promotions as well, in workplaces with strong affirmative action programs.

Not only that, there was an association between women's interactional resources and their job standing in aerospace that was missing in high tech. The aerospace workplace allowed women with higher levels of self-confidence and assertiveness to make use of those resources to secure the best positions, as it did for men. In high tech, however, having those resources helped men advance, but not women. This suggests that affirmative action contributes to a climate in which mobility is based *more* on qualifications—both technical and interactional—than on gender.

Moreover, while the women who benefited from affirmative action were aware of it, there was no evidence that they suffered a loss of self-confidence as a result. If this had been the case, we should have found lower levels of self-confidence among women in aerospace. We did not. In fact, there was no relationship between place of employment (high tech vs. aerospace) and technical self-confidence. Our data instead suggest that the success facilitated by affirmative action may enhance, or at least protect, self-confidence. Women working in the more sexist interactional climate of aerospace showed no erosion of their technical self-confidence over time. For women in high tech, however, the longer they had been in their jobs, the lower their self-confidence levels.

None of our respondents attributed their promotions solely to affirmative action. Most felt that it helped, but that their own qualifications were the most important factor in their success. Success breeds its own compensations. Most winners attribute their success to their own abilities, and it is not surprising that women in these situations do likewise.

Redefining Work-Family Relationships

Expanded and more strictly enforced laws are only part of what is necessary to ensure equality for women. As feminists recognized in the 1960s and 70s, there is also a need to change social definitions. As long as liberation means only that women are allowed to behave like men, it will remain incomplete. This point applies both to the workplace and the family. We need to foster greater self-confidence and assertiveness in young women, but we also need to devalue the cutthroat competitiveness and aggressive posturing that prevails in the male-dominated workplace. Only then will women have an equal chance to rise on the basis of ability. We need to encourage career-orientation among women, but also to encourage greater family-orientation in men. Only then will women be free to pursue their careers and have families too. In short, true gender equality must be a "two-way street."

We believe there are policy options that could move us in the direction of that two-way street, not just for engineers, but for the work force generally. In particular, changes in the definition of work-family relationships could be brought about by policies affecting both spheres. These in turn could lead to changes in behavior and values among both men and women. We need only look at other indus-trialized countries for some suggestions. The U.S.A. lags behind the rest of the industrialized world in the provision of social services of all kinds, including day care for the children of employed parents. In most industrialized countries, the government either provides or sub-sidizes day care. While shortages of facilities are commonplace in these countries, quality care is far more available—and affordable—than in the U.S.A. (Kammerman 1980).

The U.S.A. also lags in the development of public policies de-signed to make work-family integration easier for women. Virtually every industrialized country today—capitalist and socialist—man-dates maternity leave for women with newborn babies. In most, the leave is with pay, for an average of six months, with an additional one year of unpaid leave. Employers are required to guarantee the em-ployee's job, pension, and seniority. In a growing number of coun-tries, part or all of the leave is defined as "parental leave," which can be used by the mother *or the father*. The U.S.A. has yet to mandate even an *unpaid* leave for mothers as national policy. Moreover, when leaves are granted, they are most often for the mother only, reinforc-ing the ideology that it is she alone who is suited to care for her child (Kammerman 1986; Allen 1988).

We have the resources to follow the lead of a country like Swe-den, which has made conscious use of public policy to make it easier for women to be employed *and* to attempt to alter traditional family structures as well. Through generous leaves, parents can care for infant children while they receive nearly full pay, and retain full job security. Parents of young children are also eligible to work six-hour days instead of eight. These policies provide incentives for men to become more involved in family responsibilities, which of course frees women for greater career involvement. Moreover, Swedish par-ents have access to the highest quality day care in the world: govern-ment subsidized, with highly trained, well-paid staff.

We could develop other innovations to increase the participation of men in family work. Public and corporate policies could provide positive incentives for men to take time off to care for their children, and undermine the stigma now attached to such behavior. A poll of top corporate executives found nearly 40 percent believed that men who participate actively in child rearing could not hold a senior position in their organizations (McBroom 1986). Men who take their family roles seriously are often seen by colleagues and supervisors as deviant, not sufficiently career-oriented, and even of questionable masculinity (Doyle 1989). Given this reality, it is not surprising that most men have little inclination to become "househusbands" or even to participate more actively in child care. Why should they? They have little to gain, and social status and a career to lose.

But what if men—and women—who took parental leave or a reduction in hours in order to care for their children, were *rewarded* rather than penalized for their behavior? What if they were given a bonus in pay, extra points in their next evaluation, or priority in promotions? Just as men who serve their country through military duty receive preferential treatment in civil service hiring, men and women who serve their society by helping to raise the next generation would find their careers furthered as well.

A policy like this would send a clear message to both men and women that their work in the family is socially valued and carries status. It would allow men to derive status and career advancement from a sphere where they have not found it before. It would help to free women from the burden of sole responsibility for the family, as well as rewarding them for the responsibility they still carry. In the process, it would encourage the development of new values in the workplace—values that challenge the current emphasis on single-minded devotion to the career, and the view of career as antithetical to family. If combined with generous leaves, opportunities for part-time professional work, flexible scheduling, and government funded day care, such a policy could be a significant step in the direction of greater equality for women, both in the workplace *and* in the family. It would be more effective than a "mommy track" (Schwartz 1989), which would legitimate the slower career progress of women with children, by creating a separate track for them. A mommy track could help women combine family and career, it is true. But it would do so in a way that reinforces women's traditional role in the family, rather than redefining it; and that legitimizes inequality in the workplace, rather than challenging it.

Changing Power Relations

We have identified a number of institutional changes that could increase the participation of women in engineering. In particular, we have suggested ways to improve the mathematical and mechanical backgrounds of young women, to facilitate both the perception and the reality of engineering as a good profession for women, and to make family roles more compatible with career advancement. The likelihood that these changes will occur in meaningful ways, however, is limited. Institutional reforms always presuppose power relationships consistent with them. We have advocated changing schools, workplaces, and family structures in order to provide women equal access to a profession dominated by men, in a society dominated by men. That is unlikely to occur, unless other forces are able to counter those power relations.

We see two possible forces that could have such an effect. First, if the U.S.A. continues to lose competitiveness in the world economy, and to suffer increasing shortages of engineers, the need to actively recruit and retain women and minorities will become more pressing. That need is being discussed today, but concerted action has yet to occur, because the problem is not yet serious enough to force the institutional changes required.

More than thirty years ago, the Soviet launching of a space satellite created a crisis in the U.S.A. that led to the kind of action needed today. Resources were mobilized, curricula revised, and special programs created to encourage young people (mostly white men) to choose science and engineering careers. If the economic problems we face today reach crisis proportions, they could generate these kinds of efforts for women and minorities. In simplest (and most cynical) terms, it would be because political and economic elites see greater equality for women and minorities as the only way to maintain a viable economic system, and their own privileged positions within it.

A second force that could contribute to serious institutional change would be a revitalized feminist movement. The gains women have achieved in the past two decades have been due in part to the social movements of the 1960s and early 70s. Those gains will be neither protected nor expanded unless further pressure is brought to bear on elected and corporate officials. When groups have little formal power—when they are absent from the highest levels of government and corporations—having a just and rational cause is not enough. Neither new laws nor new social definitions will arrive without social activism. Without it, no matter how sensible our—or anyone else's—recommendations, they will remain just that: recommendations.

In addition to valid demands, a powerless group needs numbers, organization, and visibility. Only then do they stand a chance of being heard. Power relations are not altered by convincing arguments. They are altered by countervailing powers. In a democratic political system with an open press, a social movement can become such a countervailing power. The pressure it can place on elected officials and corporate leaders can bring about institutional change. We saw that in the 1960s and 70s. More of the same will be needed in the 1990s if we are to bring greater equality to the workplace.

IMPLICATIONS FOR THE STUDY OF WOMEN IN NONTRADITIONAL OCCUPATIONS

We believe that the conflict-structural perspective developed in this book is useful, not just for the study of women in engineering, but for understanding women's experiences in nontraditional occupations more generally. The literature in this area has tended to champion either structural or gender role explanations. We believe our approach offers an advantage over this simple partisanship. Structural factors are primary, but they operate through, and are influenced by, individual attitudes and resources. Structures of power in the workplace give certain groups the ability to define workplace culture and relations. Depending on the particular culture created, individual and gender-based behaviors will constitute either interactional resources or liabilities.

Our understanding of the relationship between structure and gender role involves a redefinition of both. On the one hand, structure must be conceived in human terms. That is, social structure is not an immutable force operating outside human interactions, but in and through them. Too often structuralist discussions of women's workforce status have implied impersonal forces working behind the backs of real people. Concepts like tokenism, organizational uncertainty, and opportunity structures often convey the sense that these things were created by no one in particular, and benefit no one in particular—they just exist. This approach often leads either to unfounded pessimism or naive optimism about the possibility of change. On the one hand, the stress on structures gives institutional relations a sense of necessity and inevitability; on the other hand, it may imply the possibility of a purely technical solution. In our view, structures can be changed, but to do so requires more than just technical knowledge and the right policy.

This is because structures constitute relations of power, created by real people with specific interests. They work to the advantage of some groups and the disadvantage of others, providing the former with both the resources and the incentive to maintain the structures as they are. Structures create the context in which individuals struggle to advance, and to change or maintain the status quo. They define the terms and rewards of those struggles as well. Change is possible, and usually occurs when groups inside the organization acquire new resources, or are rendered more powerful by changes outside the organization.

Seeing structures in human terms also means paying attention to interactional processes. Most structuralist theories simply ignore this issue. As our research suggests, however, gender-based interactional styles do contribute to difficulties in nontraditional work settings. The ability to present the proper professional image is a significant resource in the struggle for advancement and status inside the workplace. Structures and relations of power manifest themselves in interactional relations. This is an area that needs further exploration.

Just as we redefine structures, we also conceive of gender roles in a different way. They are both more variable and less deterministic than they are often seen by gender-role theorists. In much of the gender-role literature, we get a sense that gender behaviors, once learned, are invariant and context-independent. They become the central force determining men's and women's lives from childhood on. But human behavior is more complex than this. Gender roles are tendencies, comfortable styles of response, emotional orientations. They do not by themselves predetermine behaviors and outcomes.

We are making two distinct points here. First, attributes like self-confidence and assertiveness are not simply scratched into our personalities in childhood. They are maintained, strengthened, or diminished by social situations. Women enter the engineering workplace with less technical self-confidence than men. But in some workplaces (e.g., high tech) their self-confidence erodes further over time, while in others, it grows stronger. Second, the *impact* of resources like self-confidence and assertiveness depends on the social context. In college, women may be less confident about their technical skills and less assertive in displaying them than men. But those are not the resources that determine success there; theoretical knowledge is more important. Similarly, technical self-confidence and assertiveness are more crucial to success in the workplace than in college, but not uniformly so. In aerospace and mechanical engineering, these resources count for less than in high tech and electrical engineering.

Finally, to understand the relationship between structure and gender role we must see how they intersect in the culture of the workplace. A work culture is the set of practices that mediate between organization structure on the one hand, and interactional resources on the other. It is the culture to which individuals must conform in their attempts to achieve status and power in the organization. In order to do that, particular interactional skills and styles are necessary. The interactional resources most valued are those held by the group defining the culture. This typically means males, but the content of occupational cultures varies, and some are more strictly male-defined than others. To the extent that the image, activities, and interactional styles of an occupation are male-identified, women will have a harder time conforming to the cultural expectations of their peers and superiors.

As we have seen, engineering carries with it a strongly male-defined culture. Its association with tinkering, with hands-on mechanical activities, links it more directly to male-gender socialization than do the activities of other professions. Lawyers, doctors, managers, and accountants have traditionally been men, but the activities they engage in are not so exclusively male-identified. Their work involves interaction with—and often helping—other people. Beyond that, they read, write, calculate, and administer. The power and prestige of these professions are associated with masculinity, but the work itself is not incongruous with popular perceptions of femininity.

Discussions of women in nontraditional occupations commonly refer to the "male culture" that permeates the work organization and holds women back. What they fail to do, however, is to look at the *varieties* of male culture that exist, and their differential impact on women's careers. We have seen that some engineering workplaces are imbued more strongly with the culture of engineering than others. We believe that the specific features of workplace culture will vary, depending on the power relations involved, and the attitudes and interests of the groups with most power. Some of these cultural environments will be more hostile to women than others. Rather than positing an undifferentiated, one-dimensional "male culture," research on women in nontraditional occupations could benefit from greater attention to the particular types of work culture that exist in given settings, and the power relations that created and maintain them.

Just as there is no single male culture dominating all workplaces, so there is no unitary structure of male power confronting women in nontraditional occupations. While organizations are generally dominated by men, they also consist of different occupational groups vying with each other for power. Managers, engineers, technicians, and assembly line workers are typically male groups, yet they vary considerably in their share of organizational power. Each group has an interest in maintaining its position against intruders—women, minorities, the noncredentialed. But each group also seeks a greater share of organizational power vis-à-vis the other (male) groups.

The power of a particular group within an organization will affect its ability to protect itself from outsiders. Male mechanics may resist the entry of women into their ranks, but if management is determined to bring women in, they will be able to do little about it. Managers, however, have greater resources to keep women out of their own ranks, unless they are subject to the greater power of government affirmative action regulations. Therefore, women's prospects in a particular occupation or organization will be affected by the balance of power and self-interest that exists there.

In addition, conditions external to the organization can make new resources available to previously powerless groups within it. For example, when historical conditions create labor shortages in strategic occupations—as in wartime, or when a new industry is growing rapidly—excluded groups gain leverage because of the scarce skills they can provide. This has happened in engineering in recent years, with the U.S.A. facing a shortage of engineers that threatens to undermine its ability to compete in the world economy. As a result, we have seen efforts to increase the participation of women and minorities in the field. Similarly, when government imposes affirmative action requirements on employers, they hand an important resource to women and minorities as they struggle to succeed in organizations dominated by white men.

In summary, we believe that the conflict-structural perspective is useful for understanding not just the experiences of women in engineering, but in nontraditional occupations more generally. Its major contributions are two: first, it synthesises structural, gender-role, and cultural variables; and second it recognizes the complex and situation-specific nature of all three variables. They do not exist in some pure, ideal-typical state. Rather, each acquires form and relevance in a particular historical and organizational context, and in interaction with the others.

Appendix A

RESEARCH METHODS

Throughout this book we have interwoven quantitative and qualitative data. This is no accident. We believe that the most fruitful area of sociological investigation is the intersection between the two. Sociology as a discipline is distinguished from journalism by its concern for good, rather than merely interesting, data. The numbers keep us honest: they make it less likely that we will engage in easy partisanships or shallow passions. But our responsibility for description and explanation does not end when we have achieved statistical significance; it only begins there. We must look carefully at the meaning of events and structures to the individuals involved. We must tie broad patterns and historical trends to the talk and activities of real people. We must investigate the manifestation of social structures and power relations in the everyday lives of our subjects. When sociologists merely repeat street corner conversations, we trivialize the discipline, but when we ignore them altogether, we trivialize the people we are trying to understand.

We believe that we live up to this ideal only partially. Our data are not as good as we wish, and our descriptions do not always do our respondents justice. We believe that a discussion of methods should be more than just a description of what we did. It should also be an honest statement of what we wish we had done. What follows is a little of both.

We divide our discussion into two parts. First we describe the general approach of our study; then we look at the specific measures we have used.

GENERAL METHODOLOGICAL ISSUES

Our research was conducted in 1986. Our population consisted of the engineering graduates of two public universities in southern California. We originally attempted to gain access to engineer workplaces through employers, but failed. We had two tentative commitments, but the numbers and kinds of workplaces were so limited that we abandoned this approach. We wanted a larger number of workplaces because most recent research on engineers had focused on one or two employers, and we felt this limited the generalizability of the results.

Without a large number of employers willing to participate, university graduates became our focus. Graduates were easy to contact, and diversity of employer was assured. What turned necessity into virtue, however, was the fact that this approach allowed us to compare the work experiences of similarly educated men and women.

A random sample of a thousand graduates from the electrical and mechanical engineering programs at the two schools were sent an eight-page questionnaire to fill out and return. Women were oversampled, given their small numbers in this population. Two follow-up mailings were sent to encourage respondents to return their questionnaires. One hundred sixty-seven questionnaires were returned to us as undeliverable, leaving 833 potential respondents. Of this number, 545 returned questionnaires, a response rate of approximately 65 percent. Most of the literature on mailed surveys considers 50 percent adequate, and anything over 60 percent very good (Babbie 1989; Dillman 1978; Horowitz and Sedlacek 1974).

For purposes of this study we limited our focus to respondents who had graduated between 1976 and 1985. There were so few women in earlier classes that any meaningful comparison between men and women was impossible prior to 1976. This narrowing of the sample decreased its size to 406.

Two hundred sixty-three respondents indicated willingness to participate in a follow-up interview. From this group, we randomly selected a subsample of 30 men and 52 women. This oversampling of women was a conscious choice on our part, reflecting our desire to explore in depth the experiences of as many women engineers as our resources would allow. The interviews were structured and open-ended, averaging an hour and a half in length. All interviews were conducted personally by the authors. We pursued issues from the questionnaire in greater depth, and explored experiences and attitudes relating to women in engineering. The questionnaire and interview schedule are reproduced in Appendix B.

Concerns about sample bias due to self-selection are common in the literature on mailed surveys (Babbie 1989; Horowitz and Sedlacek 1974). Consequently, we compared the sample to the original population in regards to two variables for which we had data: the number of years since graduation and the proportion of minorities. In neither comparison did we find a statistically significant difference between the sample and population.

In addition, we made other checks for reliability that have been suggested in the literature. Babbie (1989) advocates assessing the randomness of a mailed sample by comparing the last returned questionnaires to those first returned, under the assumption that people who do not return questionnaires are similar to late returners. When these two groups were compared, no significant difference was found between them. Since our questionnaire also asked for volunteers for a follow-up interview, we compared those who volunteered for the interview with those who did not. We assumed that the latter group would be similar to those who did not return questionnaires at all. Once again, no significant difference was found between the two groups.

We were particularly interested in comparing these groups in terms of job satisfaction. There is always the risk with self-selected samples that either highly satisfied or highly dissatisfied respondents will be more likely to return questionnaires. This possibility was particularly worrisome because of our oversampling of women. Our fear was that the gender difference in occupational standings we found could have been an artifact of sampling error. Let us explain.

Because we oversampled women, there was a risk that our sample of women was more representative than our sample of men. If this was so, and if there was a tendency for highly satisfied engineers (particularly those satisfied because of their high job standing) to return their questionnaires, this would have disproportionately affected the male sample. That is, we would have a larger proportion of highly satisfied *and* more occupationally advanced respondents in our male sample than in our female sample.

Because of our concern about this possibility, we compared satisfaction levels of early and late returners, and of interview volunteers and nonvolunteers. We found no significant differences between these groups.

We were also concerned about one other potential source of sampling error: differences in the length of time since graduation for our male and female respondents. Since women have only recently entered the profession of engineering, it seemed possible that a larger proportion of women than men might be found among the most recent graduates. If this were so, the lower job standings of women could be due to their shorter average time in the work force. The risk of this error was minimized, at least in part, by our decision to focus only on engineers who had graduated between 1976 and 1985. To be sure, however, we compared women and men controlling for year of graduation, and found the same pattern of occupational differences reported in chapter 5.

Even if our sample is an accurate reflection of our population, there are questions about the representativeness of the population itself. Our respondents come from two schools in southern California. As such they reflect the peculiar nature of the region and of these schools. This area is heavily dependent on defense and high tech firms. While we had respondents who were employed in other industries, their percentage was smaller than in the profession as a whole.

The advantage of studying this particular population is that both the high tech and defense industries have been among the most rapidly growing segments of the U.S. economy, and are likely to continue to be of strategic importance in the future. The engineers in our sample may not fully represent the profession as a whole, but they do represent a large and important sector of that profession, today and in the decades to come.

The schools from which we drew our respondents also constitute a specific niche in engineering education. Our engineers come neither from the very top of the profession nor from the bottom. While CEU ranks itself among the best universities in the nation, its engineering program is not in the same league with those at MIT and Stanford. The PSU engineering school is a significant step down from CEU, but it is far from being a low-status program. There are many other schools where engineering preparation is even more practical and less theoretical than at PSU.

In addition, our sample excludes engineers who arrived at the profession via mobility through the technical ranks (most often a technician who is promoted to engineer), rather than through the educational system. Their numbers are fast shrinking today, but they still constitute a visible segment of the engineering work force, especially in traditional manufacturing. Thus, our sample contains neither extremes of the engineering profession: it can best be thought of as representing the solid middle.

Our respondents are also younger than the average engineer: all graduated after 1975. The obvious strength of this fact is that we are comparing similar groups of men and women, and those who will dominate the profession in the next few decades. The limitation is that the attitudes and experiences we found were those of engineers in the early stages of their careers. It is possible, for instance, that the interactional styles of male engineers change with age. We doubt this, however. For the men in our sample, self-confidence and assertiveness tended to increase with time in the work force. Moreover, our female respondents came in contact with engineers who were older than the members of our sample. Many of their managers and colleagues were further along in their careers, yet there seemed to be little difference in interactional styles between these men and the men in our sample.

We should also briefly restate our reasons for focusing on electrical and mechanical engineers. There are, of course, a large variety of engineers besides these: civil, industrial, aeronautical, chemical, automotive, and mining engineers, among others. Though these specialties share much in common, they are also distinct.

The best way to have tapped this diverse population would have been to draw a national sample. Unfortunately, our resources were not sufficient for such an undertaking. As an alternative, we could have used existing data—the Quality of Employment Survey, for example. This would have given us a greater diversity of engineers, but would have severely limited the kind of data available to us. We had many questions to ask that do not appear in existing surveys, and we wanted in-depth interview data as well. We resolved our dilemma by focusing on the two most common and rapidly growing forms of engineering: electrical and mechanical. Incidentally, two earlier studies of engineers focused on these same specialties for similar reasons (Zussman 1985; Whalley 1986).

Given all these qualifications, we must be tentative about the generalization of our findings to the engineering work force as a whole. As we have seen, the nature and extent of the culture of engineering and women's position in it vary with industry and specialty. Nevertheless, our sample represents the mainstream of engineering graduates, the most common engineering specialties, some of the most important industries in which they work, and the work force of the future. For these reasons, while we consider our conclusions provisional, we also believe we have substantial grounds to argue that they are valid.

SPECIFIC MEASURES[15]

Job Standing

Much of our discussion in this book revolves around our finding that women are rising more slowly in the engineering hierarchy than are men. We discussed the validity of our occupational rankings in chapter 5. Given the centrality of this issue, however, we want to say a little more about it here.

As we said in chapter 5, we constructed our occupational hierarchy in light of previous discussions of engineering. These indicated that prestige in engineering is a function of both technical and organizational responsibility. Our rankings are, however, generalizations across a variety of employers. There is always the risk that the status of a particular engineering title will vary from one company to another. For example, a design engineer at company X may have less technical responsibility than a manufacturing engineer. We compensated for this in part by ranking individuals according to their *actual* work activities, rather than relying on job title alone. In both the questionnaire and the interviews we asked respondents to describe their work activities, and it was from these descriptions that we ranked them.

Interactional Resources

We had not intended to study interactional resources like self-confidence and assertiveness when we began this research. The issue was forcefully brought to our attention by our interview respondents. So many women and men made unsolicited comments about these characteristics that we felt we had no choice but to devise a post hoc measure of interactional resources.

We coded our interview respondents for the extent to which they displayed technical self-confidence and assertiveness. Each respondent was assigned a score (0=none, 1=some, 2=a great deal) for technical self-confidence, and for interactional assertiveness. Scores were based on two criteria: (1) how the respondent behaved in the interview, as judged by the author-interviewer; and (2) the respondent's accounts of her or his own behaviors, as judged in independent readings of the transcript by both authors. Each respondent's scores for technical self-confidence and assertiveness were added together, producing a five-point "interactional resource scale" (0=none, 4=a great deal).

The choice to make this an additive scale was somewhat arbitrary. It was less cumbersome to present a single measure, and the patterns of association were the same, whether the variables were combined or treated separately.

The important thing to keep in mind about this scale, however, is that it is a retrospective recoding of our interview data: an analysis of respondents' descriptions and presentations of self. Without a predesigned measure administered to the entire sample, we knew there was potential for bias. To achieve as much objectivity as possible, we based each ranking on the independent judgments of both authors, and on both the behavior and self-descriptions of respondents. The length of the interviews—about two hours for women, one hour for men—gave us a good sense of the interactional styles of the respondents, and we feel reasonably confident of the reliability and validity of our coding.

We are not happy, however, with the number of cases so coded. Because the measure was limited to our interview respondents, the numbers are small. This is particularly true of men. We interviewed only thirty men, and once we began to control for employer (high tech vs. aerospace), or specialty (electrical vs. mechanical) the cell sizes became extremely small. This is less true for women, of whom we interviewed fifty-two, but it is still a concern. For this reason, we have emphasized the qualitative analysis of interactional resources, rather than the quantitative measures. The latter serve primarily as supplementary evidence, and as reassurance that we were not being carried away by a few moving descriptions.

Multivariate Analysis

One of the drawbacks of our use of both qualitative and quantitative data is the limitation it imposed on our ability to employ multivariate analysis. We discuss a number of factors (education, time in the work force, specialty, company, interactional resources) that influence our dependent variable of occupational standing, and some form of multivariate technique would seem appropriate for evaluating the relative importance of each of these factors. Yet the fact that some of these variables came solely from the interviews meant that multivariate analysis would have to be based on the much smaller size of our interview sample.

We performed a regression analysis to see if it was useful, despite the small numbers involved. Time in the work force (measured by time since graduation), level of education (BS, postgraduate), specialty (ME or EE), company (high tech or aerospace), marital status (married or unmarried), and interactional resources were all regressed on occupational standing (measured by our engineering hierarchy). All but time in work force and company size were coded as dummy variables. For men, time in work force, company, specialty, and interactional resources were significantly related to job standing (in that order). For women, only company and interactional resources influenced job standing (also in that order).

The adjusted R squared was not large for either men (.3) or women (.2). Adding this problem to the small numbers involved, this data seemed too weak to report, even though it supported our general conclusions. Instead, we focused on the qualitative data in our in-depth interviews, presented in the two case studies (CDI and UM) in chapter 6. We felt that this conveyed a sense of the relative weight of these variables, but in a way that better reflected the qualitative nature of the data.

In conclusion, we believe that our use of qualitative and quantitative data in this study contributes both to its strengths and weaknesses. On the one hand, our understanding of the forces shaping women's careers in engineering is both richer and more accurate because of it. On the other hand, the combination of the two made analysis more difficult and less rigorous than we would have liked. On balance, however, we feel that we learned more, and that what we learned has greater validity, by combining the two. Had we used only the quantitative data, our explanations would have been more strictly structural. The attitudinal measures from the questionnaires indicated only minor gender-based differences between men and women. Differences in organization type and occupational specialty stood out most strongly. We were forced to take gender-related interactional variables more seriously by the interview data. However, without the quantitative data we would have been less able to see the structural variables that proved so important. We are brought back once more to the importance of listening neither just to numbers nor to individuals. We have tried in this study to do both.

Appendix B

QUESTIONNAIRE AND INTERVIEW SCHEDULES

QUESTIONNAIRE

*First, We Have a Few Questions About Your Occupation
and Occupational Background.*

1. What is the official name of the company or organization you work for?

2. What kind of business or industry is it? (What do they do or make?)

3. Does the company or organization you work for have more than one location—that is, other divisions, branches, plants, or offices?

4. Roughly how many people are employed in your workplace (the entire plant, factory, or office)?

5. Roughly how many engineers are employed in your workplace (the entire plant, factory, or office)?

6. Besides yourself, how many engineers are working on your current project?

7. What were the last two jobs you held before you came to work for your present employer? Begin with the most recent.

Most Recent Job
Job title_____
Length of time in that job_____
Why did you leave that job?_____

Second Most Recent Job
Job title_____
Length of time in that job_____
Why did you leave that job?_____

8. How long have you worked for your present employer?

9. What is your current job title?

10. What are your main duties and activities on the job?

11. When you first came to work for this company, was it in the same job you have now, or was it in a different job?
IF IT WAS IN A DIFFERENT JOB:
11a. What other job titles have you held *at this company* and how long did you hold them? Begin with the most recent (job title and length of time in job).

Now, We Have Some Questions About Your Attitudes Toward Your Current Job.

12. All in all, how satisfied are you with your job?
_____1. Very satisfied   _____3. Not too satisfied
_____2. Somewhat satisfied   _____4. Not at all satisfied

13. If you had to decide all over again whether to take the job you now have, what would you decide?
_____1. I would take the same job without hesitation
_____2. I would have some second thoughts about it
_____3. I would definitely not take the same job

14. Do you think you will try hard to find a new job (with another company) in the next year?
_____1. Very likely
_____2. Somewhat likely
_____3. Not at all likely

Please indicate how important each of the following concerns are to you personally. Circle the number on each scale below that best reflects your feelings about the corresponding statement. The alternatives range from 0 (not important at all) to 10 (extremely important).

```
0-------------------------------10
Not                   Extremely
Important             Important
At All
```

15. To have the opportunity to help the company build its reputation as a first-class organization.   0--1--2--3--4--5--6--7--8--9--10

16. To have the opportunity to help the company increase its profits.   0--1--2--3--4--5--6--7--8--9--10

17. To work on projects that have a direct impact on the business success of your company.   0--1--2--3--4--5--6--7--8--9--10

18. To participate in decisions that set the direction of technical effort in the company.   0--1--2--3--4--5--6--7--8--9--10

19. To work on projects that you yourself have originated.   0--1--2--3--4--5--6--7--8--9--10

20. To have the opportunity to explore new ideas about technology or systems.   0--1--2--3--4--5--6--7--8--9--10

21. To work with others who are outstanding in their technical achievements.   0--1--2--3--4--5--6--7--8--9--10

22. To work on projects that utilize the latest theoretical developments in your specialty.   0--1--2--3--4--5--6--7--8--9--10

23. To become a first-line manager in your line of work.   0--1--2--3--4--5--6--7--8--9--10

24. To learn how the business is set up and run.   0--1--2--3--4--5--6--7--8--9--10

25. To learn administrative methods and procedures.   0--1--2--3--4--5--6--7--8--9--10

26. To establish a reputation outside the company as an authority in your field.   0--1--2--3--4--5--6--7--8--9--10

27. To receive patents on your technical ideas.   0--1--2--3--4--5--6--7--8--9--10

28. To publish articles in technical journals.   0--1--2--3--4--5--6--7--8--9--10

29. To be evaluated only on the basis of your technical contributions.   0--1--2--3--4--5--6--7--8--9--10

30. To have the respect of your colleagues because of your technical achievement.   0--1--2--3--4--5--6--7--8--9--10

31. To have stability in your life and work.   0--1--2--3--4--5--6--7--8--9--10

32. To work in a well-ordered job situation where requirements are clear.   0--1--2--3--4--5--6--7--8--9--10

33. To be treated as a professional by superiors.   0--1--2--3--4--5--6--7--8--9--10

34. A number of engineers have expressed an interest in starting their own business. How important is such a goal to you?

_____1. very important   _____3. not important at all
_____2. somewhat important

How often are you bothered by the following:

	1. usually	2. some- times	3. seldom	4. almost never
35. Feeling that you have an important job to do but not being able to carry it through, because you lack the authority to make sure the right steps are taken.	---	---	---	---
36. Knowing a better way to get the job done but not being able to get management to listen.	---	---	---	---

37. Not knowing what opportunities for advancement or pro-
motion exist for you.   ___   ___   ___   ___

38. Feeling that your technical
training is becoming out of date. ___   ___   ___   ___

39. That people at your level
have no say in larger matters.   ___   ___   ___   ___

40. That for people in your line
of work there are few important
projects.   ___   ___   ___   ___

41. Feeling that you have become classified by management as
a person who cannot handle broad-
er responsibilities.   ___   ___   ___   ___

42. That your company has no
need for sophisticated theoretical
contributions from people like you. ___   ___   ___   ___

43. That opportunities are be-
coming fewer for people like you. ___   ___   ___   ___

How often do you feel the following:

	1. usually	2. some- times	3. seldom	4. almost never
44. That you have participated in decisions that affect the future business of your company.	___	___	___	___
45. That your project offers you a real chance to show what you can do.	___	___	___	___
46. That you are free to choose the project on which you want to work.	___	___	___	___

47. That your position has allowed you to make the decisions

that were necessary to ensure the best technical course of action for your company?   `___`   `___`   `___`   `___`

48. That your manager asks for your assistance in establishing goals and schedules for your work.   `___`   `___`   `___`   `___`

49. That your manager gets the opinion of his men before he commits the department to a goal or schedule.   `___`   `___`   `___`   `___`

Finally, We Have a Few Questions About You and Your Family.

50. What is your sex?

51. What is your current marital status?

IF MARRIED: (all others please skip to question #57)

52. Is your (husband/wife) currently employed?
IF YES:
53a. What is your husband or wife's occupation?
53b. What are (his/her) main duties and activities on the job?
53c. If you were offered a significantly better job in a city 100 miles away, would you:
_____1. Take the job only if your spouse could be *sure* of obtaining a satisfactory position in the same area?
_____2. Take the job if your spouse had *some chance* of obtaining a satisfactory position in the same area?
_____3. Take the job *whether or not* your spouse had prospects for a satisfactory position in the same area?

54. Would you say your *main* satisfaction in life comes from:
_____1. your work   _____3. both equally
_____2. your family   _____4. something else
(specify)_____

55. Do you ever feel any conflicts between your family life and your work?
IF YES:
55a. What are they?
55b. How much of a problem is this for you?
_____a serious problem   _____a minor problem
_____somewhat of a problem   _____no problem at all

56. Do you spend as much time with your family as you'd like to?
IF NO:
56a. How much more time would you like to have?
56b. How much of a problem is this for you?
_____a serious problem   _____a minor problem
_____somewhat of a problem   _____no problem at all

57. What college degrees do you hold or are you currently working on?

58. What is your ethnic group or racial background?

59. While you were growing up, what was your father's main occupation?

60. While you were growing up, what was your mother's main occupation?

IN-DEPTH INTERVIEW

1. Let's begin by getting a history of the jobs you've held since you finished high school. Starting with the first one, tell me about each one:
Job title and brief description
Type of company
Full- or part-time
Length of time worked
Reason for leaving
Probe: Previous jobs at current employer
Breaks in work life—reasons, length

Occupational Description:

2. Can you describe for me what you do on your job?
Probe: Supervisory/technical responsibilities

3. What is the name of the company you work for?

4. (If not familiar with company): Is it part of a larger corporation?

5. What are the main activities or products of your employer (at your division or workplace)?

6. I'd like to get a sense of the authority structure at your workplace. Can you tell me which people are above you in authority, starting with your immediate supervisor and moving upward?

7. What do you do if you have a problem: do you go through the chain of authority that you just described?

8. What different types of engineer are there at this company (in your division)? (e.g., design, production, planning, R & D, etc.)
   For each: Describe the kind of work they do.

9. Are there any differences between the different types of engineer in regard to:
   pay
   how much authority they have over others
   their opportunities for promotion

10. Which of the following kinds of work done by engineers do you think is typically most admired and appreciated by other engineers at your workplace?
   1. R & D   4. Design
   2. Quality Assurance 5. Test
   3. Production   6. Sales

11. Which of the following kinds of work done by engineers do you think is most appreciated by your company?
   1. R & D   4. Design
   2. Quality Assurance 5. Test
   3. Production   6. Sales

Work Background:

12. At what age did you originally decide to go into engineering? Why was this?

13. Which people were important in influencing your original choice to go into engineering?

14. I'd like to talk a little about your college experience as an engineering major. First, what did you like most about it?

15. What did you like least about it?

16. What were your favorite courses? Why?

17. Which courses did you like least? Why? (if not mentioned, probe re lab courses)

18. Were there any people who were especially helpful to you?
   IF YES: Who?
           In what ways?

19. Were there any people who caused problems for you?
IF YES: Who?
In what ways?

20. In general, how were you received by the male students in your classes?

21. In general, how were you received by the male faculty?

22. Once you chose engineering as a major, did you ever have doubts or regrets about that decision while you were still in college?
IF YES: When?
Why?
How did you deal with your feelings?

23. Looking back, if you could have changed one thing about your college experience, what would it have been? Why?

24. Has engineering turned out to be the kind of job you thought it would be? In what ways?

25. Would you encourage your child to go into engineering?
Probe: How about a daughter?

26. Currently, women make up a very small minority of engineers. Why do you think that is?
Probe: Strengths/weaknesses of women as engineers

27. What do you think are the best fields in engineering for women? Why?

Current Job:

28. How did you get your current job?

29. If you think back to your interview for that job, do you think that being a woman gave you any particular advantages in the interview? Disadvantages?

29a. Was the interview different in any respects from any other job interviews you've had?

30. What parts of your job (that is, the actual work that you do) do you enjoy the most?

31. What parts of your job do you enjoy the least?

32. How much of your job involves using mechanical skills? (Get %) (i.e., repair, construction, physical manipulation)

IF ANY: Is that an aspect of your job that you particularly enjoy?

33. Would you like to do more of that, less, or just what you're doing now?

34. How do you think female engineers compare to men when it comes to mechanical skills?

35. How much of your job involves using mathematics? (Get %)
Probe: application of formulae vs. more sophisticated math
IF ANY: Is that an aspect of your job that you particularly enjoy?

36. Would you like to do more of that, less, or just what you're doing now?

37. How do you think female engineers compare to men when it comes to mathematical skills?

38. In the job you have now, do you find that you can pretty much do it in the way you think best?

39. Do you get as much chance as you would like to try out new ideas or new technologies?

40. Is there as much variety as you would like in your job, or do you find that you deal with the same problems over and over?

41. Are your work assignments different in any way from those of your male co-workers?
IF YES: In what ways?
How do you feel about that?
IF NO: Have they ever been different, in this or previous engineering jobs?

42. Are you ever asked or expected to do extra things at work that men are not expected to do? (i.e., coffee, social events, etc.)
IF YES: What things?
Have you tried to do anything about that?

43. Are there extra tasks or activities that you are not asked to do that you'd like to do?
IF YES: What?
Why aren't you asked?
Have you tried to do anything about that?

44. Do you think being a woman affects your job security, either positively or negatively?

45. What do you like most about the company for which you are currently working?

46. What do you like least?

47. Thinking about your current job, how would you describe your relationships with the male engineers you work around?
   Probes: Treated differently because a woman?
   Good things/bad things?
   Anything that would improve relationships?

48. Have there been any male engineers who have been particularly helpful to you at work?
   IF YES: Who?
   In what ways?

49. Have there been any male engineers who have caused problems for you?
   IF YES: Who?
   In what ways?

50. How would you describe your relationships with the male managers you work for?
   Probes: Treated differently because a woman?
   Good things/bad things?
   Anything that would improve relationships?

51. Have there been any male managers who have been particularly helpful to you at work?
   IF YES: Who?
   In what ways?

52. Have there been any male managers who have caused problems for you?
   IF YES: Who?
   In what ways?

53. Do you socialize with other people during the workday?
   IF YES: Who? How often?
   Would you like to do more socializing, less, or are you satisfied with things as they are?
   IF MORE, OR LESS: With whom?

IF NOT: Why not?
Are there people you'd like to socialize with?
IF YES: Who?
What prevents you from doing so?

54. Do you ever feel socially isolated at work?
IF YES: In what ways?
From whom?
How often?

55. Do you ever feel excluded from important information at work?
IF YES: What kinds?
How often?

56. Sexual harassment of women at work has received a lot of attention in the past few years. It is usually defined as any unwanted words, gestures, or behavior of a sexual nature. Do you think that's a problem for women in engineering generally?
IF YES: Can you give me any examples that you know about?
How serious a problem do you think it is?

57. Have you personally experienced sexual harassment in any of your jobs?
IF YES: Can you describe what happened?
How did you deal with it?

58. What would you like to be doing ten years from now?
Probe: management vs. technical and same vs. different company
What is it that appeals to you about this?
IF RESPONDENT MENTIONS MANAGEMENT:
Would your answer be the same if you could get the same pay for technical work without going into management?

59. What does it take in order to receive a promotion in your company?
Probe: personal, education, background in engineering vs. management?

60. Do you agree with those requirements?

61. Do you think being a woman affects your chances for promotion, either positively or negatively?

62. If you could change one thing about your job to make it better for you as a woman, what would it be?

Work and Family Relationships:

63. What is your current marital status? (Treat "live-ins" as married)

> IF MARRIED: How long have you been married?
> How much education does your wife/husband have?
>> Is your spouse employed?
>> IF YES: Clarify occupation and full-time/part-time status
>> How does your husband feel about being married to an engineer?
>> *Probe:* Problems/Advantages?

64. Do you have children living at home with you?
> IF YES: How many?
> What are their ages?

65. Has your career affected your decisions about marriage or having children in any way?
> IF YES: how?

If Married or a Parent, or Recently Divorced: (If Not, Skip to #85)

66. Do you ever feel any conflicts between your family life and your work?
> IF YES: What are they?

67. Do you spend as much time with your family as you'd like to?
> IF NO: How much more time would you like to have?
> What kind of things would you like to have time for?

68. What do you think of as your most important responsibilities to your family (i.e., spouse and/or children)?

69. How often do you work evenings or weekends, either at home or at the office?
> IF EVER: How many hours a week on the average?
>> Does that ever create a conflict with your family?
>> IF YES: How often?
>>> Can you give me an example?
>>> How is it usually resolved?

70. Does having a family keep you from doing more overtime work than you otherwise would?

IF YES: Does that ever create a conflict with your employer?
    IF YES: How often?
        Can you give me an example?
        How is it usually resolved?

If Married and Children at Home: (If Not, Skip to #85)

71. Who do you think of as the primary breadwinner in your family: you, your spouse, or both of you equally? Why?

72. On your questionnaire, you indicated that (answer to question #53c). Could you explain your feelings about this a little more?

73. Do any of your children require care while you're at work?
    IF YES: What kind of child care arrangements do you have?
        How much does this cost?
        How satisfied are you with this arrangement overall?
        Probe: Positive/negative aspects?
        Ideally, would you prefer some other type of care for your child(ren)?
        IF YES: What type would you prefer?

74. If someone has to be home with your child(ren) or do something for him/her/them when you are both supposed to be working, which of you is more likely to stay home? Why?

75. Does your spouse wish you'd spend more time doing things with or for your child(ren)?
    IF YES: What would she/he like you to do?

76. Do you wish your spouse would spend more time doing things with or for your child(ren)?
    IF YES: What kind of things would you like her/him to do?

77. Does your spouse wish you would spend more time doing home chores than you do?
    IF YES: what kinds of things would she/he like you to do?

78. Do you wish your spouse would spend more time on home chores?
    IF YES: which chores are you thinking of?

79. Do you hire any outside help with home chores?
    IF YES: What type?
        How often?

If Married, but No Children:

80. Who do you think of as the primary breadwinner in your family: you, your spouse, or both of you equally? Why?

81. On your questionnaire, you indicated that (answer to question #53c). Could you explain your feelings about this a little more?

82. Does your spouse wish you would spend more time doing home chores than you do?
IF YES: what kinds of things would she/he like you to do?

83. Do you wish your spouse would spend more time on home chores?
IF YES: which chores are you thinking of?

84. Do you hire any outside help with home chores?
IF YES: What type?
How often?

If Not Currently Married or a Parent:

85. How often do you work evenings or weekends, either at home or at the office?
IF EVER: How many hours a week on the average?
Does that ever create a conflict with your personal life?
IF YES: How often?
What kind of conflict?
How is it usually resolved?
Do you think you do more overtime work than you would if you had a family?
IF YES: do you think that's a good thing, or not?

All Respondents:

86. How much time do you spend socializing with co-workers off the job?
IF ANY: Are they engineers, managers, or who?
What kinds of things do you do?

87. Would you like to do more socializing with co-workers than you currently do, or less, or are you satisfied the way things are? Why?
IF MORE, OR LESS: What keeps you from doing that?

88. Is there anything we haven't covered that you'd like to bring up, in regard to your experiences in engineering?

NOTES

1. The other major approach to improving the pay levels of women has been the movement for "equal pay for work of comparable worth." Rather than attempting to move women out of their low-paid jobs into nontraditional areas, this approach focuses on increasing the pay women receive in their traditionally female jobs. Several state and local governments have already adopted this approach for their public work force. The method involves evaluating jobs and assigning points on the basis of skill requirements, responsibility, working conditions, etc. Jobs with similar point values are then awarded similar pay levels, even though the work itself may be quite different. The effect of this approach is to raise the pay for women's jobs (e.g., social service worker) to the level of comparable men's jobs (e.g., carpenter). Business groups strongly oppose this concept, and while the movement for "comparable worth" may make further inroads in the public sector, it is unlikely to be adopted on a large scale by the private sector, without a legislative or executive mandate. The Reagan and Bush administrations, however, have been openly hostile to the concept (see Treiman and Hartmann 1981; Harkess 1988).

2. Each of the perspectives we discuss here actually consists of several distinct theories. We emphasize what the theories have in common—namely, a set of underlying assumptions about the most important forces shaping occupational outcomes.

3. There is a sizable popular literature on the problems women face in nontraditional occupations, especially in corporate management. This literature relies heavily on a gender role perspective, and tells women that in order to achieve success, they need to change their own attitudes and behaviors to conform to the demands of these positions. See, for example, Foxworth 1986; Hardesty and Jacobs 1986; Harragan 1977; Hennig and Jardim 1977; McBroom 1986; Mitchell and Burdick 1985.

4. Ruth Milkman (1987) makes a similar argument in her analysis of women's work experiences in World War II. She shows that the response of (male) employers to the influx of women during the war varied with "the specific economic and political constraints facing employers in various industries" (p. 6). Moreover, male co-workers responded in different ways to women, depending on whether their gender or their class interests were more important to them at the time.

5. These percentages add up to more than 100 percent because respondents were allowed to list as many factors as they thought appropriate.

6. Our respondents were graduates of two major public universities in California. We have given them names that reflect the differences between the two. Public State University (PSU) is a large state university with a solid reputation for the quality of its undergraduate education. Its engineering school is well established, and long accredited. The students entering PSU have good, but not outstanding, academic records. The fees are moderate, making it accessible to many. In contrast, California Elite University (CEU) is known as a first-class research institution, with several Nobel laureates on its faculty. Both its entrance requirements and its fees are considerably higher than PSU's, which contributes further to its elite status. Its engineering school, however, is much newer, and only recently accredited.

7. We obtained individual GPA data on women, but not on men. The women had a mean overall GPA of 3.35. While we cannot be sure that this was higher than the men in our sample, we do know that male engineering students at CEU had a mean GPA of 3.02 during the years our respondents were in school (Lare 1988). In addition, in numerous conversations with faculty, students, and working engineers, we heard over and over that women generally outperform men in engineering classes, and are more likely to qualify for the engineering honor societies.

8. An earlier study lends support to this argument. Slaughter (1982) found that female senior engineering students at MIT were less self-confident than their male classmates. But they were also less self-confident than *freshman women*. The reverse was true for men. This suggests that the school experience itself can have a negative impact on women's self-confidence.

9. There has yet to emerge a single definition of high tech, but most definitions are based on one or more of the following criteria: (1) utilization of scientific and technical workers; (2) expenditures for research and development; and (3) a product that incorporates sophisticated electronic technology (Richie et al. 1983). We used the third criterion, since we did not have reliable information regarding the first two. Our definition of aerospace was also based on the products manufactured.

10. It is not uncommon in some companies to award the title of "senior engineer" solely on the basis of seniority. Our criteria for assigning this code, however, was whether the job involved supervisory responsibilities. We coded on the basis of respondents' job descriptions in the questionnaires and the interviews, rather than on formal job titles.

11. Even if we abandon this elaborate hierarchy and simplify our ranks, we still find significant differences between men and women. If we reduce our categories to three—below design, design, and management—we lose a little significance, but the differences remain strong (tau $c = -.12$; $p = .002$).

12. Size of employer followed this same pattern. That is, women were doing better in large corporations (tau $c = .163$; $p = .04$), and men were doing better in small corporations (tau $c = -.147$; $p = .0002$). We have chosen not to stress the importance of this variable for two reasons. First, after our in-depth interviews, we have come to suspect the accuracy of our size measurements. Many of our respondents seemed confused about what we meant by plant size—some took it to mean their workplace, while others understood it to be the size of their entire corporation.

Second, company type, and particularly the presence of affirmative action guidelines (which are more often applied to large firms), seemed to be the more profound variables. When we controlled for company type (high tech vs. aerospace), the importance of size disappeared.

13. An obvious methodological concern is whether electrical engineers are more often employed by high tech. Electrical engineers (at least in our sample) do tend to be more extensively employed in high tech, but the difference is not great. Moreover, when we control for company type (aerospace/high tech) the differences between electrical and mechanical engineers remain strong.

14. Denise, discussed below, had a son by a previous marriage. He had died a few years earlier.

15. Our questionnaire items were drawn in part from the following surveys: Ritti 1971; Quinn and Staines 1979; Wright 1982.

BIBLIOGRAPHY

Allen, Joseph P. 1988. "European Infant Care Leaves: Foreign Perspectives on the Integration of Work and Family Roles." In Edward F. Zigler and Maryl Frank (eds.), *The Parental Leave Crisis: Toward a National Policy.* New Haven: Yale University Press.

American Association of Engineering Societies. 1989a. Special Bulletin. Washington, D.C.

American Association of Engineering Societies. 1989b. "Women in Engineering." *Engineering Manpower Bulletin* 99 (Dec.). Washington, D.C.

Anderson, Karen. 1988. "A History of Women's Work in the U.S." In Ann Stromberg and Shirley Harkess (eds.), *Women Working: Theories and Facts in Perspective.* Mountain View, Calif.: Mayfield Publishing.

Babbie, Earl R. 1989. *The Practice of Social Research* (5th ed). Belmont, Calif.: Wadsworth Publishing.

Bailyn, Lotte. 1987. "Experiencing Technical Work: A Comparison of Male and Female Engineers." *Human Relations,* vol. 40, no. 5: 299–312.

Baron, James N. 1984. "Organizational Perspectives on Stratification." *Annual Review of Sociology* 10: 37–69.

Basow, Susan A. 1986. *Gender Stereotypes: Traditions and Alternatives.* Monterey, Calif.: Brooks/Cole Publishing.

Becker, Gary S. 1964. *Human Capital: A Theoretical and Empirical Analysis, with Special Reference to Education.* New York: Columbia University Press.

———. 1973. "A Theory of Marriage, Part I." *Journal of Political Economy* 81 (July/August): 813–846.

Beller, Andrea H. 1984. "Trends in Occupational Segregation by Sex and Race, 1960–1981." In Barbara F. Reskin (ed.), *Sex Segregation in the Workplace*.

Beller, Andrea H., and Kee-ok Kim Han. 1984. "Occupational Sex Segregation: Prospects for the 1980's." In Barbara F. Reskin (ed.), *Sex Segregation in the Workplace*.

Berryman, Sue E., and Linda J. Waite. 1985. "Young Women's Choice of Occupations Non-traditional for their Sex." In *Ingredients for Women's Employment Policy: Papers from the Albany Conference on Women's Employment*.

Betz, Nancy E., and Louise F. Fitzgerald. 1987. *The Career Psychology of Women*. New York: Academic Press.

Bibb, Robert, and William H. Form. 1977. "The Effects of Industrial, Occupational, and Sex Stratification on Wages in Blue-Collar Markets." *Social Forces* 55: 974–96.

Blalock, Hubert M., Jr. 1972. *Social Statistics*. New York: McGraw-Hill.

Bleier, Ruth (ed.). 1986. *Feminist Approaches to Science*. New York: Pergamon Press.

Blau, Peter, and Otis Dudley Duncan. 1967. *The American Occupational Structure*. New York: John Wiley.

Blood, Robert O., Jr., and Donald M. Wolfe. 1960. *Husbands and Wives*. New York: Free Press.

Bourdieu, Pierre, and Jean-Claude Passeron. 1977. *Reproduction in Education, Society and Culture*. Beverly Hills: Sage Publications.

Bourdieu, Pierre. 1984. *Distinction: A Social Critique of the Judgement of Taste*. Cambridge: Harvard University Press.

Boyce, Lola. 1987. Personal communication. Division of Engineering University of Texas, San Antonio.

Braverman, Harry. 1974. *Labor and Monopoly Capital*. New York: Monthly Review Press.

Broverman, Inge K., Susan R. Vogel, Donald M. Broverman, Frank E. Clarkson, and Paul S. Rosenkrantz. 1972. "Sex Role Stereotypes: A Current Appraisal." *Journal of Social Issues* 38: 59–78.

Brown, Linder Keller. 1981. *The Woman Manager in the United States*. Washington, D.C.: Business and Professional Women's Foundation.

Bryson, Jeff B., and Rebecca Bryson. 1980. "Salary and Job Performance Differences in Dual Career Couples." In Fran Pepitone-Rockwell (ed.), *Dual-Career Couples*.

Bugliarello, George, et al. (eds.). 1971. *Women in Engineering: Bridging the Gap Between Society and Technology*. Proceeedings of an Engineering Foundation Conference. Chicago: University of Illinois.

Burawoy, Michael. 1979. *Manufacturing Consent: Changes in the Labor Process under Monopoly Capitalism*. Chicago: University of Chicago Press.

Burks, Esther Lee. 1975. "Career Interruptions and Perceived Discrimination Among Women in Engineering and Science." In Mary Ott and Nancy A. Reese (eds.), *Women in Engineering*.

Burrell, Gibson, and Gareth Morgan. 1979. *Sociological Paradigms and Organizational Analysis*. London: Heinemann Educational Books.

Butler, Matilda, and William Paisley. 1977. "Status of Professional Couples in Psychology." *Psychology of Women Quarterly* 1, 4 (Summer): 307–18.

Calvert, Monte A. 1967. *The Mechanical Engineer in America: 1830–1910*. Baltimore: Johns Hopkins University Press.

Chafetz, Janet S. 1984. *Sex and Advantage*. Totowa, New Jersey: Rowman & Allanheld.

Chen, Meredith. 1989. "Women at Work: A New Debate is Born." *Los Angeles Times*, March 19: 3,6.

Cicourel, Aaron V., and Hugh Mehan. 1985. "Universal Development, Stratifying Practices, and Status Attainment." *Research in Social Stratification and Mobility* 4: 3–27.

Cline, Carolyn Garrett, et al. 1986. *The Velvet Ghetto: The Impact of the Increasing Percentage of Women in Public Relations and Business Communication*. San Francisco: International Association for Business Communication Foundation.

Cole, Jonathan R., and Harriet Zuckerman. 1987. "Marriage, Motherhood and Research Performance in Science." *Scientific American* 256, 2 (Feb.): 119–125.

College Placement Council. 1986. *Starting Salary Offers for Bachelor's Degree Candidates*.

College Placement Council. 1990. *Starting Salary Offers for Bachelor's Degree Candidates*.

Collins, Randall. 1975. *Conflict Sociology: Toward an Explanatory Science*. New York: Academic Press.

———. 1979. *The Credential Society*. New York: Academic Press.

———. 1981. "The MicroFoundations of MacroSociology." *American Journal of Sociology* 86, 5: 984–1014.

———. 1982. *Sociological Insight: An Introduction to Non-Obvious Sociology*. New York: Oxford University Press.

———. 1985. *Sociology of Marriage and the Family: Gender, Love and Property*. Chicago: Nerlson-Hall.

———. 1991. "Women and Men in the Class Structure." In Rae L. Blumberg (ed.), *Gender, Family and Economy: The Triple Overlap*. Newbury Park, Calif.: Sage Publications .

Crozier, Michel. 1964. *The Bureaucratic Phenomenon*. Chicago: University of Chicago Press.

Davis, Kingsley, and Wilbert E. Moore. 1945. "Some Principles of Stratification." *American Sociological Review*. 10: 242–49.

Deaux, Kay, and Joseph C. Ullman. 1983. *Women of Steel*. New York: Praeger Publishers.

Deaux, Kay. 1984. "From Individual Differences to Social Categories: Analysis of a Decade's Research on Gender." *American Psychologist* 39:105–16.

DeJong, Peter Y., Milton J. Brawer, and Stanley S. Robin. 1971. "Patterns of Female Intergenerational Occupational Mobility: A Comparison with Male Patterns of Intergenerational Occupational Mobility." *American Sociological Review* 36: 1033–42.

Derber, Charles. 1979. *The Pursuit of Attention: Power and Individualism in Everyday Life*. London: Oxford University Press.

Dillman, Don A. 1978. *Mail and Telephone Surveys: The Total Design Method*. New York: John Wiley.

Donald, Marjorie N. 1960. "Implications of Nonresponse for the Interpretation of Mail Questionnaire Data." *Public Opinion Quarterly* 24: 99–114.

Doyle, James A. 1989. *The Male Experience*, 2nd ed. Dubuque: Wm. C. Brown Publishers.

Dresselhaus, M. S. 1985. "Reflections on Women Graduate Students in Engineering." *IEEE Transactions on Education*. E-28 (Nov.): 196–203.

Edwards, Richard. 1979. *Contested Terrain*. New York: Basic Books.

Eisenstein, Zillah R. 1979. *Capitalist Patriarchy and the Case for Socialist Feminism*. New York: Monthly Review Press.

Ellis, Richard A. 1990. Personal communication. American Association of Engineering Societies.

England, Paula. 1984. "Socioeconomic Explanations of Job Segregation." In H. Remick (ed.), *Comparable Worth and Wage Discrimination: Technical Possibilities and Political Realities*. Philadelphia: Temple University Press.

England, Paula, and George Farkas. 1986. *Households, Employment, and Gender: A Social, Economic and Demographic View*. New York: Aldine de Gruyter.

Epstein, Cynthia F. 1974. "Bringing Women In: Rewards, Punishments and the Structure of Achievement." In Ruth B. Knudsin (ed.), *Women and Success: The Anatomy of Achievement.* New York: Morrow Publishers.

————.1983. *Women in Law*. Garden City, New York: Anchor Press.

Etzioni, Amitai. 1969. *The Semi-Professions and Their Organization*. New York: Free Press.

Etzioni, Amitai, and Paul Jargowsky. 1984. "High Tech, Basic Industry, and the Future of the American Economy." *Human Resource Management* 23: 229–40.

Fairhurst, G. T., and B. K. Snavely. 1983. "Majority and Token Minority Group Relationships: Power Acquisition and Communication." *Academy of Management Review* 8: 292–300.

Featherman, David L., and Robert M. Hauser. 1976. "Sexual Inequalities and Socioeconomic Achievement in the U.S., 1962–1973." *American Sociological Review* 41 (June): 462–83.

Finn, Michael G. 1983. "Understanding the Higher Unemployment Rate of Women Scientists and Engineers." *The American Economic Review* (Dec.): 1137–40.

Fox, Mary Frank, and Catherine A. Faver. 1985. "Men, Women and Publication Productivity: Patterns Among Social Work Academics." *Sociological Quarterly* 26, 4: 537–549.

Fox, Mary Frank, and Sharlene Hesse-Biber. 1984. *Women at Work*. Palo Alto, Calif: Mayfield Publishing.

Foxworth, Jo. 1986. *Boss Lady's Arrival and Survival Plan*. New York: Warner Books.

Frazier, Nancy, and Myra Sadker. 1973. *Sexism in School and Society*. New York: Harper & Row.

Freeman, Jo. 1979. "How to Discriminate Against Women Without Really Trying." In Jo Freeman (ed.), *Women: A Feminist Perspective*, 2nd ed. Palo Alto, Calif.: Mayfield Publishing.

Gardner, Robert E. 1975. "Women: The New Engineers." In Mary Ott and Nancy A. Reese (eds.), *Women in Engineering*.

Gartman, David. 1986. *Auto Slavery*. New Brunswick: Rutgers University Press.

Giddens, Anthony. 1987. *Sociology: A Brief but Critical Introduction*. New York: Harcourt Brace Jovanovich.

Gillespie, Dair L. 1971. "Who Has the Power? The Marital Struggle." *Journal of Marriage and the Family* 33: 445–58.

Gilligan, Carol. 1982. *In a Different Voice: Psychological Theory and Women's Development*. Cambridge: Harvard University Press.

Gitelson, I., A. Petersen, and M. Tobin-Richards. 1982. "Adolescents' Expectancies of Success, Self-evaluations, and Attributions about Performance on Spatial and Verbal Tasks." *Sex Roles* 8: 411–19.

Glenn, Evelyn N., and Roslyn L. Feldberg. 1979. "Clerical Work: The Female Occupation." In Jo Freeman (ed.), *Women: A Feminist Perspective*.

Goffman, Erving. 1959. *The Presentation of Self in Everyday Life*. Garden City, N.Y.: Doubleday.

———. 1967. *Interaction Ritual*. New York: Anchor Books.

———. 1979. *Gender Advertisements*. New York: Harper and Row.

Goldner, Fred, and R. R. Ritti. 1967. "Professionalization as Career Immobility." *American Journal of Sociology* 72: 489–502.

Gordon, David. 1972. *Theories of Poverty and Underemployment*. Lexington, Mass.: D.C. Heath.

Gordon, David, Richard Edwards, and Michael Reich. 1982. *Segmented Work, Divided Workers*. Cambridge: Cambridge University Press.

Gornick, Vivian, and Barbara K. Moran (eds.). 1971. *Woman in Sexist Society: Studies in Power and Powerlessness*. New York: Basic Books.

Gusfield, Joseph R. 1972. *The Symbolic Crusade*. Urbana: University of Illinois Press.

———.1981. *The Culture of Public Problems*. Chicago: University of Chicago Press.

Hacker, Sally L. 1981. "The Culture of Engineering: Woman, Workplace and Machine." *Women's Studies International Quarterly* 4: 341–53.

————. 1983. "Mathematization of Engineering: Limits on Women and the Field." In Joan Rothschild (ed.), *Machina Ex Dea*. Elmsford, N.Y.: Pergamon Press.

Hansen, Ronald D., and Virginia E. O'Leary. 1985. "Sex Determined Attributions." In Virginia E. O'Leary, Rhoda K. Unger, and Barbara S. Wallston (eds.), *Women, Gender and Social Psychology*. Hillsdale, N.J.: Erlbaum Publishers.

Hardesty, Sarah, and Nehama Jacobs. 1986. *Success and Betrayal: The Crisis of Women in Corporate America*. New York: Franklin Watts.

Harkess, Shirley. 1988. "Directions for the Future." In Ann H. Stromberg and Shirley Harkess (eds.), *Women Working*.

Harlan, Sharon, and Brigid O'Farrell. 1982. "After the Pioneers: Prospects for Women in Traditionally Male Blue Collar Jobs." *Work and Occupations* 9: 363–86.

Harragan, Betty L. 1977. *Games Mother Never Taught You*. New York: Warner Books.

Hartmann, Heidi. 1976. "Capitalism, Patriarchy, and Job Segregation." In Martha Blaxall and Barbara Reagan (eds.), *Women and the Workplace*. Chicago: University of Chicago Press.

————. 1981 "The Family as the Locus of Gender, Class and Political Struggle: The Example of Housework." *Signs* 6: 366–94.

Hartnett, Oonagh. 1977. "Sex-Role Stereotyping at Work." In Jane Chetwynd and Oonagh Hartnett (eds.), *The Sex Role System: Psychological and Sociological Perspectives*. London: Routledge & Kegan Paul.

Hennig, Margaret, and Anne Jardim. 1977. *The Managerial Woman*. New York: Pocket Books.

Hewlett, Sylvia Ann. 1986. *A Lesser Life: The Myth of Women's Liberation in America*. New York: William Morrow.

Hochschild, Arlene R. 1973. "A Review of Sex Role Research." *American Journal of Sociology* 78: 1011–29.

Hochschild, Arlene R., and Anne Machung. 1989. *The Second Shift: Working Parents and the Revolution at Home*. New York: Viking Press.

Hodson, Randy. 1983. *Worker's Earnings and Corporate Economic Structure*. New York: Academic Press.

———. 1985. "Working in High Tech: Research Issues and Opportunities for the Industrial Sociologist." *Sociological Quarterly* 26: 351–64.

Horowitz, Joseph, and William Sedlacek. 1974. "Initial Returns of Mail Questionnaires: A Literature Review and Research Note." *Research in Higher Education* 2: 361–67.

Huber, Joan, and Glenna Spitze. 1981. "Wive's Employment, Household Behaviors and Sex-Role Attitudes." *Social Forces*, vol. 60, no. 1 (Sept.): 150–69.

Ireson, Carol, and Sandra Gill. 1988. "Girls' Socialization for Work." In Ann H. Stromberg and Shirley Harkess (eds.), *Women Working*, 2nd ed. Mountain View, Calif.: Mayfield Publishing.

Ivey, Elizabeth S. 1987. "Recruiting More Women into Science and Engineering." *Issues in Science and Technology*, vol. 4, no. 1 (Fall): 83–87.

Jagacinski, Carolyn M., and William K. LeBold. 1981. "A Comparison of Men and Women Undergraduate and Professional Engineers." *Engineering Education* 72: 213–20.

Jagacinski, Carolyn M. 1987. "Engineering Carers: Women in a Male-Dominated Field." *Psychology of Women Quarterly* 11: 97–110.

Joffe, C. 1971. "Sex Role Socialization and the Nursery School: As the Twig is Bent." *Journal of Marriage and the Family* 33: 467–75.

Johnson, Terence J. 1972. *Professions and Power*. London: MacMillan.

Kammerman, Sheila B. 1980. *Parenting in an Unresponsive Society: Managing Work and Family Life*. New York: Free Press.

———. 1986. "Maternity, Paternity and Parenting Policies: How Does the United States Compare?" In Sylvia Ann Hewlett, Alice S. Ilchman, and John J. Sweeney (eds.), *Family and Work: Bridging the Gap*. Cambridge, Mass.: Ballinger Publishing.

Kanter, Rosabeth M. 1977. *Men and Women of the Corporation*. New York: Basic Books.

———. 1983. "Women Managers: Moving Up in High Tech Society." Pp. 21–36 in Jennie Farley (ed.), *The Woman in Management: Career and Family Issues*. Ithaca: Cornell University Press.

———. 1989. *When Giants Learn to Dance: Mastering the Challenge of Strategy, Management and Careers in the 1990's*. New York: Simon & Schuster.

Keller, Evelyn Fox. 1985. *Reflections on Gender and Science*. New Haven: Yale University Press.

Kessler-Harris, Alice. 1982. *Out to Work: A History of Wage-Earning Women in the United States*. New York: Oxford University Press.

Kohn, Melvin, and Carmi Schooler. 1983. *Work and Personality: An Inquiry into the Impact of Social Stratification*. Norwood, N.J.: Ablex.

Kornhauser, William. 1962. *Scientists in Industry: Conflict and Accommodation*. Berekeley: University of California Press.

Lare, Cosette. 1988. Data provided by university registrar's office, "CEU."

Larson, Magali Sarfatti. 1977. *The Rise of Professionalism: A Sociological Analysis*. Los Angeles: University of California Press.

Lasch, Christopher. 1977. *Haven in a Heartless World: The Family Besieged*. New York: Basic Books.

Latour, Bruno. 1987. *Science in Action*. Cambridge: Harvard University Press.

Layton, Edwin T., Jr. 1986. *The Revolt of the Engineers*. Baltimore: Johns Hopkins University Press.

Lever, Janet. 1976. "Sex Differences in the Games Children Play." *Social Problems* 23: 478–87.

———. 1978. "Sex Differences in the Complexity of Children's Play and Games." *American Sociological Review* 43: 471–83.

Maccoby, Eleanor E., and Carol Jacklin. 1974. *The Psychology of Sex Differences*. Stanford: Stanford University Press.

Marini, Margaret M., and Mary C. Brinton. 1984. "Sex Typing in Occupational Socialization." In Barbara F. Reskin (ed.), *Sex Segregation in the Workplace*.

Martin, Thomas W., Kenneth J. Berry, and R. Brooke Jacobsen. 1975. "The Impact of Dual-Career Marriages on Female Professional Careers: An Empirical Test of a Parsonian Hypothesis." *Journal of Marriage and the Family* 37 (Nov.): 734–42.

Martin, Ben R., and John Irvine. 1982. "Women in Science: The Astronomical Brain Drain." *Women's Studies International Forum* 5, 1: 41–68.

Mathaei, Julie A. 1982. *An Economic History of Women in America: Women's Work, the Sexual Division of Labor and the Development of Capitalism*. New York: Schocken Books.

McBroom, Patricia A. 1986. *The Third Sex: The New Professional Woman*. New York: William Morrow.

McClendon, McKee. 1976. "The Occupational Status Attainment Process of Males and Females." *American Sociological Review* 41 (Feb.): 52–64.

McGregor, Douglas. 1967. *The Professional Manager*. New York: McGraw-Hill.

McIlwee, Judith S. 1981. "Organization Theory and the Entry of Women into Non-Traditional Occupations." *Western Sociological Review* 12: 33–52.

———. 1982. "Work Satisfaction Among Women in Non-Traditional Occupations. *Work and Occupations* 9, 3: 299–335.

———. 1988. "Reducing Occupational Sex Segregation: Explaining Failure and Success." *Sociological Focus* 21, 1: 35–51.

Metcalfe, Alban. 1985. *The Effects of Socialisation on Women's Management Careers*. W. Yorkshire, England: MCB University Press.

Meyer, Herbert H., and Mary D. Lee. 1978. *Women in Traditionally Male Jobs: The Experience in Ten Public Utility Companies*. R & D Monograph no. 65. U.S. Dept. of Labor ETA. Washington, D.C.: U.S. Government Printing Office.

Milkman, Ruth. 1987. *Gender at Work: The Dynamics of Job Segregation by Sex During World War II*. Urbana: University of Illinois Press.

Mincer, Jacob, and Solomon Polacheck. 1974. "Family Investments in Human Capital: Earnings of Women." *Journal of Political Economy* 82 (March/April): 76–111.

Mitchell, Charlene, and Thomas Burdick. 1985. *The Right Moves*. New York: Macmillan.

Model, Susanne. 1982. "Housework by Husbands: Determinants and Implications." In J. Aldous (ed.), *Two Paychecks: Life in Dual Earner Families*. Beverly Hills: Sage Publications.

Morgan, Robin (ed.). 1970. *Sisterhood is Powerful: An Anthology of Writings from the Women's Liberation Movement*. New York: Vintage Books.

Morrison, Ann M., R. White, and E. Van Velsor. 1987. *Breaking the Glass Ceiling: Can Women Reach the Top of America's Largest Corporations?* Reading, Mass.: Addison-Wesley.

Namenwirth, Marion. 1986. "Science Seen Through a Feminist Prism." In Ruth Bleier (ed.), *Feminist Approaches to Science*.

National Science Foundation (NSF). 1986. *Women and Minorities in Science and Engineering*. Washington, D.C.

Nieva, Veronica. 1985. "Work and Family Linkages." In Laurie Larwood, Ann H. Stromberg, and Barbara A. Gutek (eds.), *Women and Work: An Annual Review*, vol. 1. Beverly Hills: Sage Publications.

Noble, David F. 1977. *America by Design*. New York: Alfred A. Knopf.

Oppenheimer, Valerie Kincade. 1970. *The Female Labor Force in the United States: Demographic and Economic Factors Governing its Growth and Changing Composition*. Population Monograph Series, no. 5. Berkeley: University of Calif., Institute of International Studies.

Ornstein, Michael. 1976. *Entry into the American Labor Force: Quantitative Studies in Social Relations*. New York: Academic Press.

Ott, Mary, and Nancy A. Reese (eds.). 1975. *Women in Engineering: Beyond Recruitment*. Ithaca: Cornell University Press.

Parkin, Frank. 1979. *Marxism and Class Theory: A Bourgeois Critique*. New York: Columbia University Press.

Parsons, Talcott, and Robert Bales. 1955. *Family, Socialization and Interaction Process*. Glencoe, Ill.: Free Press.

Pepitone-Rockwell, Fran (ed.). 1980. *Dual-Career Couples*. Beverly Hills: Sage Publications.

Perrow, Charles. 1970. *Organizational Analysis: A Sociological View*. Belmont, Calif.: Wadsworth Publishing.

―――. 1979. *Complex Organizations: A Critical Essay*, 2nd ed. Glenview, Ill.: Scott, Foresman.

Perrucci, Carolyn C. 1970. "Minority Status and the Pursuit of Professional Careers: Women in Science and Engineering." *Social Forces* 49, 2 (Dec.): 245–59.

Perrucci, Robert, and Joel E. Gerstl. 1969. *Profession Without Community: Engineers in American Society*. New York: Random House.

Perrucci, Robert, and Robert A. Rothman. 1969. "Obsolescence of Knowledge and the Professional Career." In Robert Perrucci and Joel Gerstl (eds.), *Engineers and the Social System*. New York: Wiley and Sons.

Perrucci, Robert. 1973. "Engineers: Professional Servants of Power." In Elliot Friedson (ed.), *The Professions and Their Prospects*. Beverly Hills: Sage Publications.

Pleck, Joseph. 1977. "The Work-Family Role System." *Social Problems*, vol. 24, April: 417–27.

―――. 1988. "Fathers and Infant Care Leave." In Edward F. Zigler and Maryl

Frank (eds.), *The Parental Leave Crisis: Toward a National Policy*. New Haven: Yale University Press.

Quinn, Robert, and Graham Staines. 1979. *Quality of Employment Survey, 1977: Cross-Section*. Ann Arbor: Inter-university Consortium for Political and Social Research.

Ratner, Ronnie S. 1980. "The Policy and Problem: Overview of Seven Countries." In Ronnie S. Ratner (ed.), *Equal Employment Policy for Women: Strategies for Implementation in the United States, Canada and Western Europe*. Philadelphia: Temple University Press.

Regan, Mary C., and Helen E. Roland. 1985. "Rearranging Family and Career Priorities: Professional Women and Men of the Eighties." *Journal of Marriage and the Family*, Nov.: 985–92.

Reskin, Barbara F. (ed.). 1984. *Sex Segregation in the Workplace: Trends, Explanations, Remedies*. Washington, D.C.: National Academy Press.

Reskin, Barbara F., and Heidi Hartmann (eds.). 1986. *Women's Work, Men's Work: Sex Segregation on the Job*. Washington, D.C.: National Academy Press.

Rheingold, H. L., & K. V. Cook. 1975. "The Contents of Boys' and Girls' Rooms as an Index of Parents' Behavior." *Child Development* 46: 459–63.

Richie, Richard W., Daniel E. Heckers, and John U. Burgan. 1983. "High Technology Today and Tomorrow: A Small Slice of the Employment Pie." *Monthly Labor Review* 106, 11: 50–58.

Ritti, R. Richard. 1971. *The Engineer in the Industrial Corporation*. New York: Columbia University Press.

Robin, Stanley S. 1969. "The Female in Engineering." In Robert Perrucci and Joel Gerstl, *Engineers and the Social System*.

Robinson, J. Gregg, and Judith S. McIlwee. 1989. "Women in Engineering: A Promise Unfulfilled?" *Social Problems* 36: 455–72.

Rogers, Evers M., and Judith K. Larsen. 1984. *Silicon Valley Fever*. New York: Basic Books.

Rosenfeld, Rachel A. 1984. "Academic Career Mobility for Women and Men Psychologists." In Violet B. Haas and Carolyn C. Perrucci (eds.), *Women in Scientific and Engineering Professions*. Ann Arbor: University of Michigan Press.

Rossi, Alice S. 1965. "Women in Science: Why So Few?" *Science* 148 (May): 1196–1202.

Salaman, Graeme, and Kenneth Thompson (eds.). 1980. *Control and Ideology in Organizations*. Cambridge: MIT Press.

Salembier, Olive. 1971. "Women Engineers." In Bugliarello, et al., (eds.) *Women in Engineering: Bridging the Gap Between Society and Technology*.

Sario, T., Carol Jacklin, and C. K. Tittle. 1973. "Sex Role Stereotyping in the Public Schools." *Harvard Educational Review* 43: 386–404.

Sawhill, Isabell V. 1973. "The Economics of Discrimination against Women: Some New Findings." *Journal of Human Resources* 8 (Summer): 383–95.

Scanzoni, John. 1972. *Sexual Bargaining: Power Politics in the American Marriage*. Englewood Cliffs, N.J.: Prentice-Hall.

———. 1975. *Sex Roles, Life Styles and Childbearing: Changing Patterns in Marriage and the Family*. New York: Free Press.

Schreiber, Carol T. 1979. *Changing Places: Men and Women in Transitional Occupations*. Cambridge: MIT Press.

Schwartz, Felice N. 1989. "Management Women and the New Facts of Life." *Harvard Business Review* Jan.-Feb.: 65–76.

Sells, Lucy. 1978. "Mathematics: A Critical Filter." *Science Teacher* 45, 2 (Feb.).

Sewell, William H., and Robert M. Hauser. 1975. *Education, Occupation and Earnings*. New York: Academic Press.

Slaughter, E. M. 1982. "Career Goals, Attitudes and Interpersonal Relationships of MIT Undergraduates." Bachelor's thesis, MIT.

Sokoloff, Natalie. 1981. *Between Money and Love: The Dialectics of Women's Home and Market Work*. New York: Praeger.

Sprey, Jetse. 1979. "Conflict Theory and the Study of Marriage and the Family." In Wesley R. Burr, Reuben Hill, F. Ivan Nye, and Ira L. Reiss (eds.), *Contemporary Theories about the Family: General Theories/Theoretical Orientations*, vol. 2. New York: Free Press.

Stake, Joan E. 1979. "The Ability/Performance Dimension of Self-Esteem: Implications for Women's Achievement Behavior." *Psychology of Women Quarterly* 3: 365–77.

Stockard, Jean, and Miriam H. Johnson. 1980. *Sex Roles: Sex Inequality and Sex Role Development*. Englewood Cliffs, N.J.: Prentice-Hall.

Strober, Myra H. 1984. "Toward a General Theory of Occupational Sex Segregation: The Case of Public School Teaching." In Barbara Reskin (ed.), *Sex Segregation in the Workplace*.

Stromberg, Ann H., and Shirley Harkess (eds.). 1988. *Women Working: Theories and Facts in Perspective*. Mountain View, Calif.: Mayfield Publishing.

Taylor, Alex, III. 1986. "Why Women Managers are Bailing Out." *Fortune* Aug. 18: 16–23.

Taylor, Patricia A. 1988. "Women in Organizations: Structural Factors in Women's Work Patterns." In Ann H. Stromberg and Shirley Harkess (eds.), *Women Working*.

Thurow, Lester. 1970. *Investment in Human Capital*. Belmont, CA: Wadworth Publishing Co.

Treiman, Donald J., and Kermit Terrell. 1975. "Sex and the Process of Status Attainment: A Comparison of Working Women and Men." *American Sociological Review* 40 (April): 174–200.

Treiman, Donald J., and Heidi Hartmann (eds.). 1981. *Women, Work and Wages: Equal Pay for Jobs of Equal Value*. Washington, D.C.: National Academy Press.

U.S. Bureau of the Census. 1987. *Current Population Reports*, Series P-60, no. 157.

U.S. Dept. of Labor, Bureau of Labor Statistics. 1980. *Perspectives on Working Women: A Databook*. Bulletin 2080. Washington, D.C.: U.S. Government Printing Office.

U.S. Dept. of Labor. 1982. *Equal Employment Opportunity for Women: U.S. Policies*. Washington, D.C.

U.S. Dept. of Labor, Bureau of Labor Statistics. 1983. *Time of Change: 1983 Handbook on Women Workers*. Bulletin 298. Washington, D.C.: U.S. Government Printing Office.

U.S. Dept. of Labor, Bureau of Labor Statistics. 1988. *Projections 2000*. Bulletin 2302 (March). Washington, D.C.: U.S. Government Printing Office.

U.S. Dept. of Labor, Bureau of Labor Statistics. 1990. "Weekly Earnings of Employed Full-Time Wage and Salary Workers." Unpublished data.

Vetter, Betty. 1981. "Women Scientists and Engineers: Trends in Participation." *Science* 214 (Dec. 18): 1313–21.

Vetter, Betty, and Eleanor L. Babco. 1989. *Professional Women and Minorities: A Manpower Data Resource Service*, 6th ed. Washington, D.C.: Commission on Professionals in Science and Technology.

Waite, Linda J. 1981. "U.S. Women at Work." *Population Bulletin*, vol. 36, no. 2. Washington, D.C.: Population Reference Bureau.

Walshok, Mary Lindenstein. 1981. *Blue-Collar Women: Pioneers on the Male Frontier*. New York: Anchor Books.

Weber, Max. 1978. *Economy and Society*. Berkeley: University of California Press.

Weitzman, Lenore. 1979. *Sex Role Socialization: A Focus on Women*. Palo Alto, Calif.: Mayfield Publishing.

Whalley, Peter. 1986. *The Social Production of Technical Work*. Albany: SUNY Press.

Wheatley, Meg. 1982. "High Tech: The Fast Tracks and Dead Ends in the Job Market of the Future." *MS*. July/Aug.: 166–69.

Wilkie, Jane Riblett. 1988. "Marriage, Family Life and Women's Employment." In Ann H. Stromberg and Shirley Harkess (eds.), *Women Working*.

Wright, Eric Olin. 1982. *The Questionnaire on Class Structure, Class Biography and Class Consciousness*. Working Paper Number 2. Department of Sociology, University of Wisconsin.

Zey-Ferrell, Mary, and Michael Aiken (eds.). 1981. *Complex Organizations: Critical Perspectives*. Glenview, Ill.: Scott, Foresman.

Zimmer, Lynn. 1988. "Tokenism and Women in the Workplace: The Limits of Gender-Neutral Theory." *Social Problems* 35, 1(Feb.): 64–77.

Zussman, Robert. 1985. *Mechanics of the Middle Class*. Berkeley: University of California Press.

SUBJECT INDEX

A

Academic performance
  data gathered on, 218n7
  of women, 47–49
Academic skills, as reason for entering engineering, 26
Aerospace firms, 80
  culture of engineering in, 126–135
    affirmative action and, 127–128
    organizational structure and, 128–131
    women and, 131–135
  high tech firms versus, 135
  sexism in, 103–107
  women's success in, 182
Affirmative action
  culture of engineering and, 127–128
  strengthening, 182–184
Assertiveness. *See also* Self-promotion
  gender roles in workplace and, 88–93
Autonomy, at high tech firm, 113–114

C

California Elite University (CEU)
  description of, 218n6
  theoretical orientation at, 54
Career continuity
  gender roles in workplace and, 84
  withdrawal from work force and, 148, 161–163
Children, 154–167
  career change and, 163–165
  career-oriented women and, 165–167
  day care for, 185
  perception of responsibility for, 155, 173
  withdrawal from labor force to care for, 148, 161–163
College experiences, 46–78. *See also* California Elite University; Engineering education; Public State University
  of Ginger, 70–75
  interactional structure of engineering school and, 56–70
    faculty and, 57–61
    female students and, 68–70

H

I

J

L

M

Males
engineering school students
interaction with female engineering students, 61–68
skepticism and resentment among, 66–68
gender role of, power achievement and, 16
increasing participation in family work, 185–186
mechanical experience of, 24, 25, 26, 52, 276
parental backgrounds of, 28–30
patronization of women by, in workplace, 97–98
power and priorities in marriage and, 145–145
with professional wives, 146–150
reasons for entering engineering, 24, 25–26
Management
in aerospace firm, 130
collegiality encouraged by, at high tech firm, 112
engineers encouraged to resist, at high tech firm, 115
factors hindering women from moving into, 14–15
interactional style and, 140
middle, 81
relations between engineers and, at high tech firm, 112–113
technical knowledge and, 20
upper, 81
Manufacturing firms, employment by, 80
Marketing
attractiveness to women, 123
low status of engineers in, 115, 121
Marriage, 150–154, 177–178
atypical status relationships in, 168–172

importance of spouses' careers in, 153–154
power and priorities in, 145–146
professional women and, 146–150
women married to engineers and, 151–154
Maternity leave, 185
Math
importance in engineering education, 27–28
providing women with opportunities in, 180, 181
Mechanical engineering
electrical engineering versus, 135–138
growth as profession, 2
women entering, 106–107
Mechanical skills. *See also* Tinkering
providing women with opportunities in, 180–182
women's lack of self-confidence about, 49
Medicine, reasons for choosing engineering over, 31
Mentors
in college, 64–66
husband as, 152–153
in workplace, 98
Mid-management, 81
Mother. *See also* Children
importance of role of, 155
Multivariate analysis, 199–200

N

Nontraditional occupations, implications for study of women in, 188–191

O

Occupational segregation
attempts to decrease, 8

Occupational segregation (*cont.*)
human capital theory and, 10
pay gap and, 7–8
resegregation and, 8–9, 82–83
status attainment theory and, 10
Organizational structure, culture of
engineering and, 128–131

P

Parental background, entry into engineering profession and, 28–30, 32–34
Parental leave, 185
Patronization, by males, in workplace, 97–98
Power relations, 15–17, 189
changing, 186–188
culture and, 16–17
of engineering, 19–20
male gender role and, 16
in marriage, 145–145
sexism and, 95
Practical orientation, entry into engineering profession and, 30–32
Project engineers, 81
Promotions
in aerospace firm, 129
in high tech firm, 126
Public policy. *See also* Affirmative action
sex discrimination in educational institutions and, 51
work-family relationships and, 185–186
Public State University (PSU)
description of, 218n6
practical orientation at, 54

Q

Questionnaire, order of return of, 195–196

R

Reliability, checks for, 195
Research and development (R & D), in engineering hierarchy, 80–81
Research methods, 193–200
general methodological issues and, 194–198
specific measures and, 198–200
of interactional resources, 198–199
of job standing, 198
multivariate analysis and, 199–200
Resegregation, occupational, 8–9, 82–83
Romance, among engineering school students, 63–64

S

Salaries, 2–3
engineering hierarchy and, 81
gender gap in, 7–8, 13
of women, improving, 217n1
Sample bias, 195
School systems, career information in, 179
Science
competition in, 141–142
importance in engineering education, 27–28
reasons for choosing engineering over, 31–32
Segregation, occupational. *See* Occupational segregation
Selection interview, for lab engineers, 114, 120
Self-confidence
affirmative action and, 184
building, 54–56, 181–182
college experience and, 48–50, 54–56, 218n8

U

United Missile (UM)
Computer Devices Incorporated compared with, 135
culture of engineering at, 126–135
affirmative action and, 127–128
organizational structure and, 128–131
women and, 131–135
Upper management, 81
Utility companies, employment by, 80

W

Women's Educational Equity Act of 1974, 51
Women's movement, 38–40
changing power relations and, 187–188

Workplace, 79–108
culture of engineering in. *See* Culture of engineering, in workplace
employment patterns in, 80–82
gender roles in, 82–93
career continuity and, 84
education and, 83–84
self-confidence and assertiveness and, 88–93
work values and, 84, 87–88
male domination of, 17
sexism in, 93, 95–107
career patterns of women and, 103–107
exclusion of women and, 100–101
job assignments and, 101–103
mentors and, 98
patronization and, 97–98
sexual harassment and, 99–100
teasing and joking and, 96–97
Work values, gender roles in workplace and, 84, 87–88

NAME INDEX

S

Salembier, Olive, 3
Sario, T., 11
Sawhill, Isabell V., 10
Scanzoni, John, 145, 146
Schooler, Carmi, 13
Schreiber, Carol T., 8, 15, 95
Schwartz, Felice N., 186
Sedlacek, William, 194, 195
Sells, Lucy, 180
Sewell, William H., 9
Slaughter, E. M., 218n8
Snavely, B. K., 15
Sokoloff, Natalie, 11, 16, 18, 145
Stake, Joan E., 11
Strober, Myra H., 13

T

Taylor, Patricia A., 14
Terrell, Kermit, 10
Thurow, Lester, 10
Tittle, C. K., 11
Tobin-Richards, M., 11
Treiman, Donald J., 8, 10, 14, 217n1

U

Ullman, Joseph C., 8, 95
U. S. Bureau of the Census, 8

U. S. Department of Labor, 3, 7, 8, 13, 51

V

Velsor, E. Van, 9
Vetter, Betty, 2
Vogel, Susan R., 11

W

Waite, Linda J., 37
Walshok, Mary Lindenstein, 8, 37
Weitzman, Lenore, 11
Whalley, Peter, 20, 81, 197
White, R., 9
Wilkie, Jane Riblett, 145
Wright, Eic Olin, 219n15

Z

Zey-Ferrell, Mary, 16
Zimmer, Lynn, 15
Zuckerman, Harriet, 149
Zussman, Robert, 20, 81, 197